Routedge Revivals

Kidnappers in Philadelphia

Kidnappers in Philadelphia
Isaac Hopper's Tales of Oppression
1780-1843

Daniel E. Meaders

First published in 1994 by Garland Publishing, Inc.

This edition first published in 2018 by Routledge
2 Park Square, Milton Park, Abingdon, Oxon, OX14 4RN
and by Routledge
52 Vanderbilt Avenue, New York, NY 10017, USA

Routledge is an imprint of the Taylor & Francis Group, an informa business

© 1994 Daniel E. Meaders

All rights reserved. No part of this book may be reprinted or reproduced or utilised in any form or by any electronic, mechanical, or other means, now known or hereafter invented, including photocopying and recording, or in any information storage or retrieval system, without permission in writing from the publishers.

Publisher's Note
The publisher has gone to great lengths to ensure the quality of this reprint but points out that some imperfections in the original copies may be apparent.

Disclaimer
The publisher has made every effort to trace copyright holders and welcomes correspondence from those they have been unable to contact.
A Library of Congress record exists under ISBN:

ISBN 13: 978-0-367-10968-4 (hbk)
ISBN 13: 978-0-367-10971-4 (pbk)
ISBN 13: 978-0-429-02412-2 (ebk)

STUDIES IN AFRICAN AMERICAN HISTORY AND CULTURE

edited by
GRAHAM HODGES
COLGATE UNIVERSITY

A GARLAND SERIES

KIDNAPPERS
IN PHILADELPHIA

ISAAC HOPPER'S TALES OF OPPRESSION
1780–1843

DANIEL E. MEADERS

GARLAND PUBLISHING, INC.
NEW YORK & LONDON / 1994

Copyright © 1994 Daniel E. Meaders
All rights reserved

Library of Congress Cataloging-in-Publication Data

Hopper, Isaac T. (Isaac Tatem), 1771–1852.
    Kidnappers in Philadelphia : Isaac Hopper's Tales of oppression, 1780–1843 / [compiled by] Daniel E. Meaders.
      p.   cm.
    Studies in African American history and culture
    Originally published in the National anti-slavery standard as a column entitled Tales of oppression, beginning Oct. 22 1840.
    Includes bibliographical references (p.   ) and index.
    ISBN 0-8153-1776-X (alk. paper)
    1. Fugitive slaves—Pennsylvania—Philadelphia—History—Sources.
2. Afro-Americans—Pennsylvania—Philadelphia—History—Sources.
3. Philadelphia (Pa.)—History—Sources. 4. Philadelphia (Pa.)—Race relations—Sources.   I. Meaders, Daniel, 1945–   . II. Title.
F158.9.N4H67   1994
974.8'1103—dc20   94-10190
                                                                         CIP

Printed on acid-free, 250-year-life paper
Manufactured in the United States of America

This book is dedicated to Wayne Gibbons, Charles Williams, Andy Gill, Fred Wallace, Tarina Meaders, and the memory of Gloria Williams.

"I most sincerely believe that slavery is the greatest sin the Lord Almighty ever suffered to exist upon this earth. As sure as God is good and just, he will put an end to it; and all opposition will be in vain."

Isaac Hopper

Contents

		Page
ACKNOWLEDGMENTS		xi
INTRODUCTION		1
TALES:		
I.	Haitian Slave	33
II.	Peter Johnson	37
III.	A Child Kidnapped	41
IV.	Cyrus Field	47
V.	Peter	49
VI.	Kidnapped into Slavery	55
VII.	Romaine	59
VIII.	A Maryland Fugitive	65
IX.	Richard Allen	69
X.	Daniel Benson	75
XI.	Samuel Curtis	79
XII.	A Kidnapping Ring	83
XIII.	Samuel Clark	89
XIV.	Reuben Moore	93
XV.	Phebe	95
XVI.	Thomas Hughes	99
XVII.	Emery Sadler	105
XVIII.	Stephen Lamaire	111
XIX.	Wagelma	117
XX.	William Bachelor	121
XXI.	Prince Hopkins	127
XXII.	Germaine	129
XXIII.	Joe	133
XXIV.	Pegg	137
XXV.	Sarah Roach and Child	143
XXVI.	George Cooper	147
XXVII.	Maryland Slave	149
XXVIII.	Solomon Clarkson	157

XXIX.	Levin Smith	159
XXX.	Samuel Wilson	163
XXXI.	Philadelphia Apprentice	167
XXXII.	Ben	171
XXXIII.	Thomas Hughes and John Darg	177
XXXIV.	Anne Garrison	179
XXXV.	James Poovey	183
XXXVI.	Virginia Fugitive	187
XXXVII.	James Davis	191
XXXVIII.	Mrs. Morris	195
XXXIX.	New Jersey Slave	199
XL.	Maryland Slave	203
XLI.	East Jersey Slave	207
XLII.	Maryland Slaves	211
XLIII.	Phebe Numbers	215
XLIV.	Red Betsey	219
XLV.	James Hall	223
XLVI.	Mary Holliday	229
XLVII.	A Slave Hunter Defeated	233
XLVIII.	An Aged Bondman	237
XLIX.	James	239
L.	Uncle Beck	243
LI.	Tobias Boudinot	247
LII.	Ben Jackson	251
LIII.	Self-emancipated Couple	255
LIV.	Samuel Johnson	261
LV.	Virginia Slave	265
LVI.	The Foreign Slave	271
LVII.	The Fraudulent Indenture	275
LVIII.	Chattel Restored to Manhood	279
LIX.	Charles Webster	283
LX.	Tom	287
LXI.	What's in a Name?	293
LXII.	William Anderson	297
LXIII.	The Traitor	301
LXIV.	Tender Mercies of a Slaveholder	305
LXV.	Benjamin Clark	309
LXVI.	Poor Amy	313

LXVII.	The Patriarchal System	317
LXVIII.	William Healy	321
LXIX.	Theodore	325
LXX.	Caesar King	329
LXXI.	Maryland Slave	333
LXXII.	The Slave Trader	337
LXXIII.	William Wright	343
LXXIV.	Peter	347
LXXV.	Mary	351
LXXVI.	James Williams	355
LXXVII.	Thomas Harrison	359
LXXVIII.	Tom	371
LXXIX.	William Dixon	375

BIBLIOGRAPHY 383
INDEX OF PLANTERS' NAMES 387

Acknowledgments

John Blassingame contributed to this work by first urging me in his graduate seminars to examine "new kinds of sources viewed from different angles." I am deeply indebted to him, for he assigned me the enviable task of collecting and verifying Hopper's *Tales of Oppression*. Grateful acknowledgments to Michelle Brenner for her computer expertise, and to Madeline Himy who typed more drafts than she cares to remember. I owe a debt to Elizabeth Vasile for her editorial assistance, and to Estelle Paris who was involved in the project in its early beginnings. I owe special thanks to Dr. Martha Ashby for her thorough reading of the manuscript. Finally, I am grateful to Dr. Graham Hodges of Garland, who believed in the project and was a decisive factor in making sure that it saw the light of day.

Introduction

On November 6, 1802, the *Poulson's American Daily Advertiser*, a local Philadelphian newspaper, published an editorial, "Melancholy Effects of Slavery," that accused James Ewing, Trenton's mayor, of having ordered several blacks, including one Romaine, along with his wife and his child, all of whom belonged to a French planter, to leave New Jersey and return to St. Domingo where they had lived as slaves. After boarding a Trenton stagecoach, the blacks and their owners rode to Philadelphia where they stopped to eat. Somehow, Romaine's wife and child slipped away, but before Romaine could escape, the planter's escorts ordered him into the stagecoach. Romaine "walked a few steps, and with a pruning knife, which seemed," wrote the editor, "prepared for the purpose, cut his throat in so shocking manner that he expired in a few minutes after on the pavement."[1]

In his anonymous editorial, Isaac Hopper, a thirty-one year-old Quaker, alias Friend Hopper, who was a member of the Abolitionists, suggested that Mayor Ewing should bear responsibility, at least partly, for Romaine's death, and that the "legality of the permission granted by the mayor of Trenton, is much questioned and will be investigated."[2] On December 10, 1840, Isaac Hopper published a story about Romaine in the *National Anti-Slavery Standard* noting that the "circumstances here related occurred many years ago, but they made such a deep impression on my mind, that they are now as fresh before me as though it was but yesterday."[3]

Lydia Maria Child, the *National Anti-Slavery Standard's* editor, encouraged Hopper to write about his experiences assisting blacks pursued by their former masters, hoping that blacks such as Romaine would be immortalized. Child had arrived in New York from Massachusetts in the Spring of 1840 and needed a place to stay and "took up my abode with the family of Isaac Hopper."[4]

Because Hopper needed a job, Child hired him in June of 1840 as a treasurer and a book agent for the *Standard*, a paper that "represents itself before the world as the official organ of the American Anti-Slavery Society." On June 11, 1840, Hopper penned his first narrative, "An Interesting Case of Escape." In September of 1840, one reader in a letter to the editor maintained that Friend Hopper had an "immense fund of the most graphical interesting anecdotes, stored away in his excellent memory, and his tact in the relation of them never fails to exite the liveliest attention." Eventually, Hopper received space to print his stories serially. On October 22, 1840, Hopper penned the first of seventy-nine narratives in a bi-weekly column called the *Tales of Oppression*. The *Standard* said, "they will be read we have no doubt with deep interest."[5]

Drawn from "authentic sources, relating to the sufferings of the slaves and their efforts to escape from their fetters, and having a great abundance of such facts in my possession, I have concluded to offer them for publication in your columns," reported Hopper in his preface to the *Tales of Oppression*. The majority of the *Tales* featured black men: 55 (70%) referred to them; whereas 17 (22%) of the stories referred to black women, 4 (5%) to white men, and 3 (4%) to black children. Sixteen (29%) of the black men were free or passing for free; 10 (59%) of the women fell into the same category. Thirty-eight (40%) of the men were fugitives, as were 11 (67%) of the women. Over 90% of the blacks gave no ages or Hopper overlooked them; seven of the 11 blacks that did mention their ages were between the age of 25 and 35. About 75% of the blacks featured in the *Tales* came from Pennsylvania, New York, New Jersey, Delaware, and Maryland. Seventeen percent came from Virginia, North Carolina, South Carolina, and Mississippi. Over 90% of the blacks either had set foot at least once in Philadelphia or had been permanent residents in that city. Twenty-five percent of the blacks were skilled. In short, the typical black highlighted in the *Tales of Oppression* probably was likely to be in the prime of his life, unskilled, and a fugitive passing for free, who was either living in the North or had fled there seeking solace.

Isaac Hopper's *Tales of Oppression* captured thousands of readers' attention, including Frederick Douglass, who said these "thrilling narratives" contained the "incidents of the lives of many fugitives from republican whips and chains." In his review of Hopper's biography, Douglass had the "pleasure and the privilege of being invited to his house, and there listened to some of the admirable stories and adventures in the matter of rescuing fugitives, which abounds in the autobiography, by Mrs. Child, and I can bear testimony to the admirable accuracy and naturalness with which she has reproduced the same stories here." Nathaniel P. Rogers, editor of the *Herald of Freedom*, noted in 1841, that he "published numbers of these interesting narratives, from time to time, from the *National Anti-Slavery Standard*. Our readers find one of them on the last page of today."[6]

Because the *National Anti-Slavery Standard* published the *Tales*, scholars can easily find them; the *Standard* began publication in 1840 and has been on microfilm since 1953. Comprising some 85,000 words, Hopper's *Tales of Oppression* provided the main source for Child's *Life of Isaac T. Hopper*, published two years after Hopper's death. According to Child, "the narratives and anecdotes of fugitive slaves, which form such a prominent portion of the book, were originally written by Friend Hopper himself, and published in the newspaper, under the title of 'Tales of Oppression.' I have remodelled them all." It took over a century before a scholar discovered Hopper's narratives; John Blassingame published one narrative in his *Slave Testimony*. In his *Forging Freedom: The Formation of Philadelphia's Black Community, 1720-1840*, Gary Nash barely mentioned Hopper. In *Freedom by Degrees: Emancipation in Pennsylvania and Its Aftermath*, Gary Nash and Jean Soderlund mentioned Hopper but do not draw on the narratives.[7]

Before World War I, the American historian reluctantly drew on the slave's or the abolitionist's testimonies, fearing that to do so would challenge the nation's leading historian, U.B. Phillips, who downplayed what blacks wrote themselves or what white abolitionists wrote for them, claiming they were, for the most part, propagandists and biased.[8] If bias means that the abolitionists leaned toward the blacks, then Isaac Hopper's *Tales of Oppression* were biased accounts. If one meaning of propaganda is to circulate or disseminate ideas or thoughts, then Hopper was a masterful propagandist; he used these *Tales* to provoke indignation, anger, and bitterness, hoping to thereby undermine the planter's credibility and standing, and more importantly to undermine chattel slavery. When Romaine slashed his throat, Hopper claimed to have said, "How long! How long! Oh Lord, shall this abominable system of slavery be permitted to curse the land?"[9] A disinterested observer he was not.

Save for the official records and papers of the Pennsylvania Abolition Society, the *Tales of Oppression* offers the reader the largest body of sources concerning blacks, both free and enslaved, who either lived in Philadelphia, or were just passing through during the late eighteenth and the early nineteenth centuries. No longer does the researcher have to rely solely on the planter's runaway advertisements, diaries, memoirs, or autobiographies, to describe black resistance, especially if he wants to make sense of it as seen through their eyes. If you want to read about white men riding into the heart of Philadelphia in the 1790's, grabbing blacks off the streets, forcing them into slavery and threatening to shoot rescuers, then the *Tales* is the leading point of departure. If Philadelphia immediately brings to mind the First and Second Continental Congresses, the Constitutional Convention, the Independence Hall, the Federal Capital, then Hopper's *Tales* should make us mindful that the federal government, operating out of Philadelphia from 1790-1800, failed to protect the wayward fugitive or the unlawful seizure of blacks.[10]

Are these *Tales* verifiable? Some might not care; the question is rarely asked about the planter's documents. Charles T. Davis and Henry Louis Gates, Jr. claimed that "historians who work so painstakingly to establish verifiable records have, until recently, treated these texts either with an alarmingly irresponsible naivete, or else with a pernicious double-standard, finding 'bias' in the slave's text and 'objectivity' in that of the master."[11]

In Hopper's first *Tale*, entitled "Haitian Slave," he noted that "I begin with the following narrative, which I procured from the lips of a fugitive," who recalled how her master, a white woman, made her "rub her feet, and sometimes being weary with the labors of the day, I could not refrain from nodding, when she would kick me with great force in the breast. I was often whipped very severely, because I could not accomplish my task in the field, and my skin now bears evidence of it from my neck to my ankles." The incident took place in South Carolina, and Hopper listed the names of several planters: James Dobson, Widow Dobson, Betsey Dobson, and Samuel Read. When the Read family visited Philadelphia they brought the "Haitian Slave" with them, and it was there that she "made up my mind never to return to Carolina, if I could possibly avoid it." Hopper "spent more than an hour in her company, as she was on her way to the land of the free, and where she has doubtless arrived before now." Hopper omitted the black woman's name to prevent her owner from finding her. In Tale No. LVIII, "The Chattel Restored to Manhood," Friend Hopper stated that the "following narrative I have written down just as I received it from the lips of a very intelligent and worthy colored man, a subscriber to the *Standard*. I have thought it prudent to suppress names and dates, lest some innocent person might be brought into trouble. No one who knows the narrator (and he is known and respected by many) will have doubt of the truth of his statements."[12] Isaac Hopper refused to slight the names of certain Quaker slaveholders. In Tale No. LXIII, "The Traitor," he said that he used the "fictitious name of James Austin, because I am unwilling to wound the feelings of his respectable relations, descended from an ancient and worthy family of Friends, in New Jersey."[13]

By suppressing the blacks' names in seventeen of his *Tales*, Hopper might have made it difficult for the scholar to accept those narratives. Can any of Hopper's narratives be verified? In *Poulson's American Daily Advertiser* of November 21, 1801, the editor wrote that "In the night of Sunday, the 25th ult., the house of Samuel Clark, a free black, of West Nottingham, near the Maryland line, was attacked and broken open by five abandoned villains, who committed great outrages on the family with intent to seize these persons and send them to Georgia or Kentucky to be sold for slaves; Clark was wounded by a pistol fired at him in one of his arms. His daughter, a young woman, received a shot in the neck, which proved a mortal wound, of which, after languishing six days, she died. Her brother, a youth, who lay sick with a fever, was cruelly abused, dragged out of the house and wounded in his head..." In Tale No. XIII, "Samuel Clark," Hopper asked Joseph B. Mckean, then Attorney General, to tell his father, Thomas Kean, who was Governor of Pennsylvania, to bring the attackers to justice. But the "matter there ended, and nothing was done."[14] Much of the language found in the newspaper piece can be found verbatim in Hopper's narrative, suggesting that he sent a summarized version of the incident to Poulson who printed it.

The *American Daily Advertiser*'s reportage of Romaine's suicide was also apparently authored by Hopper because "Tale No. VII, Romaine" contains exactly the same words and sentences. While neither one of the accounts revealed Isaac Hopper's name, the incidents that befell Romaine and Samuel Clark did take place. Since Clark's neighbor mailed Hopper a summary of the attack, the Quaker abolitionist may not have based his account on a direct encounter with Clark himself. In Romaine's case, Isaac Hopper walked to the scene and saw him "lying on the pavement before me, with the throat cut almost ear to ear."[15]

On August 4, 1807, two French planters placed a runaway advertisement in the *Pennsylvania American Daily Advertiser*, offering ten dollars for the capture of a "French Indentured *Negro* Boy named *Theodore*" who "took all his clothes with him, speaks English and was about 15 or 16 years old." Hopper penned a Tale about Theodore, a mulatto boy, the son of a 31 year old Frenchman who was thrown in jail for robbery.[16]

Frederick Douglass verified Hopper's Tale entitled "Tale No. LXXIX, William Dixon," a case that brought "thousands of persons of all colors in and around the courthouse" in New York. Arrested on April 4, 1837 after fleeing from Doctor Walter P. Allender of the City of Baltimore in April 1832, Dixon denied being Dr. Allender's slave or ever living in Baltimore. Allender called some twenty witnesses from his home town who swore that Dixon belonged to Allender. Convinced that Allender could not win his case, Hopper asked Allender to abandon it, because the planter could not support Dixon's upkeep in prison. In his autobiography, *Life and Times of Frederick Douglass*, Douglass mentioned that once, after arriving in New York, he "ran into a fugitive slave whom I had once known well in slavery," who was known in Baltimore as "Allender's Jake," but in New York, he "bore the respectable name of 'William Dixon.'" Jake belonged to Doctor Allender and Tolly Allender. The doctor's son had once tried to recapture Dixon but lacked evidence to support his claim.[17]

Court records can verify some of Hopper's narratives. In "Tom," Tale No. LX, he admits he "does not remember" the slave's name, and "for convenience will call the colored man Tom." Yet he did remember the name of Tom's master, Robert Creswell, and that Tom had "left his service in Maryland" for Pennsylvania, where Creswell recaptured him. Creswell, armed with a pistol, tied Tom up in order to take him home. When Hopper learned of Tom's predicament, he swore out a warrant, charging Creswell with attempting to take Tom out of the state. The records of "Common Pleas Court Appearances" confirm this case.[18]

The Pennsylvania Abolitionist Society left letters, reports, manumission papers, pamphlets, and books presently located in the Historical Society of Pennsylvania. Among these papers are documents describing several of the blacks in Hopper's narratives. In "Samuel Curtis," Tale No. XI, Hopper tells how Curtis (whose real name was Manuel) fled from North Carolina to Philadelphia, where he found a job, saved some money, built a house, and became an upright citizen. Because he missed his enslaved children, Curtis asked Hopper's help to secure a bill of sale for himself from his master, Joseph Spears. Hopper had a friend who was going to Halifax, North Carolina, to "visit his relations" where Spears lived; Manuel gave Hopper's friend $100 and secured Manuel's freedom. The bill of sale can be found in the papers of the Pennsylvania Abolition Society. Manuel journeyed to Halifax, but Spears claimed he had sold the children to a planter in South Carolina, who had sold them to a planter in Georgia, who had sold them to someone in Tennessee. Manuel never found his children.[19]

Still another important source of corroborating evidence for Hopper's narratives lies in the Minutes of the Acting Committee, a continuous report, covering 1787-1842, of blacks who claimed that their "liberty was being denied them illegally." Isaac Hopper used these minutes as a source in nine of his *Tales*, beginning with "Steven Lamaire," Tale No. XVII, and ending with "Maryland Slave," No. XVII. These minutes, though lacking Hopper's passion and graphic character descriptions, offer the reader a terse account of the experiences of many blacks. Hopper's *Tales*, "Wagelma," published in April 1841, showed to what lengths this Quaker would go to block the kidnapping of a black. Wagelma, a ten year old black servant, was indentured to Peter de Boudee of Pennsylvania who intended to return to France. Without asking Wagelma's mother's permission, Boudee prepared to send the young servant to France by placing him on a boat. Hopper who keeps the reader riveted by showing how he rescued Wagelma referred to the Acting Committee Minutes for his source material. On August 6, 1801, the Committee Secretary, Thomas Harrison, wrote:

> Wagelma, a Black boy about 10 years old bound servant to _____ Deboudee - a Frenchman - who being about to remove Part of his Family to France, and in order to send the Boy - with his Wife had him on Board the New Castle Stage Boat - not having obtained the consent of the Boy nor his mother - agreeably to the Direction of the Law of 1788 - and the Boat - having sailed - Information was received - Isaac T. Hoper - Persued to Gloster Point & took boat. - Reached the Stage Boat near the Jersey Shore & Brought the Boy away - Delivered him to his mother - Since which time Deboudee has Brought Suit against Isaac T. Hoper. Thomas Harrison.[20]

Twelve of the *Tales* are based on Hopper's interviews with blacks. Some sort of documentation triggered his recollection of other *Tales*--an old newspaper article or pamphlet, or the Acting Committee minutes. In 1838, the pro-slavery forces burned his New York bookstore where he stored old papers and pamphlets, but fortunately the Pennsylvania Abolition Society preserved documents describing black activities. The Pennsylvania Historical Society has available on microfilm the Acting Committee minutes, including Hopper's assistance of blacks, a large body of correspondence, and thousands of indentures and manumission certificates.[21] Hopper probably used these documents in his narratives.

How can these narratives help scholars? What insights do these *Tales* offer the historian? The *Tales of Oppression*, offers a singular insight into the black's day to day world, an opportunity that eluded Kenneth Stampp, who said that because there were "few reliable records of what went on in the minds of slaves, one can infer their thoughts and feelings from their behavior, that of their masters, and the logic of their situation."[22] The planter's view should not be set aside or played down, but to make sense of the slave's world, it is necessary to listen to their testimony.

One of the most difficult things to find out is what the blacks felt about their treatment. In the "Patriarchal System," (Tale No. LXVII), Hopper maintains that he "took the following account from the mouth of the sufferer, in nearly her own language." The woman slave was born in Anderson county, North Carolina, and lived there until she was five years old, at which time she moved to York, fifty miles from Anderson. "While here, he sold my mother to New Orleans, leaving my father at home." She remained at York for three years and "during that time I was treated with great cruelty. I was frequently stripped stark naked, locked in the cellar, and while in that condition, severely whipped by my mistress; frequently for small omissions of duty, and sometimes without any fault at all. So severe were the whippings, that the blood often run down to my heels, and my clothes were stiff with it."[23]

Her master moved to Alabama, and died three years later, leaving behind unpaid bills and seven slaves, all of whom a sheriff sold, save for her father, to a creditor. She never saw her father again. She remained with the creditor for five years and felt that he was a "good master, and treated his slaves kindly." After he died, his slaves, including the nameless woman, were given to his stepdaughter, who married a man named J...A. of Mobile, Alabama. She married one of his slaves, but soon after the marriage, the "husband was sold and sent away. I never saw him afterwards."[24]

Once she left the storeroom open, and the master, "without saying one word," beat her with a cane. It hurt so much that she "screamed aloud. This provoked him. He tied me by the two wrists, and drew me up, so that my toes could just touch the ground. He kept me in that condition about fifteen minutes, whipping me at short intervals, all the time, with a cowhide." For three days the master had her locked up, and during that time "I gave birth to twins. They were both dead, and I was very near losing my own life also; I kept my bed five weeks, during which time I suffered extremely." After going through several masters, she ended up in Mobile, Alabama, where the planter's wife beat her with a bucket and "made a deep wound" on her arm. The nameless slave shoved her back to prevent the whipping, but the woman told her husband, who "became greatly enraged, and told me if I ever did the like again he would cut my hand off." Again, she was tied up and whipped. So when one master brought her to New York it was no accident that she made a dash for freedom.[25]

Scholars have long been concerned with the issue of representativeness or what is typical of the black experience under chattel slavery. Eugene Genovese maintains that "Two decades of work in the history of southern slave society have helped formed my estimates of what is and is not typical - what does not ring true." He is well aware that if you rely on planter's testimony at the expense of the black's sources, then you will end up with a distorted vision of the black experience. In the long run, Genovese maintains that all sources are "treacherous" and that one has to use his own "judgment." Blassingame argues all sources of evidence should be examined and utilized, but "sources left by slaves, and especially the autobiography" are the superior form of evidence.[26] For the early American historian, the choices of what to use in depicting the experience of the black or of the planter are limited. They lack the choice of choosing between the WPA narrative or run-away slave accounts, the folklore material or the black autobiographies. As a result, they are forced to draw heavily on the planter's testimony, especially the runaway advertisement, to depict the black experience, which is tantamount to using police files to make sense of the dreams and hopes of blacks. Hopper's *Tales of Oppression* are neither police or planter records; they are stories written by a white abolitionist Quaker, stories that are infinitely more superior than the runaway advertisement in their ability to uncover the feelings of blacks. The runaway advertisement represents the planter's world, his feelings, his anxieties; the *Tales* represent the black's world and his effort to escape from the madness of the planter's world. The *Tales of Oppression* gives the researcher the rare opportunity to compare two different classes of documentary sources and to determine which contains the greater ring of truth.

David McCallmont of Delaware published an advertisement describing a fugitive named James Payton, in the *Philadelphia Gazette* on November 11, 1801:

Thirty Dollars Reward
RAN AWAY from the Subscriber, the 1st day of August last, a Mulatto Man called James Payton, about 5 feet 7 or 8 inches in height; had on when he went away, a light coloured broadcloth coat, dimity trowsers, and round hat; when spoken to is apt to laugh, two teeth out before; - was since seen in Philadelphia, where his wife Cloe now lives: It is expected he is now about the city. Any person securing him in goal, shall be entitled to the above reward, and all reasonable charges.
David McCallmont.
New Port, state of Delaware, Oct. 30.[27]

While the advertisement shows that an act of rebellion had taken place and that these two men, McCallmont and Payton, were at odds, it excludes the black's direct testimony. Hopper's Tale No. LX, entitled "James," tells the reader why James Payton absconded. "Preferring liberty to slavery, about the year 1805, he took the liberty to walk off," leaving his master to guess that he may be in Philadelphia because that was where his wife lived. According to Hopper's Tale, the fugitive lived in the "neighborhood of Pilesgrove, Salem county, New Jersey, and lived with a farmer." Loathing his fugitive status, Payton applied for manumission. The harborer called on Hopper to assist Payton by contacting McCallmont. Hopper wrote the planter, asking for his "lowest terms" for the manumission of James Payton. In a matter of weeks, the planter, along with Levi Hollingsworth, a Philadelphia merchant, knocked on Hopper's door looking for the fugitive. Hollingsworth told Hopper that McCallmont was a "highly respectable man, and treated his slaves with great humanity, and even kindness; that James would be happier in his service, than he could be in any other situation." The Delaware planter finally agreed to sell Payton for 150 dollars. Did the black ever return to Delaware? James Payton did return to see his former master, and he was "kindly received by all the family, and spent a day or two with them very agreeable" before the planter asked the black to leave: "Well, Jim, I am glad to see you, and I am pleased to find you have a good master, and are happy; but I would rather you would not come here again, the way you have now; it will make my people dissatisfied."[28]

In August of 1800, while attending to his senatorial duties in Philadelphia, Jacob Read of South Carolina placed a runaway advertisement in the *Poulson's American Daily Advertiser*, in which he described Pat, a fifty-one year old washer-woman, her husband Sharper, her daughter Clara, and a couple named Dick and Amelia. During this period Hopper was a member of the Pennsylvania Abolitionist Acting Committee. From his account in Tale No. XLIV, "Red Betsey," we know that he was well aware of Read's presence in the Quaker city: "Jacob Read of Charlestown, South Carolina, was a member of the Senate of the United States, and as Congress then sat in Philadelphia, he went there in the latter part of the year 1797 to discharge the duties of his station, and took his family with him, and several slaves to wait upon them. Among the number was a bright mulatto, who assumed the name of Betsey." She ran away and Hopper maintained she was "not advertised and it did not appear that her master took any measures to recover her."[29]

But Amelia seems to have resembled Red Betsey, whom Hopper described as a "family servant, who was an excellent cook; but having lived amidst great affluences, she was rather too extravagant to suit my circumstances." According to the runaway advertisement, Amelia was a "dark mulatto, and she dresses with taste and imitates the French style." Hopper maintained that Betsey was "uncommonly intelligent and discreet; possessed of much sensibility, and faithful in whatever is given her in charge." Read said Amelia was "very ingenious and can turn her hand to anything." Hopper said Betsey was "much attached to a man and his wife, who were her fellow servants, and who left the master about the same time as she did." Whereas Amelia and Red Betsey seem to be one and the same, the writer maintains that Read's runaway advertisement cannot match Hopper's Red Betsey Tale. Unlike the account in the tale of "Red Betsey," the runaway ad tells us nothing about the anxieties and the efforts of its subjects. Isaac Hopper remembered Betsey saying that "She was very much depressed, and said that she should take no comfort in anything; but she could not sleep, for the dread of being apprehended was constantly pressing upon her." Clearly, Hopper's *Tales*, again, are qualitatively superior to the class of runaway advertisements; they include both the planter's and the slave's recollections, and sharply depict the forces that trigger the flight of the slave, and the publication of the fugitive advertisements. The *Tales* also trace the personalities of the subjects and their circumstances in far greater depth than the fugitive advertisements.[30]

Still another important feature of the *Tales* is that they span from the late eighteenth century to the first half of the nineteenth century and provide as much information, if not more, than any extant planter document concerning black experiences in the late 1790s and early 1800s. They include, too, a valuable narrative in Tale No. IX concerning Richard Allen, treating the reader to a glimpse of the trials and tribulations that beset him while living in Philadelphia. A former slave from Maryland, Allen had obtained his manumission, fell in love and got married. He opened up a shoe repair business; anyone in Philadelphia who wanted their shoes repaired could go to him. He had a chimney cleaning business as well; anyone who desired to have his chimney soot-free could go to Bishop Allen. He made a great deal of money as a black merchant who lived in a three-story brick house in the 1790's, but he was more than wealthy.[31] When the yellow fever struck Philadelphia, sending scores of whites and blacks to their graves, some, including a member of Hopper's family, lost heart and caught the first stagecoach heading out of that disease-ridden town. Allen and his friend, Absalom Jones, stood fast and were "unremitting in their labors for the relief of the sick, and in burying the dead." Because of their efforts, the community embraced them, the local press praised them, and the town mayor saluted them for their "diligence, attention, and decency of deportment."[32]

Richard Allen showed no fear of the white man and the black community seemed to sense this. When an enslaved black absconded, planters often saw Allen as a possible harborer, as in the case of two wealthy merchants who knocked on Allen's door inquiring about a fugitive. Allen's wife claimed the fugitive was not in her house, but the two pushed past the woman, searched the house, and came up empty-handed. After Allen's wife told her husband, Allen placed his case before the magistrate rather than send the men to jail. Allen asked that they "ask my pardon, promise not to repeat the offensive conduct, and pay the cost; or, if they prefer to pay to the overseers of the poor in the ward where they live, ten pounds each, I shall be satisfied." They complied and a stunned crowd yelled, "they have begged the Negro's pardon. They have begged the Negro's pardon."[33]

In another part of the same tale, Hopper provides us with further evidence of Richard Allen's position in Philadelphia. Two men, a planter and his two sons, residents of Maryland, rode into the city searching for a black named Dick. As the days rolled on, one of the sons found Dick standing in a doorway next to a window with the name Richard Allen written on it. He asked Allen if his name was Dick, and Allen said yes. The boy ran home and told his father who called a jailer to arrest Allen. He was released after the magistrate saw the case as one of mistaken identity. Allen demanded redress. The magistrate called Hopper, who was "soon on the spot," and he suggested that the "father and the two sons should be committed to prison for a misdemeanor until we could take advice as to the proper manner of procedure." After they paid eight hundred dollars, they finally released the family from the jail, save for the father who was put for several months in debtor's prison. Because Allen felt he had "suffered enough," the planter was released. By all accounts, Richard Allen was the most powerful black man in America.[34] These are just a few reasons why the *Tales of Oppression* should be drawn on.

The *Tales* are far from being flawless. Hopper neglected to mention that Allen himself tracked down black men who left their work sites without permission. On September 8, 1794, he published a runaway advertisement in *Poulson's American Daily Advertiser* offering ten dollars for Robert Rich, a servant who was once a slave to Captain Rich. Hopper also failed to mention that Absalom Jones, Allen's close friend, placed a runaway advertisement in the Philadelphia Gazette on July 23, 1794 describing John Creanes, a black servant man, and offered six dollars for the servant's capture.[35]

One can easily conclude from these *Tales* that the slaves were forever at war, with the planters who, as a class, owned the slaves, the land, the crops, the tools, and the livestock. How could one escape against these odds? According to Isaac Hopper's stories, a successful escape depended on the black's willingness to get away, the planter's disposition, the state, the period in history, the organizational strength of the black community, and its harboring network. It was not a matter of just strolling off the plantation; the right conditions had to be in place. Before the black decided to leave, he had to take stock of the planter's state of mind, especially if he planned to break the news to him about his yearnings to be free. Ben, "born a slave in the family of Frisby Lloyd, of Hartford county, Maryland," made "application to his master, to put a moderate price upon him, and permit him to go to Philadelphia and try to find some person who would pay the amount." An "offended Lloyd" told Ben "if he ever said another word about his freedom, he would sell him to Georgia." To soothe his master, Ben feigned obsequiousness, returned to work and waited for an "opportunity to make his escape." Lloyd feigned forgiveness before trying to sell Ben. Which illusion won out depended on who moved first. Ben escaped before Lloyd could sell him to a speculator.[36]

Some blacks kept the notion of freedom to themselves and remained at work until an opportunity presented itself. Samuel Wilson of Eastern Shore, Maryland asked his master for permission to go fishing and never returned. The master visited Wilson's fishing spot, and seeing an overturned canoe and a hat on the shoreline, thought the slave had drowned, for he published no runaway advertisements in the local newspapers.[37]

Hopper's *Tales* show that what might have worked well for the fugitive black in Maryland and Virginia, and even in Delaware, might have lost its effectiveness for those who lived in Pennsylvania, where freedom seemed to ring everywhere. After several belated attempts in 1778 and 1779, the Pennsylvania legislature passed a bill called the "Act for the Gradual Abolition of Slavery," declaring that all blacks born after March 1, 1780 were free. These newly freed blacks unfortunately saw not complete and unconditional freedom, but another kind of forced labor--twenty-eight years of indentured servitude. Real freedom came to the children of those servants, and the closest year was 1847, some sixteen years before Lincoln published his Emancipation Proclamation. The lawmakers spoke about being able to "extend a portion of that freedom to others, which has been extended to us; is a release from that State of Thraldom, to which we have now every prospect of being delivered," yet the black could not testify against a freeman and could be "corrected" if he ran away.[38]

The Gradual Abolition Act was neither a ploy, nor a play on words, nor another illusion; it warned planters in Pennsylvania, and even those outside the state, that it opposed black enslavement in the far future. This alone angered the planters, who were dead set against any interference in their affairs, especially when the Act demanded that they visit the City Clerk and list their slaves' and servants' names, age and sex, as well as their own names, occupations and residences. They had to comply with the requirement by November 1, 1780, or the enslaved black could take his master to court and sue for his freedom. Congressional officers and diplomats were exempt.[39]

The "sojourning" planter remained in Pennsylvania and made his business deals, visited the local inn, where he could sing and dance, and attend plays, but on the last day of the sixth month of their stay in that state, they had better grease their coach wheels, water their horses, load up their luggage, and make it to the state's borders or face the loss of their slaves. Who knew about these laws? The governmental officials, the local planters, the Pennsylvania Abolition Society, the black community, and the United States federal government. How could they not know when the Act took up the entire front page of the December 23, 1779 *Pennsylvania Packet*. According to Tale LIX, in 1798 Charles Webster of Virginia and his master named A.B. might not have

Introduction 17

known about the law. Looking to escape the Virginia heat, and looking to "enjoy the company and amusements of the city," A.B. and his family rode to Philadelphia--Webster was the coachman--and stayed at the celebrated inn, the Indian Queen. Within a matter of weeks Webster, "in company with a colored man of the place," found Friend Hopper and asked him if he was "not free." The Quaker abolitionist told the coachman that the "law permitted his master to take him away when he pleased, provided he did not remain *six months*.[40]

Webster, who expected his master to know the law, especially the six-month deadline provision, could have run away and asked someone to harbor him, or he could have waited out the entire six months, hoping the planter would forget about the time, or he could have returned to Virginia. Because Webster could be captured and sent further South, Hopper opposed flight. Instead, he counseled Webster to use legal means to obtain his freedom by waiting out the six-month period. After six months and a day the twenty-six year old coachman visited Hopper, and they went to see William Lewis, a noted lawyer and a drafter of the Gradual Abolition Act. Lewis gave Webster a note for A.B., stating that Webster was "free by the laws of Pennsylvania and cautioning him against any attempt to remove him out of the state." After Webster gave his master the note, he never saw him again.[41]

In town for amusement, master Wallace of Virginia and his family expected to relax in Philadelphia and then to return home, but like A.B., Wallace overstayed the six-month limit. When Wallace realized that his coachman Tom enjoyed Philadelphia and would, sooner or later, make an escape attempt, he had him jailed. After the jailkeeper informed Hopper of Tom's plight, Friend Hopper took out a habeas corpus and pressured the judges to give Tom a hearing, a hearing that eventually showed that Wallace violated the Gradual Abolition Act. The court ordered the planter to free Tom.[42]

According to Hopper's narratives, twenty-five percent of the enslaved blacks, before they became free, labored outside Pennsylvania, mostly in Delaware, Maryland and Virginia. Once they got to the Quaker state, they soon discovered that Philadelphia offered far more than the self-contained world of the plantation. Auctions, lotteries, museums, zoos, playhouses, libraries, inns, churches of every denomination, schools--even a black school--could be found in this lively city. It would not take long for the fugitive or the black passing for free to discover, too, that white men were everywhere, that they outnumbered the blacks and had the authority to demand the arrest of any black on suspicion of being a fugitive. In 1780, the white population of Philadelphia numbered 30,900, to 5,100 blacks. By 1800 that number had doubled. By 1849 the number of whites in Philadelphia was 149,000, as compared to 14,554 blacks.[43] It would take one to create havoc.

One of Hopper's themes in the *Tales* centered on the fugitive's fear of detection in any city, especially Philadelphia. If the night seemed full of unknown perils, if every white man looked like a planter in disguise, if the bark of dogs made him jumpy, then the fugitive could forget about peace of mind regardless of any other good fortune he might enjoy. Hopper tells of Manuel of North Carolina, a fugitive who escaped with nothing, and ended up making good money in his chimney business. But however he tried, he could not avoid the curiosity of one white man who once lived next door to his former master. This man eventually "apprehended him and took him to Robert Wharton who was then mayor," but Manuel got off after showing Samuel Curtis' "certificate of freedom." Was Philadelphia a city of refuge, or was it a city of danger? Manuel headed for Boston and remained there until he ran into the same white man. He returned to Philadelphia again to find solace.[44]

What the black fugitive needed was a friend or community support. What better friend to have than Frederick Douglass? What about Arthur Jones of Boston who had to trek to New York to testify on Dixon's whereabouts and successfully swayed the court to support Dixon. William Dixon left Baltimore in 1832; Douglass left in 1837. Dixon's master came close to capturing him; Douglass' master was still on his trail. Dixon told Douglass that the "colored peopled of New York were not to be trusted, that there were hired men of my own color who would betray me for a few dollars." Dixon even seemed to be wary of Douglass.[45]

The fugitive needed food, clothes, shelter, and a job, or he could freeze or starve to death. Rare was the fugitive who could go it alone and shun the harborer's services, white or black, woman or man. Even if the fugitive thought little of the black community, this community could be counted on to rush to his assistance as a matter of principle. Sarah Roach escaped from Delaware and made it to Philadelphia, but left behind, a daughter who escaped some time after. Neither the mother nor the daughter were supposed to be slaves; their owner had sold them to a sojourner who had no intentions of remaining in Delaware. Roach came to Philadelphia, found Sarah's daughter, put her in his boat, and prepared to sail for home without formally notifying the magistrate. Had not "several colored people followed the master and the girl to the vessel," had not the girl's mother found Hopper, and had not Hopper hired a boat and two black men to take him to the vessel, Sarah Roach's child would have been re-enslaved.[46]

Though he knew a great deal about harboring techniques, Isaac Hopper himself shunned the practice, because the planter expected him to know every missing black's whereabouts, or to be harboring the slave himself. "Colored friends" told Doctor Rich's female slave that she was entitled to her freedom because her master had brought her from Maryland to Philadelphia. Hopper said she needed to wait six months before the question of freedom could even be addressed. The woman ran away anyway; minutes later Doctor Rich and his father-in-law, an Episcopal clergyman, led the search for the fugitive's harborer. Tipped off by a black woman, they made their way to a black family's house where they found a "bond-box belonging to the black fugitive." After the doctor threatened them "with prosecution for harboring his fugitive slave," they confessed the fugitive had been there, but then left and went to Hopper's house. Isaac Hopper admitted seeing the fugitive, but denied knowing her whereabouts, though he confessed that he could probably find her. "I believe there were no colored persons in the city who would wish to secrete themselves from me. They all knew I was their friend." The Doctor returned to Hopper's house and claimed, "She is now in your house, and I can prove it, and if you don't let me see her, I will commence a suit against you tomorrow for harboring my slave." He hired guards to watch

Hopper's house day in and day out. Friend Hopper invited them into his house to rest, but they refused. The doctor finally gave up and returned to Maryland.[47]

Who harbored the fugitive? "Joe Hill, a colored man, who had often given shelter to the weary fugitive, protected this stranger, and in a few days he removed her into the country, five or six miles from Philadelphia, where she was employed as a servant in a respectable kind family." For ten years, this woman and her husband enjoyed their lives and certainly had nothing to fear from "Uncle Hill." But one day Hill changed. Angry with a neighbor for suing him, he turned on the blacks; he pointed out the fugitive to a kidnapper who took her to New Orleans, never to be seen again. Because these men existed, the black community had to be on guard against traitors and informers; Hopper himself needed to find reliable harborers, and black fugitives needed to choose their allies carefully.[48]

What was the use of Ben making his way from Hartford country Maryland to Pennsylvania, only to be betrayed? Ben asked a white farmer in Delaware for directions to Pennsylvania. The farmer, a Quaker named Bellerby, discovered that Ben was a fugitive and invited him into his house. There the fugitive remained until he met Peter Barker, a Quaker resident of Philadelphia, and an abolitionist, who offered Ben a job as a servant. Eventually Ben left that job and went to work for Jacob Downing, who was also a Quaker.[49]

Since Quakers played a major role in harboring and employing fugitive blacks, the planter sought to find ways to infiltrate their network. One planter from East Jersey came to Philadelphia in 1827 looking for a woman fugitive and her son. He knew that the woman had two free sons in the city who might be harboring, so he "disguised himself by procuring a suit of plain clothes, such as commonly worn by Friends, and calling upon one of the sons, passed himself off as one of that denomination, pretending great friendship for the mother and expressed a strong desire to see her." The son fell for the trick; the planter told a watchman to watch the house and called the police, but the woman and child managed to escape because a "crowd of colored people" had gathered in front of the house and some held the watchman while the fugitive "took refuge in a house occupied by colored people on Locust Street." The watchman followed them, the planter went to get another search warrant, and Hopper and his 14 year-old son went home and found them hidden in a "closet exceedingly terrified." The son managed to get the mother to go to his father's house and Hopper gave him directions to find sanctuary with a farmer 30 miles from Philadelphia. He returned home and referred the women to a "place of safety."[50]

The best place to be harbored was in the black community because it protected the fugitive and the kidnapped victims. Benjamin Clarke of Virginia had left his master in 1808, and made his way to Middle Alley in Philadelphia, a place "mostly inhabited by colored people." There he met his wife, landed a job sawing wood, and joined the Methodist church. For 10 years he remained at peace. When the constable Richard Hunt came to Clarke's house to arrest him, he showed no remorse because in his eyes Clarke broke the law, the planter's law. Clarke's wife, who saw Hunter as nothing more than a kidnapper, "ran out of the house and screamed, as loud as she could, 'Kidnappers! Kidnappers!'" Her call to arms aroused the sleepy community and by the time Hunt got Clarke out and into the street, the blacks were "prepared for war. They opened their windows, and let fly a general volley of brickbats." Hunt fell to the ground, bruised and cut, and the crowd made it to the streets and provided an opportunity for Clarke to escape. The black community stopped Hunt, but they had more difficulties with Pennsylvania's legal system because they had no black governors, no black senators, no black congressmen, no black justices, no black alderman, no black constables to represent their interests. They turned to the Pennsylvania Abolition Society and men such as Hopper for legal assistance. Clarke went to Hopper for legal help, and the dispute with Hunt was eventually settled in Clarke's favor.[51]

Attention has been devoted to the black community's heroics. In contrast, the white community eyed the treatment of blacks warily and seemed reluctant to voice their disapproval of the kidnapping raids--at least collectively. Friend Hopper credited Thomas Harrison and other individual whites, many of whom were abolitionists anyway, but nowhere in his stories did he pay tribute to the white community. When James Frazier of Maryland shot Reuben Moore, a free black, in the chest for protesting the kidnapping of a black accused of being a fugitive, the white community remained unscrupulously silent, despite the fact the shooting took place not in some sleepy backwoods town, but on Market Street in the heart of Philadelphia in 1799. After serving only three months in prison, Frazier was back in Maryland, probably before Moore's wounds had healed.[52]

Three years later, Frazier returned to Philadelphia with his partner, Joseph Ennells. Both men were bounty hunters who made their money by capturing blacks and returning them to their masters. On the surface it appears that these two men were serving the cause of justice, and anyone including Hopper could not interfere, at least according to the Fugitive Act of 1793. Under this law, Frazier and Ennells had the right to go into any part of the United States and arrest a fugitive and forcibly take him to his master. It did not matter whether it was South Carolina or New York, Virginia or Pennsylvania; as long as the black was a slave he was considered fair game because he was just a piece of property. Planters had the right to their property, and the harborers who tried to hide the fugitive could expect to be fined five hundred dollars. If the Fugitive Act had any merit, it was that it did not sanction the kidnapping of free black men or women or their children just because of their skin color. Before the planter or his agent or his lawyer could force a black to leave a state,he had to go to a judge, circuit or district, or to a county magistrate within the state and testify orally or in writing that the black "owed service of labor" to the planter. It was the judge or magistrate who made the decision about the black's status, not the planter or his agent. Without a certificate of approval, the planter could not take the black anywhere.[53]

According to Hopper's Tale entitled "William Bachelor," Ennells and Frazier seized Bachelor in the heart of Philadelphia, and they looked forward to seeing the judge, for they had brought along Sam, a black overseer who would swear that Bachelor was a fugitive slave from Maryland. If Hopper's narratives tell us anything about kidnapping, they tell us that speed and timing were everything and the bounty hunters knew this all too well. But no one seemed quicker to the draw than Isaac Hopper, because after being informed of Bachelor's seizure, he gave chase and caught Frazier and Ennells near the Schuylkill river. This was indeed a dangerous move, because the captors had no qualms about shooting blacks and unnerving and outfacing the white populace. In fact, Ennells showed Hopper the pistol's barrel and said, "I will blow out your brains if you say another word on the subject, or make an attempt to molest me." Hopper managed to convince the bounty hunters to return to Philadelphia, where Bachelor got another hearing in front of Judge Baker. This time he was able to bring witnesses who convinced the judge that he was a free man. Again, the kidnappers might have been thwarted had the white community expressed outrage, but this called for empathy, sacrifice, and audacity to ward off the kidnapper. It was 1803 before Ennells met Hopper face to face, whereupon he said, "Your name is Hopper, is it?" Friend Hopper said, "Yes it is." Ennells then stated, "I have heard of you; it is time the world was rid of you; you have done too much mischief already." Hopper expressed confusion and asked what he had done. The bounty hunter replied, "You have robbed many people of their slaves." Hopper responded that he was trying to stop "Southern marauders from robbing free people of their liberty."[54]

What manner of man was Friend Hopper? A Hicksite Quaker who believed in the "inner light," Hopper, by all accounts, was a modest and sober man who dressed plainly and who did not smoke, gamble, drink, or chase women. He had been married twice, had ten children, and he supported the family by tayloring. He never talked about politics in the narratives and showed no inclination to run for office. Hopper believed "Quakerism was synonymous with genuine Christianity," that it was a "righteous" religion, and that it would be used to fight oppression. But did the Quakers in New York believe that to be the case?[55]

Not according to the blacks. On September 20, 1837, at a convention of the New York State Anti-Slavery Society in Utica, Reverend Theodore S. Wright, a black clergyman, recalled how he was "taught in childhood to remember the man of the broad-brimmed hat and the drab-colored coat, and to venerate him." The Quakers, he said, "had lifted up their voices against slavery and the slave trade. But, ah! with but here and there a noble exception, they go but half-way. When they come to the grand doctrine, to lay the ax right down at the root of the tree, and to destroy the very spirit of slavery--there they are defective. Their doctrine is to set the slave free, and let him take care of himself." Theodore Wright claimed the Quakers did not readily admit blacks into their church: "We hear nothing about their being brought into the Friends Church or of their being viewed and treated according to their moral worth." He was "happy to see that the Annual Meeting of the Friends Society in the City of New York" had pressed for support of a "doctrine of immediate emancipation. But that very good man who signed the document as the organ of that society within the past year, received a man of color, a Presbyterian minister, entered his house gave him his meals alone in the kitchen, and did not introduce him to his family.[56]

By 1838, Hopper and a few of his associates had concluded that the New York Quakers, headed by George White, opposed the abolition of slavery and criticized the abolitionists and everything they stood for. Friend Hopper and other like-minded Quakers set up an organization called "The New York Association of Friends for the relief of those held in Slavery and the improvement of the Free people of Color." The New York Quakers opposed the new organization and criticized Hopper, his son-in-law, James Gibbons, and Charles Marriott, a Quaker friend, of trying to "disunite the Quakers," and promptly expelled them in 1841. Hopper never talked about the strife within the Friend's Society nor did he make mention of his expulsion in the narratives. In his Tale No. XVI: "Thomas Hughes," "he had ample opportunity to tell his readers why he posed a threat because it was the subject of this narrative that helped expose the divisions in the Quakers.[57] On August 29, 1838, a Louisiana planter named John Darg published an advertisement in the *New York Sun* offering one thousand dollars for a "mulatto about 21 years of age," named Hughes who had apparently taken a large sum of money from him. Having misgivings about taking the money, Hughes raced to Hopper's house for advice and protection only to find the house watched by the police. At Hopper's advice, Hughes found his way to Margaret Shoemaker's house, who harbored him. He then made contact with

Barney Corse, who arranged for Hughes to return Darg's money in return for manumission. Both Corse and Shoemaker were Quaker abolitionists.[58]

Unfortunately, the Quaker overseers opposed Hopper's role in the "Darg" case, claiming he had riled the New York police, provoked the New York Sun, and harbored Thomas Hughes, a slave accused of taking seen or eight thousand dollars (a sum later recovered by Hopper) before escaping from his master, John Darg. The court indicted Friend Hopper, his brother-in-law James Gibbons, and David Ruggles, a black Secretary of the New York Committee of Vigilance, for their role as accomplices to the crime. Hopper reported the Quakers would have disowned him then, but "as I was indicted as an accessory to a larceny after the fact, they forbore out of tenderness to me and my family, less it should prejudice the public mind, and be injurious to me on my trial." "Since the Darg case was pending for several months, the overseers could have taken up the case then" and consequently, "this assertion was false."[59]

The Quakers remained silent throughout the trial, though the district attorney tried to convict Hopper, Ruggles, Gibbons, and a fourth man, Barney Corse. The Quakers refused to speak out though Ruggles spent time in jail, where he "stood up the whole time in an underground hole intended only for animals" and where he virtually lost his sight. They ignored the *Colored American*'s warning that the pro-slavery newspaper editors were trying to "destroy those noble philanthropists." The New York Quakers tried to deal a deathblow to Hopper and everything he stood for. Hopper said of them, that they were "willing and anxious to torture and prevent what it considered one of the best acts of my life into an engine, that would crush me to pieces and blast my moral and religious character forever."[60]

Minister George White pointed out that though Thomas Hughes had been sentenced to two years of hard labor in Sing Sing prison, Hughes still chose to return to slavery with his master, and "endure all the evils of that condition rather than stay with those hypocritical workers of popular righteousness." After Hughes' sentence expired, Hopper told him he was free and promised to "protect him." But Darg brought Hughes' wife to see him at the prison, and told him "if when his time was out he would go South, he would manumit her" and would not "attempt to make a slave of him." Hughes said, "I went with Mr. Darg to get my dear Mary, whom I never expected to see again." He added that Darg had told him, "abolitionists would do nothing for me; and that I should suffer here in the North, but I went with him solely with a hope of seeing Mary." When they reached Baltimore, Darg "had sold his wife, and intended to make a slave of him" whereby Hughes left Darg, and went North.[61]

Who would have thought that the Quakers would embrace John Darg and not Thomas Hughes, that they would expel Hopper, proplanters, or that the Quaker would have walked arm in arm with the police to jail their favorite son. Why was Hopper considered a menace when Darg sold Hughes' wife?[62] Clearly, the *Tales of Oppression* is a rich vein waiting to be mined by an inquiring mind interested in understanding the black community in Philadelphia and New York, and Hopper's role in forging freedom there.

NOTES

1. *Poulson's American Daily Advertiser*, November 6, 1802.

2. Ibid.

3. *National Anti-Slavery Standard* (hereafter *N.A.S.*), December 10, 1840, 106.

4. Lydia Maria Child, *Isaac Hopper: A True Life* (London, 1853), 363; Margaret Brown, *Lamb's Warrior: The Life of Isaac T. Hopper* (New York, 1970) 107. Child noted, "If you could ever be free at a private house you could here at Isaac Hopper's." See Lydia Maria Child *Selected Letters*, 1817-1880, Milton Meltzer and Patricia G. Holland, eds. (Amherst, 1982), 145.

5. *N.A.S.*, June 11, 1840, 2; September 24, 1840, 62; October 22, 1840, 78, 79.

Introduction 27

6. N.A.S., June 17, 1841, 6; Rochester, *Frederick Douglass' Paper* (Rochester), November 11, 1853, *Herald of Freedom*, June 4, 1841.

7. John Blassingame, *Slave Testimony: Two Centuries of Letters, Speeches, Interviews and Autobiographies* (Baton Rouge, 1977); Gary B. Nash, *Forging Freedom: The Formation of Philadelphia's Black Community 1720-1840*, (Cambridge, 1988); Gary B. Nash and Jean R. Soderlund, *Freedom by Degrees: Emancipation in Pennsylvania and its Aftermath* (New York, 1991), 131-132; Child, *Isaac Hopper*, v, vi.

8. August Meier and Elliott Rudwick, *Black History and the Historical Profession, 1915-1980* (Chicago, 1986), 4-6; C. Vann Woodward, "History from Slave Sources" in *The Slave's Narrative*, Charles T. Davis and Henry Louis Gates, Jr., eds. (New York, 1985), 48-58.

9. N.A.S., November 6, 1802, 114.

10. Bacon, *Lamb's Warrior: The Life of Isaac Hopper*, 1-20. For a "Critical Essay on Sources," see John Blassingame's *The Slave Community* (New York, 1979), 367-382; for a careful account of kidnapping in Philadelphia, see Julie Winch, "Philadelphia and the Other Underground Railroad," *Pennsylvania Magazine of History and Biography*, 111 (1987), 6,7.

11. Davis and Gates, *Slave Narratives*, XI, XII.

12. N.A.S., October 22, 1840, 78.

13. N.A.S., June 23, 1842, 10; November 3, 1842, 66.

14. *Poulson's American Daily Advertiser*, November 21, 1801; N.A.S., February 11, 1841, 142.

15. N.A.S., December 10, 1840, 106.

16. *Poulson's American Daily Advertiser*, August 4, 1807; *N.A.S.*, February 16, 1843, 146.

17. *N.A.S.*, May 23, 1844, 154; Frederick Douglass, *Life and Times of Frederick Douglass/Written by Himself; His Early Life as a Slave, His Escape from Bondage, and His Complete History to the Present Time*; With an Introduction by George L. Ruffin (New York, 1881, 1962), 203-204.

18. *City Archives of Philadelphia*, Record Series 202, Common Plea Court Appearances. Pocket March 1810, Case No. 20, *N.A.S.*, September 22, 1842, 62.

19. Acting Committee: Papers relating to slaves purchased and manumitted, by M.C. Cope, Thomas Harrison, and Isaac T. Hopper; *Pennsylvania Abolitionist Society Papers*, Reel 22; *N.A.S.*, January 7, 1841, 122-123.

20. *The Papers of the Pennsylvania Abolition Society*, Acting Committee Minutes (1798-1810, 1810-1822), Vols. 3 4, Rec. 14, 5; (1798-1810), Reel 5.

21. See *A Guide to the Microfilm Publication of the Papers of the Pennsylvania Abolition Society of Pennsylvania*, Jeffrey Nordlinger Bumbrey, ed. (Phil., 1976).

22. Kenneth Stampp, *The Peculiar Institution* (New York, 1956), 88.

23. *N.A.S.*, December 27, 1842, 118.

24. Ibid.

25. *N.A.S.*, December 27, 1842, 118.

26. Eugene Genovese, *Roll Jordan Roll: The World the Slaves Made* (New York, 1974), 675-677; Blassingame, *Slave Community*, 367-368.

27. *Philadelphia Gazette*, November 11, 1801.

28. *N.A.S.*, September 22, 1842, 62.

29. *Poulson's American Daily Advertiser*, August 2, 1800; *N.A.S.*, November 25, 1841, 98.

30. *N.A.S.*, Nov. 25, 1841, 98.

31. *N.A.S.*, December 31, 1840, 118; Allen is described as a shoe dealer in *The Philadelphia Directory for 1800*, 13.

32. *N.A.S.*, December 31, 1840, 118; *Philadelphia Gazette*, March 8, 1794; Charles H. Wesley, *Richard Allen* (Washington, D.C., 1935), 59-68; Leon F. Litwack, *North of Slavery: The Free Negro in the United States, 1790-1860* (Chicago, 1961), 13-17.

33. *N.A.S.*, December 31, 1840, 118; *Philadelphia Gazette*, March 8, 1794.

34. *N.A.S.*, December 31, 1840, 118.

35. *Poulson's American Daily Advertiser*, September 8, 1794; *Philadelphia Gazette*, July 23, 1794.

36. *N.A.S.*, August 19, 1842, 42.

37. *N.A.S.*, August 5, 1841, 34.

38. Nash, *Forging Freedom*, 60-65, 91-94; *Pennsylvania Packet*, December 23, 1779; Arthur Zilversmit, *The First Emancipation: The Abolition of Slavery in the North* (Chicago, 1967), 126-138, 212-214.

39. Ibid.

40. *N.A.S.*, July 14, 1842, 22; *Pennsylvania Packet*, December 23, 1779.

41. *N.A.S.*, July 14, 1842, 22.

42. *N.A.S.*, February 29, 1844, 154.

43. Nash, *Forging Freedom*, 135-137, 143.

44. Nash, *Forging Freedom*; *N.A.S.*, January 7, 1841, 122-123.

45. Frederick Douglass, *Life and Times*, 203-204.

46. *N.A.S.*, June 10, 1841, 2.

47. *N.A.S.*, July 8, 1841, 18.

48. Ibid.

49. *N.A.S.*, August 19, 1841, 42.

50. *N.A.S.*, November 4, 1841, 86.

51. *N.A.S.*, February 24, 1842, 150.

52. *N.A.S.*, May 6, 1841, 190.

53. Stanley W. Campbell, *The Slave Catchers: Enforcement of the Fugitive Slave Law, 1850-1860* (New York, 1970) 7-9; See Thomas P. Morris, *Free Men All: The Personal Liberty Laws of the North, 1780-1861* (Balt. 1971) 19-21; William M. Wiecek, *The Sources of Antislavery Constitutionalism in America, 1760-1848* (Ithaca, 1977), 97-100.

54. *N.A.S.*, May 6, 1841, 190.

55. Child, *Life of Isaac Hopper*, 325-333; *N.A.S.*, June 24, 1841, 11.

56. Herbert Aptheker, *A Documentary History of the Negro People in the United States* (4 vols., New York, 1951-1973), I, 169-173; Benjamin Quarles, *Black Abolitionists* (New York, 1969), 46-47;

Introduction 31

See Thomas E. Drake, *Quakers and Slavery in America* (New Haven, 1950).

57. *N.A.S.*, March 25, 1841, 166; *New York Journal of Commerce*, August 18, 1835.

58. *New York Sun*, August 29, 1838; *N.A.S.*, March 25, 1841, 166.

59. *New York Sun*, August 29, 1838; *N.A.S.*, March 25, 1841, 166.

60. Herbert Aptheker, "The Quakers and Negro Slavery," *Journal of Negro History*, 25 (July, 1940), 331-362; Darold D. Wax, "Quaker Merchants and the Slave Trade in Colonial Pennsylvania," *Pennsylvania Magazine of History and Biography*, 86 (1962), 143-159.; *Narrative of the Proceedings*, 30-31; Child, *Isaac Hopper*, 50; *The Colored American*, September 15, 1838; *N.A.S.*, March 25, 1841, 167; Dorothy Porter, "David M. Ruggles, An Apostle For Human Rights," *Journal of Negro History*, 28 (1943), 23-50.

61. *Narrative of the Proceedings*, 30-31; *N.A.S.*, March 25, 1841, 166; September 2, 1841, 50.

62. *N.A.S.*, August 12, 1841, 38.

No I.
Haitian Slave[1]

Respected Friend:--I have thought that the readers of the Standard would be interested with facts, from authentic sources, relating to the suffering of the slaves and their efforts to escape from their fetters; and having a great abundance of such facts in my possession, I have concluded to offer them for publication to your columns. I begin with the following narrative, which I procured from the lips of a fugitive:

"I was born a slave, in Cape Francois. My mother belonged to a Mr. Leigh, and I remained in his family until I was about 12 or 14 years old. When I was about 8 or 10 years old, my master burnt on my breast, with oil of vitriol, the letters W.L. When he first applied the vitriol, I wiped it off, but as soon as he discovered that I had done so, he tied my hands behind my back and again applied the vitriol, which made the letters above-mentioned, and which yet remain on my breast. My master died and left my mistress a widow with six children, two of whom were not more than six or seven years old. A captain of a vessel, who lived in Philadelphia and traded to Cape Francois, brought his wife with him to the Cape, and she and my mistress became very intimate, and my mistress concluded to go with them to Philadelphia. She accordingly went on board the vessel, and took me and a boy that she held as a slave, with her. In the afternoon of the day that we sailed from Cape Francois, we were hailed by an English privateer, who passed between our ship and the shore, and kept behind us until we got out of sight of land, when he came alongside our ship and boarded us. We became very much frightened, thinking it probable he would not only rob us, but murder us also; but they offered us no personal harm. My mistress gave her money to the captain of our ship, for safe keeping, and by that means saved it, as the privateer did not take any thing that belonged to him, but took all he could find that belonged to the French passengers. After staying with us till the next day after they captured us, they left our ship, and took me and two other colored people, who were slaves, with them to Bermuda; but, before they reached the ___, they fell in with two other vessels, which they also plundered. Some days after we arrived at Bermuda, they divided the plunder, and I was given to Thomas Hutchins, one of the officers of the privateer. I lived with him about a year in Bermuda, and was treated kindly, particularly by my master, who endeavored to seduce me from the path of virtue. Failing to accomplish his object by persuasion, he attempted to coerce me to comply with his wishes; but he did not succeed, and I informed my mistress. This greatly enraged him, and he sold me to Capt. Salter, who lived in South Carolina, and he took me home with him. I remained with him about a month, when he sold me to James Stone, who had married a widow Dobson. In about three years after James Stone bought me, he died. I lived with his widow about a year after his death, when she also died. I then fell into the possession of her daughter, Betsey Dobson, and I lived with her several years, when she married Samuel Read, who died about four years ago. He had a son Samuel, a doctor, who married a Miss Brett, of Boston, and my old mistress Read lived with them. The doctor and his wife treated me kindly, when I was in the family taking care of their children; but I found very different usage when at work in the fields, and my old mistress was very severe. I was obliged every night to rub her feet, and sometimes being weary with the labors of the day, I could not remain from nodding, when she would kick me with great force in the breast. I was often whipped very severely, because I could not accomplish my task in the field, and my skin now bears evidence of it from my neck to my ancles."

"About six or seven weeks ago, my master went with his family to Philadelphia, and stayed there about three weeks, and then went to Bristol, about 20 miles north of that city, where he remained near two weeks. As the weather began to get cool, my master concluded to return home to South Carolina, and began to make preparations for the journey. I had not been long in Philadelphia before I made up my mind never to return to Carolina, if I could possibly avoid it; and on the evening of the 8th instant I left

Bristol, hoping to find some friend who would afford me protection from the wrongs I had suffered for more than fifty years, and I was not disappointed. I have had eight children, six of whom are dead; the other two are slaves, and I expect will remain so as long as they live. I have sometimes heard the slaves talk of rising upon their oppressors and obtaining their liberty by violence, and I am inclined to think they would make the attempt, if it was not that they believe such a procedure would be inconsistent with the spirit of the gospel."

I saw the individual who gave the foregoing relation, which I penned from her own lips. I spent more than an hour in her company, as she was on her way to *the land of the free,* and where she has doubtless arrived before now. The letters on her breast, which are about an inch and a half long, and the scars on her back, &c., bear ocular testimony to the truth of her narrative. The former I have seen, and the latter were examined by a respectable female. New York, 10th mo. 21st, 1840.

NOTES

1. *National Anti-Slavery Standard*, October 22, 1840, 78. (Hereafter cited as *N.A.S.*)

No. II.
Peter Johnson[1]

In the summer of 1811, a man by the name of T.I. Moses came to Philadelphia, took lodgings in Cherry, near Eighth street, and hired a colored boy, by the name of Peter Reuben Francis Johnson, to wait upon him. After the boy had been with him a few days, he proposed going to Jersey to get cherries, and asked the lad to accompany him, to which he readily assented, and they proceeded together to Market street wharf, and went on board the New castle packet-boat. He directed the lad to go into the cabin, and remain there till he was ready to start for Jersey. The boy did so, and after the lapse of perhaps an hour, he became uneasy, and went on deck to see what had become of his master. To his astonishment, he found that the boat had sailed and was then several miles down the river; and before the evening of the next day, they reached the city of Baltimore! There Moses sold the boy to a man by the name of J. Roach. The landlord of the hotel where they put up, observing the child crying, and appearing in great distress, inquired of him the cause of his grief; and upon being informed immediately sent for Elisha Tyson,[2] whose character for benevolence was well known in Baltimore. E.T. lost no time, but promptly proceeded to the inn, and upon investigating the circumstances in relation to the lad, became satisfied that he had been kidnapped. He took measures to have him secured, and addressed the following letter to me at Philadelphia

Baltimore 6 Mo 27th, 1811
Isaac T. Hopper.
Esteemed Friend--I have taken the liberty to ask thy assistance in detecting a monster of a man, by the name

of T.I. Moses, who, it appears, a few days past hired a mulatto boy, by the name of Peter Robin Francis Johnson, about nine years old, from his mother in your city. She formerly lived with Benjamin Chew as a cook. Her name was formerly Isabella Douglass, but is now Stephens, and at present lives with her mother in Middle Alley, Sixth street, and follows sewing for a livelihood.

Immediately on the fellow's arrival here, he lost no time in selling the boy to one of the dealers in human flesh, for two hundred and fifty dollars. But, fortunately for the boy, he was accidentally secured from being made a slave for life, and is now here safe, of which I wish thee to inform his mother. The fellow has made his escape.

I wish some person or document to be sent on here, sufficient to identify the boy, so that he may return to his mother and friends again.
ELISHA TYSON

The foregoing letter was laid before the acting committee of the Abolition Society. I was well acquainted with the boy and his mother, and found no difficulty in procuring the necessary documents to identify him and establish his freedom. They were forwarded to Baltimore, and he was liberated and sent to Philadelphia.

In the tenth month following, T.I Moses made his appearance in Philadelphia, and was soon recognized as the person who had kidnapped P.R.F Johnson. He was arrested and committed to prison for the offence. A letter was addressed to E. Tyson, requesting him to inform the committee what evidence could be had to prove the sale of the boy by Moses. An answer was received, in which stated that the boy had been sold to J. Roach, and that he (Roach) was willing to come to Philadelphia and testify to the fact, if his expenses were paid. The committee agree to pay his expenses; but, as it afterwards appeared, he is an accomplice in the transaction, and did not come to Philadelphia according to his promise. However, testimony sufficient was procured, and Moses was convicted of kidnapping the boy in the same month that he was committed to prison, and the court sentenced him to pay a fine of ___ hundred pounds to the overseers of the poor, and be imprisoned at hard labor in the Penitentiary in the city of Philadelphia for one year; this being the utmost extent of the punishment prescribed by the law.

Roach was a systematic kidnapper. In the summer of 1812, he decoyed four colored men from Philadelphia to Baltimore, and delivered them to Henry Bruvington, who sold them to a speculator in slaves, for twelve hundred dollars. But before the purchaser paid the money, the men alleging that they were free, Elisha Tyson interfered and had them taken before Judge Scott. Bruvington and Roach were examined separately, and differed widely in their account respecting the alleged slaves; whereupon the judge committed the colored men to prison for safe keeping, until their real situation could be ascertained, and Roach was committed for kidnapping. Thomas Canby of Philadelphia went to Baltimore, and testified to the freedom of the men, and they were set at liberty. Three of those belonged to Philadelphia, and one to the State of Delaware. Roach voluntarily offered to turn state's evidence, disclose the whole affair, and give the names of his accomplices; for several persons were concerned in this business; but, by some means, they all escaped and were not arrested.

NOTES

1. *N.A.S.*, October 29, 1840, 82.; *The Papers of the Pennsylvania Abolition Society*, loose. Correspondence, incoming: (1796-1819), Reel 12, June 24, 1811. (Hereafter cited as *P.P.A.S.*); See Acting Committee Meeting Book Vol. 4 (1810-1822) 37. Reel 5.

2. A member of the Maryland Abolitionist Society, a key figure in the Acting Committee, and Quaker, Tyson played a major role in assisting the black fugitive, John Tyson. *Life of Elisha Tyson the Philanthropist* (Baltimore, 1825).

No. III.
A Child Kidnapped[1]

In England, where their laws are probably more extensive than in any other country, they are still without one to punish the inhuman and unnatural crime of stealing children. Of this, some years ago, we had authentic information, deduced from the trial of a woman who had stolen a child, and who could only be prosecuted for stealing clothes! It was never supposed a human being could find sufficient inducement to plunder a parent of his offspring, and therefore, no provision was made to punish so monstrous a crime. In this country, however, nay, in the city of Philadelphia, and in this city also, we have witnessed, with regret, instances of this nature, which stamp with indelible disgrace the authors, and indeed reflect discredit on the community. One of these instances I shall give an account of; and I trust no person, because the child was black, will conceive the crime less infamous. Parental feelings are not acquired; they are natural, and therefore, no doubt, as poignant in the breast of a black, as a white mother.

Some time in the 3rd month, 1801, a certain Capt. Dana had engaged his passage in a schooner, then in the port of Philadelphia, bound to Charleston, South Carolina. On the day he expected to sail, he went to the house of a colored woman, who had a son about nine or ten years old, and with the most deceitful and false professions of regard for the child, and of a wish to serve the mother, told her that he had lately had a suit of clothes made for his son, but that they were too small for him, and that, if she would permit him to take the lad home, he would make them a present to him. Upon saying this, he gave the child a piece of ginger-bread, took him by the hand, threw his cloak about him and left the house. He went immediately with the lad on board the schooner, in which he had taken his passage, and which then lay in the stream. Here he left the child under the care of the captain, and said he would come on board as the vessel was on her way down the river.

Is there a parent in the United States, who would not commiserate the situation of the woman, who was thus bereft of her only child? Is there one who, after this circumstance, would require additional proof of this sinful inhumanity of a system, which, by holding out a prospect of gain, has thus, and will still, excite unprincipled men to the commission of deeds which humanity shudders to contemplate?

This circumstance acquires additional aggravation from the fact, that the perpetrator was himself the father of several children. He, however, stifled the voice of nature, and relinquishing himself to the dominion of avarice, was rendered callous to the misery he inflicted on the unfortunate mother.

The schooner lay in the stream, opposite Walnut street, when the child was put on board; but about the time she was ready to sail, a severe storm commenced, and the wind blew with such violence, that she dragged her anchor, and hauled to at Gurling's wharf, near the Swedes' church, in the district of Southwark. Joshua Humphreys, a respectable inhabitant of that neighborhood, was standing on the wharf at the time, and hearing the child cry, inquired of the cook, a colored man, what child that was, and why it was crying. He was informed that it was a child the Captain Dana, a passenger, had brought on board, and *the child* said that Dana had stole him from his mother. This information was conveyed in a note, signed "A Citizen," to Thomas Harrison, whose active zeal on behalf of the oppressed, was exceeded by none in the United States. Thomas Harrison was unwell, and sent the note to my house. I had gone to a meeting, and stopping to see a friend on my way home, did not get the note till after 10 o'clock at night. I immediately called upon Samuel Smith, who readily accompanied me; and taking George Gass,[2] a constable, with us, we proceeded to the schooner. Upon arriving there, we called up the captain, who had retired to bed, and inquired for the boy. He assured us that there was no person on board but himself, telling us all the hands had gone on shore. We called for a light, and he produced a lantern. We then asked the captain to open the forecastle and let us see if there was no person there. This he peremptorily

A Child Kidnapped

refused to do, alleging that his positive declaration ought to satisfy us. I saw an axe lying on the deck, and taking it up, told him, if he did not instantly open the door, I would do it. Finding resistance useless, he unlocked the forecastle, and there we found the cook and the boy! We requested them to follow us, and told the captain that he must also go with us, to which, after much hesitation, he assented. In the midst of the rain, we went to the Mayor's. There were at that time no lamps in Southwark, and it was extremely dark. Sometimes we were stumbling over cellar doors, and at other times, we were nearly knee-deep in the gutters. At length, we arrived at the Mayor's, John Inskeep's, who then lived on the west side of Front street, a few doors above Mulberry street. We rang the bell, and a servant soon came to the door. I requested him to inform the Mayor, that Isaac T. Hopper wished to speak with him at his chamber door. I was accordingly invited upstairs, and found him wrapped up in his cloak. After apologizing for disturbing him at that unseasonable hour, (it being after 12 o'clock,) I briefly stated the case, and told him, that we merely wanted his verbal order to put the captain and cook in prison till morning, when they should be brought before him. He replied "It is a matter of too much importance to be disposed of in that way. I will come down and hear the case." He then ordered the servant to invite us into the parlor, where we found a large hickory log embedded in ashes, which, being removed, we had a good fire-- and a great comfort it was, for we were wet and cold.

The Mayor, on entering his parlor, was surprised to find in the person of Captain Watson, the prisoner, an old acquaintance, and expressed his regret at seeing him under such disagreeable circumstances. He was also acquainted with the owner of the vessel. The captain was required to enter into recognizance to the sum of $3,000 and to appear at his office the next morning at 9 o'clock. The cook was committed to prison, as a witness, and the lad was placed under my care, with directions to have him at the office at 9 o'clock.

The next morning I sent to the boy's mother, to let her know her lost son was safe; but she had gone in search of him, and was not to be found. As I was on the way, however, to the Mayor's office, we met her in the street. Upon seeing her child, she cried out aloud, "My son, my son, I thought you were lost forever," and immediately embraced him in her arms and kissed him. The scene was most affecting. Upon arriving at the office, the captain of the vessel said that Capt. Dana had brought the boy on board, but strongly denied that *he* had any knowledge of their being anything wrong in the business. The Mayor, after hearing his account of the matter, ordered him to enter into heavy recognizance to appear at the next Mayor's court, to answer the charge of kidnapping. The captain now became greatly alarmed, and in order to extricate himself from so serious a charge, informed the Mayor that Dana had gone into Jersey, and was to come on board his vessel as she was going down the river; and that, if an officer was put on board, he could apprehend him. George Gass, a constable, was employed for the purpose. When about three miles below the city, opposite Gloucester Point, she cast anchor, and after waiting about two hours, Dana was seen coming from the Jersey shore in a small boat. As soon as he came on board, the officer arrested him and took him to my house in Philadelphia, which he entered in a great passion, and rudely inquired of me what all this meant; protesting his innocence, and threatening vengeance against those who had caused his detention. I inquired of him if he had a family, and he informed me that he had a wife and several children. Although I had but little sympathy for the man, I felt most keenly for his family, and was almost ready to wish he had escaped. It was about 4 o'clock, P.M. when he was brought to my house, and the Mayor's office was then closed. Dana was, therefore, lodged in jail till the next morning, when he was arraigned before that magistrate. Being aware that my presence was not necessary, I did not attend, apprehending his wife would probably be present, and I did not wish to witness her distress. She, however, did not attend. Dana, finding his case desperate, made a full confession, and offered his poverty as an excuse. He was a man of education, and had sustained a fair reputation. He was required to enter into recognizance in the sum of fifteen hundred dollars, and to find two sureties in the like sum. James Brown and Joseph Wildes became his bail, and he was liberated. Not appearing at court, his recognizance was forfeited, and suits were instituted against Brown and Wildes, and judgments obtained for fifteen hundred dollars,

A Child Kidnapped 45

but were never enforced.

A considerable part of the foregoing narrative is taken from a pamphlet entitled, "Reflections on Slavery," &c. by Humanitas, published in Philadelphia, in 1803. It was written from notes furnished by myself.

NOTES

1. *N.A.S.*, November 5, 1840, 86.

2. George Gass was a constable. *Philadelphia Directory (1800)*, 5. (Hereafter cited as *P.D.*)

No. IV.
Cyrus Field[1]

Cyrus Field, and Alice his wife, resided in the lower part of Philadelphia. He followed sawing wood, and she went out to wash; and being very expert at the business, she always had as much as she could do. For several years, she was employed one day in the week in my family. She was a sprightly, tidy person, and much esteemed by all who employed her. Cyrus was also industrious, and by their united industry and frugality, they had things comfortable about them. Their house was neatly, but not extravagantly furnished, and there were few, if any, who seemed to enjoy the comforts of life to a greater extent than they did. In the autumn of 1816, they laid in a good store of provision and fuel for the winter, as was their custom, and were as independent in their circumstances as the Governor of the State. I have often heard her recount their numerous blessings with a grateful heart. But in an instant, when they least expected it, all their hopes were forever blasted, as regarded their earthly comforts.

Cyrus, at the time above referred to, had his saw sharpened, and the person who did it brought it home. Not having the change to pay for it, Cyrus stepped out to get a bank note changed, and requested the man to wait until he should return; but he never returned to his home and the bosom of his wife again! It was a final separation! His wife became greatly distressed and alarmed at his absence, and the next day she called to consult with me as to the best course to pursue in the case. After waiting a day or two, I made a summary statement of the case, and advised her to take it to the editor of one of the daily papers, and ask him to give it one or two insertions. Alice said Cyrus always spent his evenings at home, and she was sure something very extraordinary must have happened.

Not many days had elapsed before it was announced in one of

the daily papers, that a colored man had been found dead on the Haverford road about seven miles west from Philadelphia. Upon seeing this account, I advised Alice to go there and have the man disinterred, and see whether she could recognize in him her husband. She went accordingly, without delay, but returned the same day, with information that they would not permit her to have him taken up! I then wrote a few lines to a magistrate, who lived in the neighborhood where he was interred, remonstrating with him upon the impropriety of their conduct in refusing to permit Alice to satisfy herself upon a matter that so deeply interested her. After the reception of this letter, the grave was ordered to be opened when her worst apprehensions were awfully and painfully realized. The dead man was ascertained to be Cyrus Field. Upon examining his person, it was discovered that his wrists had been so tightly bound with cords that his skin was cut. No doubt now remained that he had been decoyed out of the city, under some plausible pretense, and there seized and bound, in order to take him to the South and sell him as a slave. It is supposed that he resisted, and in consequence received a blow which terminated his existence. Alice possessed keen sensibility, and was for some weeks so depressed that she was incapable of attending to any kind of business; but, after some time, she recovered and lived several years in the capacity of a domestic, in the family of James Abercrombie,[2] a well known Episcopal minister in Philadelphia.

NOTES

1.   *N.A.S.*, November 12, 1840, 90.

2. James Abercrombie (1758-1841) was a prominent minister who headed the American Protestant Episcopal Church in Philadelphia; Henry Simpson, *The Lives of Eminent Philadelphians Now Deceased Collected From Original Sources* (Philadelphia, 1859), 2.

No. V.
Peter[1]

About the year 1809, a colored man, by the name of Peter, and a slave for life, went to the city of Philadelphia, with permission, in writing, from his mistress, who resided in Newcastle county, in the State of Delaware. This paper stated, that the price of Peter was two hundred dollars. He had been in Philadelphia but a short time, when he found a person, John Miller, jr.,[2] who agreed to pay the amount demanded, and take an indenture upon him for a few years; but when the money was about to be paid, Joseph Taggart, the agent of the mistress, declined receiving it, saying that she had given directions that he should return home. John Miller was a respectable merchant, and a man of humanity and benevolence, and he concluded to make an effort to compel the mistress to carry into effect the agreement she had voluntarily made with Peter, not so much with an eye to his own interest, as from a desire that Peter might get his liberty. He called upon me, and exhibited the paper given to Peter by his mistress. He also informed me of what had occurred between him and the agent. I became convinced that Peter could not be removed to Delaware without his consent, for the reasons mentioned in the letter published below, from Miers Fisher.[3]

John Miller placed two hundred dollars in my hands, with which I proceeded to the counting-house of the agent. I was kindly received, but was informed by him that all attempts to negotiate respecting Peter were useless, as he had positive directions to send him home, and that he should act accordingly. Finding remonstrance of no avail, I gave him to understand, that if he attempted to have Peter arrested, I should defend him. After tendering him two hundred dollars, I withdrew, and returned home. This occurred in the afternoon, a short time before sunset.

About 9 o'clock the same evening, I was informed that Peter had been taken into custody, and was then on his way to Alderman Hillegas,[4] in charge of an officer. I went immediately there. The case was so plain, that I did not anticipate any difficulty; but John Miller had gone out of town, and I was not prepared to prove the authenticity of the document purporting to be a permit from the mistress, for Peter to go to Philadelphia; and I found the magistrate disposed to make short work of the business, by surrendering him to be taken to Delaware. This decision I strongly protested against, believing it to be palpably illegal and oppressive. After much hesitation, the magistrate said he would adjourn the further hearing of the case until next morning at 5 o'clock, and unless the witnesses were then produced, he would surrender Peter to the agent. He was informed that no benefit to Peter could be expected from such a postponement, as it would be impossible to procure the attendance of witnesses at so early an hour. Peter was then sent to prison, and the parties left the office.

Miers Fisher was an attorney, though he did not practice as a lawyer; but being an old acquaintance of Alderman Hillegas, and highly respectable, and possessed of considerable influence in the community, I determined to call upon him for advice, and to endeavor to enlist his influence in favor of Peter. After stating the case, he wrote the letter which will be found below, and gave it to me to deliver. At 5 o'clock, I went to the magistrate's office and gave it to him. After reading it, he threw it upon his table and exclaimed, "I would rather have found five hundred dollars than had any thing to do with this business." I observed, "There is a very easy way by which thou mayest get rid of it. Commit the man, and give us an opportunity to take out a habeas corpus." After some hesitation, he acceded to this proposition, and accordingly remanded Peter to prison.

I immediately applied to John Inskeep,[5] one of the judges of the court of Common Pleas, for a Habeas Corpus, and having procured it, I left it with the keeper of the prison. It had been customary to get the writ, and leave it with the keeper of the prison, and when he appeared with the prisoner before the judge, procure his signature to be affixed to it. This mode saved some trouble. But, in this instance, it had like to proved fatal to Peter's liberty; for the counsel of the agent called at the jail, and upon discovering that the writ was not signed by Judge Inskeep, he made application to Thomas Smith,[6] one of the Associate Judges of the Supreme Court, who issued a Habeas Corpus, and had the prisoner taken before him. The keeper produced the writ issued by Judge Inskeep, but Judge Smith pronounced it void, because it was not signed by that magistrate, and proceeded to hear the case; and no one being present to defend Peter, he was delivered over to the agent. This occurred while I was gone to a meeting, and as soon as the meeting broke up, I found a person waiting at the door who informed me of what had been done. I was also informed that Peter had been put on board the Newcastle packet, and was then, probably, on his way down the river. I lost no time in calling upon the Judge, stated the case, and suggested to him that I thought he had been too precipitate. He then gave me an order for re-hearing; but on going to the wharf, I found the boat had sailed. Without delay, I mounted a horse, and proceeded to Greenwich Point, about three miles below the city, and arrived there just in time for the boat, which I saw slowly sailing down the river. I hired a man, who lived at the Point, to put me on board, which being done, I exhibited the order for a re-hearing, and the Captain, under whose care Peter was placed, ordered him to be put on shore, and I proceeded with him to Judge Smith, who lived in High street, near Twelfth. After hearing the case, and all the circumstances being laid before him, Peter was set at liberty; but not being disposed to take any undue advantage of his mistress, he nobly and magnanimously went directly to John Miller, jr., and indented himself for the time of five years; at the expiration of which he was to be free. It is not possible for those who have not witnessed it, to conceive how rejoiced the slaves are, when they find a limit is fixed to their bondage; and I have often felt the most exquisite gratification in being instrumental in promoting such an object. By permission of the Alderman, I took possession of the letter of Miers Fisher, and now have it in my possession. It is without date, as follows:

RESPECTED FRIEND:—
I am called on at the hour when I usually retire to rest,

to hear a case to which, if I did not give to it what attention is in my power, I could scarcely expect to enjoy the comfort of a sleeping pillow.

It is stated to me, that a negro man of the name of Peter has been committed to jail, by the mittimus, this afternoon, as a runaway slave, from Newcastle County; that the Widow of _____ Grantham, Esq. of Newcastle County, (a gentleman long well known to me,) was his mistress; that she had given Peter a note in writing, mentioning that his price was two hundred dollars, with permission, for him to seek a master; that, under this permission, he came to this city, and has found a master willing to give the price set on him by his mistress, and to relieve him from slavery by a short, temporary servitude. This note in writing is stated to me by two witnesses, under their hands, (Wm. J. Miller and John Miller, jun., both gentlemen of character,) to be of the proper hand writing of the mistress; and Isaac T. Hopper informs me, that the sum of two hundred dollars has been tendered to the agent of the widow. Under these circumstances, there can be no manner of doubt of the right of Peter to his freedom, (perhaps even without payment of the money,) for by his coming into Pennsylvania, with permissions of his mistress and *not as a fugitive,* he becomes immediately free, unless he accompanies his master as a sojourner for six months only. This, however, will not be insisted on, if her agent is willing to accept the money which the bearer, Isaac T. Hopper, assures me he will pay him.

But the object of this letter is, to inform thee, that it is represented to me, that thou hast informed the bearer, that thou wilt grant a permission to the Agent of the widow to take this man out of the State, unless witnesses are produced, before five o'clock to-morrow morning, to authenticate the facts above stated. From my long acquaintance with thee, and thy general character, I can scarcely believe it possible, that a magistrate could exercise so peremptory, so arbitrary a power, to anticipate the usual hours of business, and prevent the benefit of the writ of Habeas Corpus in favor of Peter's liberty. I say I cannot believe this to be true of a man I have so long known, and hope that nothing more will be heard on the subject. Should I, however, from prejudice in thy favor, be mistaken in the conduct thou shalt pursue on this occasion, I shall lament the declension of the magisterial character in my native city and State.

Thy respectful friend,
MIERS FISHER
Michael Hillegas, Esquire

NOTES

1. *N.A.S.*, November 26, 1840, 98.

2. John Miller was a merchant. 1805 *P.D.*, 3.

3. Miers Fisher (1748-1819), a Quaker, a lawyer, was a city council member in Philadelphia from 1789-1791 and a member of the House of Representatives in 1791. Fisher spent the remainder of his life in the business world; he was the Director of the Bank of North America and of the Insurance Company of Pennsylvania. Simpson, *Lives of Eminent Philadelphians*, 359.

4. Alderman Michael Hillegas (1729-1804) was a member of the Provincial Assembly in Pennsylvania from 1765 to 1775, treasurer of the Continental Congress in 1776, and an alderman in Philadelphia during 1793-1804. *Who Was Who in America: Historical Volume 1607-1896* (Chicago, 1963, 1967), 252.

5. John Inskeep was a president of the North American Insurance Company, *Pennsylvania Trade Directory*, (1809) 29.

6. Thomas Smith was born in Scotland in 1745 and attended the University of Edinburgh (Scotland). He migrated to America in 1769 and earned a law degree in 1772. He became a member of the House of Representatives in Pennsylvania during 1776-1780, a Continental Congress member between 1780-1782, and a Supreme Court Judge during 1794 and 1809. He died three years later. *Who Was Who in America*, I, 493.

No. VI.
Kidnapped Into Slavery[1]

In the early part of 11th mo. 1802, John Folwell,[2] merchant of Philadelphia, was riding into that city from his country place, and when near Gray's Ferry, he met a close carriage with five colored persons in it, driven by a white man. It was certainly a novelty to see a carriage with a white driver, while those inside were colored; and upon getting into the city, he called upon me and expressed his apprehensions that there was something wrong in the business, and proposed that we should pursue them, and endeavor to ascertain what were the real circumstances of the case. Not many minutes elapsed after he called upon me, before we were in pursuit of them. In less than half an hour, we arrived at the Blue Bell tavern, on the road to Baltimore, where we found the black men, with the driver, seated at the dinner table. We inquired where they had come from, and where they were going. The driver, with perfect composure, informed us that the colored people were from the West Indies; and, in New-York, had entered into articles of agreement with A.G. Hammond, to live with him in Baltimore, for the term of two years, as servants in a hotel, which he said he kept in that city. He had furnished them with some clothing, and was to give them thirty dollars each, at the expiration of the two years. The driver, whose name was Thomas Kirk, said that he was a witness to the agreement, and that he fully believed there was nothing improper in the business. We informed him that we thought otherwise, and that he must return to the city, for we were determined to investigate the matter. He then took a letter out of his pocket, and said, "Here is a letter, given to me by Mr. Hammond, that will explain the whole affair. I will open it." He was requested not to do so till we went before a magistrate; but, confident that the letter would prove his innocence, he broke it open, and I read it before all the company. It was as follows.

"29th of October, 1802
SIR—You will receive the black men from the bearer, and, with the first opportunity, send them to their *own country,* where *they wish to go.* I have been at some expense for them, but being [am] acquainted with some gentlemen who will bear part of the expense.

Their masters, no doubt, will refund the money so paid. They were in a miserable state in New York. I think it an act of charity to assist them. Whatever may be the laws of any individual State, I think no man of *feeling* will wish to prevent their going where they may get an immediate passage home.

Yours with respect,
A.G. HAMMOND"

The men had just taken their seats at the table, when we entered the room; and although they understood the English language very imperfectly, they comprehended enough to discover that they were in jeopardy; and upon the letter being read, they all rose and looked upon one another, and upon us, with amazement; and on its being made known to them, that we had come to their rescue, they stepped up to us, and took us by the hand, and made all the manifestations in their power of their gratitude for deliverance. T. Kirk informed us, that all his money was expended, and that Hammond had agreed to meet him at this place, and furnish him with an amount sufficient to defray his expenses to Baltimore. Being satisfied that Kirk was guiltless in this business, and finding he was pennyless, we paid his fare at the Blue Bell, gave him money to defray his expenses home, and then returned with him to the city, and called upon Michael Hillegas, an alderman, when Kirk made the following affidavit, viz.

"Thomas Kirk, a person employed as a stageman, part of which belongs to himself, says—that about a week ago he was applied to by a person, who called himself A.G. Hammond, in New York, to carry in the said stage three black men and two mulatto men to Baltimore, and a letter which he would furnish him with, which is hereunto annexed, and endorsed with the name of Thomas Kirk. The said letter is directed to John Matinea, Baltimore, per M. T. Kirk.

"That, on Friday, the 29th day of October last, the said Thomas Kirk was at the place where A.G. Hammond appointed to meet him in New York, where also were the blacks and mulattoes: and there he was evidence to a paper of agreement, which was drawn up by the said A.G. Hammond, and signed by A.G. Hammond and all the blacks and mulattoes—the purpose of which was, that they should serve him, the said A.G. Hammond two years in Baltimore, whither he was going to reside, and there keep a tavern. That the instrument covenanted, that the said A.G. Hammond should find them sufficient meat, drink, wearing apparel, washing and lodging, and at the expiration of the two years, give them thirty dollars each. That on Sunday morning, the 30th of October last, the said Thomas Kirk crossed the North river, with the said five persons, and the said A.G. Hammond overtook them near Newark where he advanced to him fifteen dollars and fifty cents, and informed him he would return to New York; and directing the said Thomas Kirk to travel on with his cargo to Trenton, where he expected to overtake him; but should that not be the case, that he there overtook him, then he directed that he should stop at the sign of the Blue Bell, about three and a half miles from Gray's Ferry.

"City of Philadelphia, ss.

"Thomas Kirk being sworn according to law, did depose and say, that the facts above stated are just and true, to the best of his knowledge and belief.

THOMAS KIRK."

"Sworn and subscribed before me,
MICHAEL HILLEGAS.
November 3d, 1802."

We waited at the Blue Bell till near sundown, hoping to meet Hammond there; but we had reason to believe, that he had, but some means, discovered that his plans had been intercepted, and would not come. We were afterwards informed, that he had stopped for a short time at a tavern in Market street, the next day, but we could get no further intelligence of him.

Upon inquiry, we found that Hammond had lived in Baltimore, and at one time had sustained the character of a respectable man, but there was not the slightest evidence that he had any intention of keeping a hotel. Hammond's letter, in this narrative, precedes Kirk's affidavit. It will appear evident, that it was intended to deceive, in case it should fall into other hands than the individual to whom it was directed, but the scheme was too palpable not to be easily seen through. He speaks of *their masters:* the men were free, and, of course, had no masters. He also speaks of their *miserable state:* the fact was, they were intelligent smart men, and were by no means in need of the extension of his philanthropy. They resided, after this event, in Philadelphia, and conducted reputably. His object was, there can be no doubt, to send them to the West Indies and sell them as slaves; but his plan was happily frustrated.

The details of this case were published in the newspapers, one of which I forwarded to Thoroughgood Smith, who was then Mayor of the city of Baltimore, and in the course of a few weeks I received a letter from him, informing me that Hammond was in custody. He was, on trial, convicted and sentenced to hard labor on the public road for the term of three years; but, I was informed, that after serving about one year, he was pardoned by the Executive of Maryland, on condition of leaving the State not to return.

NOTES

1. *N.A.S.*, December 3, 1840, 102.

2. John Folwell was a shopkeeper. *P.D. for 1800*; N.P.

No. VII.
Romaine[1]

DEATH PREFERRED TO SLAVERY—Anthony Salaignac removed from St. Domingo, in the West Indies, to the State of New Jersey, and took with him several slaves, and among the number ROMAINE, the subject of the following notice. After remaining in that State some years, he concluded to send Romaine, and his wife and child, back to the West Indies; and as Romaine manifested great reluctance to return there, he confined him in prison some time previous to that fixed upon for sending him. After he had been a few days in confinement, a man was engaged to take him, with his wife and child, in a carriage, to Newcastle, in the State of Delaware, from whence they were to be shipped to the West Indies. They left Trenton late in the evening of 11th mo. 3d, 1802, and arrived in Philadelphia, at the inn kept by P. Howell, in Second street, between Mulberry and Sassafras, about 4 o'clock the next morning, in custody of a Frenchman, and John Musgrave, a constable of the city of Trenton, who had undertaken to see the colored people delivered at Newcastle. They appeared to be in great haste, having travelled all night. While at the inn, several persons remarked that Romaine and his wife appeared very much dejected. When breakfast was offered them, they declined eating, and the wife rose from the table, and making an excuse to go out, soon disappeared. Search was immediately instituted, but without effect. At length, Romaine was ordered to get into the carriage, and he proceeded as far as the step at the front door, where he saw the carriage door open to receive him. The constable was on one side of him, and the Frenchman on the other. Here he paused, and looking around him, asked, "Must I go?" The reply was, Yes, "And alone!" Yes, you must. At that instant, he took a pruning knife that he had in his pocket, and stepping on to the foot-way, drew it across his throat with such force as to sever the jugular vein. He fell upon the pavement, and, in a very little time, was a corpse.

As they had travelled all night, and manifested great hurry and trepidation, several persons at the inn apprehended that there was some scheme in agitation, that would not hear the light of day; and, about sun rise, a man came and informed me of the case, and requested me to inquire into it. I went immediately to the inn. Upon arriving there, I saw the lifeless body of Romaine lying on the pavement before me, with the throat cut almost from ear to ear. My whole soul was filled with horror, and as I stood viewing the corpse and ruminating on the awful spectacle, I exclaimed within myself, How long! How long! O Lord, shall this abominable system of slavery be permitted to curse the land? My mind was introduced into sympathy with the sufferer. I thought of the agony he must have endured before he could have resolved upon the desperate deed. By his sufferings he was driven to desperation, and he preferred launching into the unknown regions of eternity, to an endurance of slavery. He knew what he had to expect, from what he had experienced when in the West Indies before, and he was determined not to submit to the same degradation and misery again.

The coroner made his appearance in a short time after the fatal catastrophe had occurred, when a jury was called, and the following proceedings were had.

> *William Beaton, the coachman, sworn*—Says he was the driver of the carriage, was employed to go as far as New Castle—arrived in town this morning about 4 o'clock, with the deceased, who, with his wife and child, *were in custody of a constable*—had his carriage ready to carry them to Newcastle—saw him on the pavement, immediately after he cut his throat—no person was near him.
>
> *John Musgrave, constable, sworn*—Says he accompanied deceased, a woman and child, from Trenton, at the desire of a Mr. Salaignac, with whom he agreed to see them as far as Newcastle, from whence, he understood, they were to be shipped to the West Indies—did not wish to

undertake it at first, but applied to the Mayor, who told him he might do it, if well paid for it--did not know who to deliver them to at Newcastle--got no provisions for them on the road.

The French gentleman sworn--Declares he was travelling towards Baltimore--had no interest whatever in the slaves in question--undertook to see them delivered at Newcastle, to serve his friend Mr. Salaignac, who obtained the Mayor's authority in a certificate, and without which, would have had nothing to do with them--did not supply them with any provisions on the road, but Mr. Salaignac had furnished them with some loaves of bread, that were in the stage--did not know the name of the vessel or captain by whom the Negroes were to be conveyed to the West Indies--would have delivered them in the case of the Mayor of Newcastle. To the best of his belief, the deceased was actuated to the commission of the deed by a dread of slavery--saw the deceased cut his throat and fall on the pavement; he drew the knife across his throat three times--no person was near him. (In conversation with this man afterwards, he admitted to me that he was on one side of Romaine and the constable on the other.)

The following is a copy of the certificate of the Mayor to which was attached the seal of the city of Trenton, and which was handed to the Inquest.

"State of New Jersey. City of Trenton, ss.

To all whom it may concern, I, James Ewing, Mayor of said city, do hereby certify, that Monsieur Anthony Salaignac, late an inhabitant of the island of St. Domingo, in the West Indies, now resident in the said city of Trenton, did bring with him, when he came to this place, the following negro slaves, viz. Romaine, aged about twenty-seven years, Marie Navel, and Clementine, aged about twenty-six years, and that he had born in his family, during his residence here, the following slaves, viz: Anna, now aged five years and Garcin, aged three years, children of Marie Navel, and Charlotte, daughter of Clementine, now about three years old, and that it is the opinion of counsel learned in the law, that he hath full power, agreeably to the laws of this State and the United States, to remove the abovementioned slaves together with the remainder of his family, back to his own country.

In testimony whereof I have hereunto set my hand at seal, this 19th day of October, 1802.

JAMES EWING, *Mayor*

The jury, after short consultation, rendered the following verdict:

"Suicide, occasioned by the dread of slavery, to which the deceased knew himself devoted."

Great excitement prevailed among the people generally and much sympathy was manifested for the wife and child of Romaine, who had escaped. It was evident that both the Frenchman and the constable were doubtful of the legality of their proceedings; and, I was informed, that the inquest were clearly of opinion, that the procedure was unauthorized by law, and strongly urged that those men should be taken before the proper authority, that the affair might be inquired into.

An officer was sent for, and the Frenchman was arrested and taken before Alderman John Douglass, not so much from a desire to punish him, as to procure the manumission of the woman and child. Upon getting to the magistrates, he stated, with much confidence, that if we would accompany him to a house in Spruce street, a few doors above Fifth, he could satisfy us that he was innocent in the affair, and we concluded to comply with his request—and we left the office, (that is, two members of the Abolition Society beside myself, and the Frenchman). Upon arriving at the place designated, we were introduced into the back parlor which we found filled with Frenchmen, some of whom stopped in between our prisoner and us, and let him out the back way, without attempting any explanation. They soon showed signs of violence, and my two companions withdrew, when they laid hold of me and carried me out and deposited me upon the step of the front door, and immediately closed it. We returned to the magistrate and reported the result of our mission, and then separated to go to our respective homes. As I was walking deliberately down Spruce street, at the corner of Third street, I came in contact again with the Frenchman, who had been a few minutes before rescued, and before he was aware of it, I took him by the button of his coat, and observed, "We have met again." He was very much alarmed, and at once said he would do anything I desired. He accordingly procured the manumission of the woman and child, when he was set at liberty.

Romaine and his wife were under middle age, and were very good looking; their features were regular, and gave evidence of considerable intelligence, and I was informed they had been faithful slaves.

It will be seen that the circumstances here related occurred many years ago, but they made such a deep impression on my mind, that they are now as fresh before me as though it was but yesterday.

We often hear it said that the slaves are contented and happy. This case is but one, among many, that has come to my knowledge, where they have preferred death to slavery.

NOTES

1. *N.A.S.*, December 10, 1840, 10.

No. VIII.
A Maryland Fugitive[1]

In the 7th month, 1802, a man by the name of David Lea went to Philadelphia to hunt up runaway slaves. He had been there but a few days before he arrested one, who was claimed by Nathan Peacock, an inhabitant of Maryland, where, it appeared, Lea belonged. The slave was taken before John Hunter, a Justice of the Peace in Moyamensing. I was sent for, and, upon arriving at the magistrate's, I found Peacock, with his witnesses, prepared to identify the poor captive, and to prove his legal claim to him. After a thorough investigation, the poor fellow seeing no chance of escape, acknowledged that he was the slave of Peacock, and that he had left his master's service without his consent; alledging, as a reason for doing so, that he wished to be free. He had been in Philadelphia several years, where he married. He had taken a lot of ground in the Northern Liberties, and had erected a small house on it. Rather than permit him to be separated from his wife and children, some friends concluded to make an effort to purchase his freedom, and after much entreaty, the master fixed a price; I do not now remember what the sum was, but it was very large. The man was then committed to prison.

Lea was a very ill looking fellow, filthy in his person, and bore the appearance of being intemperate. I enquired of him if he had any business in Philadelphia; he replied, no. I asked him if he had any money; he answered, no. Then, addressing the magistrate, I observed, "Here is a stranger without money, and he admits that he follows no stated means for a livelihood. I would suggest whether it is proper that he should be permitted to go at large; for, if we may judge from his appearance, we may safely conclude he is a dangerous man." The magistrate interrogated him as to the cause of his being there, but his answers being unsatisfactory, (for he was ashamed to avow the real object of his coming,) he was committed to answer at the next Court of Sessions. It was customary at the prison, before the prisoner was locked up, to search him, and take whatever he had about him and lay it by carefully, to be returned to him when he should be discharged. To this operation, as I was informed the next day, upon calling at the jail, he strongly objected. It was nevertheless accomplished, when it was discovered that he had in his pockets *advertisements for more than fifty fugitive slaves!* It was now evident, that his business in Philadelphia was, to seek them out, inform their masters, and get a reward for apprehending them. The slave informed us that he owned a house in the Northern Liberties of Philadelphia, but that he owed some ground rent. We, however, concluded it probable, that we might raise some money on it. I called at the jail and inquired of Lea how much money he was to have for looking up Peacock's man; he replied, forty-five dollars. I then told him, if he would give me an order on Peacock for that sum, to be applied to assist in purchasing the man's freedom, he should be discharged from confinement, upon condition that he would enter into bonds to leave the city forthwith, and not return. He readily agreed to this proposition, gave me the order, and I received the money. Upon inquiry, we found the poor slave was in debt to a greater amount than his house would sell for, and as the price his master demanded for him was extravagantly high, we were compelled, though with great reluctance, to give up the idea of purchasing his freedom. I called at the prison and informed Lea how we were circumstanced, and offered him the $45 I had received from Peacock, but he declined receiving it, and said I might do what I would with it; that it was a fair bargain I had made with him, and I ought to stand by it; but he was willing to take three dollars of it to pay his expenses home. He then gave me a document, a copy of which is as follows. I now have the original paper, viz:

"I request Isaac T. Hopper to pay the money received upon the order which I gave him upon Nathan Peacock, to the Managers of the Pennsylvania Hospital, or to any other charitable institution he may judge proper.
Philadelphia, 7th mo. 16th, 1802.

	his	
		DAVID
	X	LEA.
Witnesses present.	mark.	
ROBERT EDWARDS,		
JOSEPH EDWARDS."		

Lea was taken to the magistrate that had committed him, where he entered into bonds, agreeably to his contract, and was discharged.

I paid the money received of Peacock to the Managers of the Pennsylvania Hospital, and in their accounts, published the next year, was the following item, viz:--Received of David Lea, a noted negro catcher, by the hands of Isaac T. Hopper, forty-two dollars; he having received forty-five dollars for taking up a runaway slave, of which he afterwards repented, and directed this sum to be paid to the Hospital, after deducting three dollars to pay his expenseses home."

The slave was taken to Norfolk and there he managed to escape, and immediately started for Philadelphia. After encountering many difficulties and great hardships, travelling by night, and lying by in the day, he arrived safely at Baltimore; but, almost as soon as he entered that city, he was taken up on suspicion of being a runaway, and lodged in prison. Isaac Proctor, a merchant of Baltimore, was informed of his case, and called to see him. The slave alledged that he was a free man, that he had served his time in Chester County, Pennsylvania, and in proof of this he indented him to me. Some time after his first elopement, he resided at "the Valley," about twenty-five miles from Philadelphia, where he became, illegally, a father; and to indemnify the township from expense on that account, he tended himself to Isaac Walker for the term of three years. I. Proctor wrote to me in relation to his case, and in reply I informed him, that I knew the man, and that he had served three years, as stated by him, and that I held the indenture. At the bottom of the letter, I observed, "there are some circumstances attending this case that it will not do to explain here." This I requested my friend to cut off before presenting it to the court; but, by some means, he overlooked it, and handed the whole to the court. The omission of my friend defeated the whole plan, and the wretched man was ordered to be sold. The day arrived, and he was put up for sale. It is not necessary to detail the circumstances attending the sale, further than to say, that a plan was devised, and successfully carried into effect, by means of which he was purchased for the sum of one dollar. This sum, with a small amount for prison fees, &c., was promptly paid, and in less than twenty-four hours from the time of his discharge, he was in Philadelphia. A day or two after his arrival in that city, he hired himself to a brick-maker, and, in a reasonable time, deposited in my hands the amount expended on his account by my friend in Baltimore. He was never troubled afterwards.

NOTES

1. *N.A.S.*, December 12, 1840, 114.

No. IX.
Richard Allen[1]

Richard Allen was born in Maryland, a slave to Benjamin Chew[2] of Philadelphia. After some years of servitude, he purchased his manumission, and went to that city, where he married and settled. For many years, he kept chimney-sweeps, and did considerable business in that line. At length, he commenced the business of shoe-making, and had several apprentices, though he was ignorant of the business himself, and carried it on through a "foreman." He was very generally known, and respected for his integrity and close application to business. In the summer and autumn of the year 1793, when the city of Philadelphia was visited with the Yellow Fever, Richard, with his contemporary, Absalom Jones,[3] a much respected colored man, and minister of the Episcopal Church in that city, were very useful, being unremitting in their labors for the relief of the sick, and in burying the dead. At that awful period, it was extremely difficult to procure assistance, on account of the contagious character of the disorder; and those who were willing to render their services, generally charged such extravagant prices as to make it impossible for a large number, who needed them, to obtain their aid.

Richard, and his friend and colleague, Absalom Jones, it is believed, on no occasion hesitated to go wherever they could be useful, making compensation a secondary consideration; and after the disorder had subsided, the Mayor furnished them with a certificate, of which the following is a copy, viz.

"Having, during the prevalence of the late malignant disorder, had almost daily opportunities of seeing the conduct of Absalom Jones and Richard Allen, and the people employed by them to bury the dead, I with cheerfulness give this testimony of my approbation of their

proceedings, so far as they came under my notice. Their diligence, attention and decency of deportment, afforded me, at that time, much satisfaction.
MATTHEW CLARKSON, *Mayor*
Philadelphia, Jan. 23, 1794"

Richard Allen resided many years in Dock street, where he attended to his business as a chimney-sweep and a shoemaker. One day, when he was from home in pursuit of his business, P.S., a wealthy and respectable citizen of Philadelphia, called at his house, in company with J.C., a dry goods merchant, and informed Richard's wife that his colored boy had eloped, and wished to know if he had not been there. She assured him that he had not. But, not being satisfied, he and his friend proceeded to search the house, disregarding the remonstrances of the woman, whom he treated with much insult and abuse. Upon Richard's return, his wife informed him of what had transpired during his absence.

Richard resolved to seek redress, and applied to Alderman Todd,[4] who resided in the neighborhood, and laid the matter before him. The magistrate addressed a note to the offending parties, requesting them to attend at his office the next day. The circumstance excited considerable curiosity, and a large number of people collected at the office, it being rather a novelty to see a wealthy merchant arraigned on the complaint of a colored man. Richard stated his case, which was not denied by the defendants, when the magistrate let them know that they had made themselves amenable to the law. Richard Allen magnanimously observed, that he did not wish to be vindictive, and he would make a proposition, which, if those persons would accept, he was willing the matter should be dropped. After describing the conduct of which he complained, on pretty strong terms, he made the following proposition, viz:--"If those gentlemen will ask my pardon, promise not to repeat the offensive conduct, and pay the cost; or, if they prefer it, pay to the overseers of the poor, in the ward where they live, ten pounds each, I shall be satisfied." The accused were fully aware that they had committed themselves, and concluding that it would be the cheapest mode of settling the business to comply with the first proposition, they asked permission of the magistrate to retire into a back room, which was granted, and thither they all went, where ample acknowledgements were made. As soon as they returned, Richard, addressing the Alderman, said--"Squire Todd, I am now willing this business should be dismissed. Those gentlemen have asked my pardon, promised not to repeat the offence, and will pay the costs." Almost as soon as the words were uttered, the people who had collected on the occasion, cried out, "they have begged the negro's pardon! they have begged the negro's pardon!" This covered P.S. and J.C. with confusion, and greatly provoked them, and P.S. exclaimed, "I did not think you would have served us so. I would rather have paid five hundred dollars than be treated in this way." They withdrew through a back way to avoid being mobbed!

Richard Allen, by industry and economy, became possessed of considerable property. He purchased a lot in Spruce, above Fourth street, and erected a good three story brick house on it, where he spent the remainder of his days. He was the chief instrument in organizing the first congregation of colored people in Philadelphia, and was their pastor from the commencement of it to the time of his death, but he never demanded or received any compensation for his services. And during several of the last years of his life, he was Bishop of the colored Methodist Episcopal Church.

While he resided in Spruce street, a man who lived in Maryland, bought a slave *running*--that is, one who had runaway--and sent one of his sons to Philadelphia to ferret him out. In passing along one of the streets of that city, this man saw the name of Richard Allen on a window, and a colored man standing in the door. He stepped up to him, asked if his name was Richard Allen, and was answered in the affirmative. After a short interview, the stranger walked away, and immediately returned home, and informed his father that he had found Dick. The father and his two sons mounted their horses without delay, and were soon in Philadelphia, where they made application to Alderman Todd for a warrant to apprehend a runaway slave by the name of Dick. Upon getting it, they procured an officer, and proceeded to Richard Allen's house, and walked in. The front room was occupied as a shop, where were employed four or five colored boys, apprenticed to the business of shoemaking. They inquired for Richard Allen, who was called. Upon his entering the shop, the stranger advanced towards him and accosted him with--"Well, Dick, do you know me?" Richard replied, "No, I do not know you." "Well, I will soon make you know me. Seize him constable." The officer inquired, "Is this the man you have got a warrant for?" "Yes," was the answer. The constable then informed Richard that he had a warrant for him, as the slave of the stranger; and then, addressing the pretended master, observed, "We will walk down to the magistrate,"--and added, "Mr. Allen, you will come down to Alderman Todd's soon, will you?" Richard assured him that he would. The pretended master became much alarmed that the officer should be willing to trust him to go alone, and threatened him with the consequences if he should not appear agreeably to his engagement.

In a short time, they all appeared before the magistrate, who, addressing the stranger, asked him if this man was his slave? He replied, with much confidence, that he was. He then asked, how long it was since he had left his master's service? The man replied, four years. The magistrate observed, that there must be some mistake about the business, for that he had known Richard Allen for more than twenty years, and he knew he was a free man. Notwithstanding this positive declaration, the unprincipled fellow offered to swear, and so did his two sons, that the prisoner was the identical slave he had bought, and for whom they had come to Philadelphia. This impudent conduct drew from the magistrate a severe rebuke, and he immediately discharged the prisoner. Richard then inquired whether redress was not to be had for this outrage upon him, and said, that if it had not been for the kindness of the officer, he might have been dragged through the streets like a felon. The Alderman was at a loss what to advise in the case, and proposed that I should be sent for; and as I lived but a short distance from the office, I was soon on the spot. The magistrate related all the circumstances, when I proposed that the father and two sons should be committed to prison for a misdemeanor until we could take advice as to the proper manner of procedure. This was done, and the next day a civil suit was commenced, and two thousand dollars bail demanded. Upon application to Judge John D. Coxe, the bail was reduced to eight hundred dollars for the father, and the two young men were set at liberty. The father remained in confinement, in the debtors prison, about three months. Richard Allen, concluding that he had suffered enough to deter him from taking up free people again, had him discharged, and he returned home to his family.

NOTES

1. *N.A.S.*, December 31, 1840, 118; Richard Allen (1760-1831), an ordained minister at age twenty-four, began preaching in 1786 at the St. George Methodist Church in Philadelphia. He organized an independent Methodist Church for blacks. In 1788, he was chosen to be the first black bishop at the African Methodist Church. *Who Was Who in America*, 20; Charles H. Wesley, *Richard Allen, Apostle of Freedom* (Washington, D.C., 1935).

2. Benjamin Chew (1722-1810), the son of Dr. Samuel Chew, was admitted to the Philadelphia Bar in 1754, appointed City Recorder in 1765, and stepped down from that post in 1777. Chew was a member of the Pennsylvania Executive Council during 1775-1776 and a judge of the High Court of Errors and Appeals during 1791-1801. Burton A. Konkle, *Benjamin Chew (1722-1810)* (Philadelphia, 1932); head of the Pennsylvania Judiciary System Under Colony and Commonwealth (Phil., 1932).

3. For details concerning Jones's role during the yellow fever epidemic in Pennsylvania, as well as his role in organizing an independent black denomination, see Wesley, *Richard Allen*, 101.

4. Alexander Todd was an alderman. *P.D.* (1800).

No. X.
Daniel Benson[1]

Daniel Benson was a slave to Perry Boots of Newcastle County, State of Delaware. His master for several years hired him to the neighboring farmers and received his wages. Benson was married to a free woman, who mostly supported herself and children, of whom they had several, by her own industry, while the earnings of her husband were appropriated to the support of his master. Benson's mother was also a slave to Perry Boots--she was old and entirely incapable of doing any kind of labor, so that her master was obliged to support her--this he found rather burdensome, and proposed to Benson to take charge of his mother, and pay him forty dollars a year and go where he pleased. This offer he gladly accepted, and in the year 1805 or 6 removed to Philadelphia and took his ancient mother and his family with him; here he followed sawing wood for a livelihood--he was honest and faithful in his business and soon had many friends and customers among the white citizens, and when those wanted wood Benson was employed to purchase and saw it;--and he regularly paid his master twenty dollars every six months.

Among his numerous customers was Alderman Alexander Todd; and on one occasion, when Benson called on him for his pay for sawing wood, the Alderman suggested to him whether he had not charged him too high--he replied that he had charged no more than the customary price, and that he could not afford to work for less, and gave as a reason, that he was a slave and was obliged to pay his master forty dollars a year, besides supporting his family and aged helpless mother. A. Todd's sympathy was excited, which led him to enquire somewhat particularly into his condition, which he briefly explained to him. A.T. then wrote a note and sent him with it to me, requesting that I would examine into the circumstances of his case, and gave it as his opinion, that Benson was free; he soon called and handed me the note, saying Squire Todd says he thinks I am free. I asked him to give me a history of his case. After hearing his narrative, I told him to go home and get any receipts for the money he had paid his master since he resided in Philadelphia--he immediately went and in less than half an hour returned--by those receipts it appeared that he had made several payments in that city. After I had become possessed of all of the facts of the case I advised him that he need not pay his master any more money, and by his residing in Philadelphia six months, with his master's consent, he became free. Benson was overjoyed, the tears started in his eyes, but yet he could hardly believe but that there must be some mistake--his mind was agitated between hope and fear. I assured him there was no mistake--he was certainly free, he then left me, but in a little time returned bring his wife with him. I cannot find language which would adequately describe the joy that _____ both their countenances, and, with hearts warmed with gratitude, they expressed their thankfulness to God for his goodness, manifested on this occasion.

Soon after I addressed a letter to P. Boots, informing him that he need not expect to receive any more money from Daniel Benson, for that he was a free man. P.B. came immediately to Philadelphia and called to see me, and enquired where he could "find Dan, the ungrateful villain, I will take him home in irons." I informed him that I thought he would find himself relieved from such an unpleasant task and explained the case fully to him, and shewed him the law under which Benson became entitled to his liberty. But he was not satisfied, and said he would advise with counsel and left me. After a short time he returned and found Benson waiting to see him. He had now become convinced that Benson was no longer under his control and began to upbraid him with ingratitude. Benson replied, I did not know when I came here that I would be free any more than you did, Master Perry-- It was not justice that made me your slave, it was the law and you took advantage of it, but now the law makes me free, and you ought not to blame me for taking the advantage which it gives me. But when would you be willing to take and manumit me if I was free? P. Boots then said, I always intended to set you free some time or other. Benson replied, I am now forty years old and if I am ever to be free I think it is near time for it, and then repeated the question, what would you be willing to take for me? Why, Benson, I think you ought to give a hundred dollars--would that satisfy master Perry? P. Answered, yes. Well, master Perry, I can pay you a hundred dollars. I then interfered and observed, that certainly Benson owed him nothing, and that justice was done in the case. Perry Boots ought to pay Benson for his services from the time he was twenty-one years old. Benson's reply to this surprised and gratified me, and exhibited a magnanimity and nobility of mind rarely to be found in those of a different complexion from himself. He said, I was a slave to master Perry's father and he was kind to me--master Perry and myself are about the same age--we were brought up together and more like brothers than like master and slave;--I can afford to give him one hundred dollars better than he can afford to do without me. I will go home and get the money, and then addressing me said, make out the papers while I am gone. He went home and soon returned with one hundred silver dollars; the papers were ready and P.B. signed the manumission, which also contained a receipt for the money.

After the business was thus finished, Benson invited his master to dine with him, and added, we are going to have a pretty good dinner--he also invited me to make one of the guests; but I excused myself by telling him it was not convenient, but that I would call and see them after dinner. After I had dined I went to Benson's and found they had not yet risen from the table. They had a turkey and a ____ and a variety of vegetables, and also a decanter of wine. I was pressed to take my seat at the table. I could not suppress a smile at Benson's remarks. He said that master P., he knew, loved a little brandy, but he did not like to ____ brandy, but had got a quart of "Mr. Morris's" best wine and thought perhaps that would do instead of brandy--He added, "I never drink any thing but water myself."

Not long after Benson's freedom was effected he abandoned the business of sawing wood and opened a store for the sale of second hand clothes, in which he was very successful--and maintained his family comfortably and reputably. He was many years a class-leader among the Methodists, and several times within the last ten or fifteen years came to this city to attend their meetings, and on those occasions, always called to see me--he deceased two or three years since. I should have mentioned that P.B. wanted it inserted inthe deed of manumission that he shold not be responsible for the support of the old woman; but Benson objected to this, and offered as a reason, that such an agreement would imply thathe would not do so voluntarily. He took care of his mother and supported her comfortably to the end of her days without any expense to her master. New York, 1st mo., 1841.

NOTES

1. *N.A.S.*, January 7, 1841, 122.

No. XI.
Samuel Curtis[1]

Samuel Curtis was a slave to Joseph Spear, at North Carolina. He was an active, intelligent man and was employed in transporting tar that was manufactured by his master, and other matters, the produce of the place, down Tar river to a town called Tarborough. After some time Samuel came to the conclusion, if possible, to be free, and he accomplished his object in the following manner. His name, while he resided in North Carolina, was Manuel but there was a free colored man who lived in the same neighborhood by the name of Samuel Curtis, and he proposed to him to get a pass, and he would buy it of him. Curtis accordingly applied to the Clerk of the county where he resided, and procured a certificate of his freedom, duly authenticated, with the county seal attached, and sold it to Manuel for two dollars, who now determined to make the best of his way to Philadelphia. The next trip he made to Tarborough, after delivering his cargo as was customary, he left his boat at that place and started for the North. He now assumed the name of Samuel Curtis, and was afterwards known by it. Having "*a free paper*," he had no difficulty on his journey. Some months after he arrived at Philadelphia he commenced the business of a chimney sweep--had several boys, and soon laid by money. After being in that city a year or two, he met, in the street, one of his master's near neighbors, who was well acquainted with him. The stranger accused Curtis with being a runaway, apprehended him and took him to Robert Wharton[2] who was then Mayor. Upon appearing before that magistrate, the stranger informed him that the prisoner was a fugitive slave, who had eloped from one of his neighbors. Curtis denied that he was a slave, and exhibited his certificate of freedom. The stranger admitted the authenticity of the document, and observed that he knew the signature was in the proper hand-writing of the Clerk, and said the seal affixed was the seal of the county, but he informed the Mayor that the name of the man he had arrested was Manuel, and not Samuel Curtis--that he also knew Samuel Curtis, who was a free man then living in North Carolina. The Mayor remarked that he could not receive parole evidence on contradiction of a public record, and accordingly set Curtis at liberty. Curtis considering himself no longer safe in Philadelphia, went to Boston, and he had been there but a few days, when he met the man in the streets of that city, who had arrested him in Philadelphia. Fearing he might not succeed as well there as he had in the place he had but a little time before left, he determined to return to Philadelphia. While in Boston, during his absence from his lodgings, his trunk was broken open and about one hundred and fifty dollars stolen. He now began to conclude his lot was hard, and that he should never find a place of safety; however, he returned to Philadelphia, and there pursued his business with diligence and industry, and every year saved some money, which he regularly put out to interest, in safe hands. At length he took a lot on Powell street, in that city, and erected a good three story brick house on it, in which he resided as long as he lived.

About the year 1807 he called upon me and informed me that he had left two children in North Carolina, who were slaves, and that he was very desirous of purchasing their freedom, but that he also was a slave himself, and as a preliminary step, he would first endeavor to secure his own manumission, and solicited my aid. About this time a friend of mine was about going to visit his relations in the neighborhood where J. Spear, Curtis's master, lived; and I commissioned him to negotiate for the freedom of the latter, and it was not long before one of Spear's neighbors was going to Philadelphia to buy goods, and he sent, by him, a bill of sale, conveying his property in the person of Manuel to me, for the sum of one hundred dollars. I communicated information of this to Curtis, and the same evening he called and gave me the amount demanded by his master, who, I understand, was highly pleased to get the money--it seemed like so much found, as his slave had been absent so many years, he had no expectation that he would ever hear from him again.

Curtis was now a free man, and his first object was to secure the freedom of his children. The necessary documents were procured and duly authenticated; they consisted of his manumission and certificates of his good character; the latter of which was signed by a considerable number of the most respectable citizens, and certified by the Mayor; and also "a pass" stating the object of his journey and commending him to the protection and kind attention of all among whom he might find it necessary to travel. Being thus prepared, he called to take his leave of me, when he remarked, "I know I am going in the midst of danger, and perhaps I may be seized and sold into slavery; but I am willing to hazard even my own liberty, as I can only secure the freedom of my children. I was a slave myself, and I know what slaves suffer."

Samuel Curtis was now considerably advanced in years, and when he came to take his leave of me, the tears run copiously down his cheeks, and clasping my hand in his, with a tremulous voice he said, "farewell, farewell may God bless you and give me my children, and then I shall be a happy man." He then set off on his journey and went straightaway to see his old master. Upon arriving there, he was so much altered since he had left that neighborhood, that his master did not know him; however, when Curtis had satisfied him that the person then standing before him was the identical Manuel, who was once his slave, he appeared glad to see him, entertained him kindly, enquired how he had fared and how he had made out to get so much money. The real Samuel Curtis was now dead, so there was no danger of his suffering in consequence of the part he had taken in assisting Manuel, now Samuel Curtis, to make his escape--and he related all the circumstances that attended his flight and how he had lived since his departure from Carolina.

Curtis then enquired for his children, whom he had left with his master. J. Spear informed him that he had sold them to a person in South Carolina, and he went in pursuit of them--when he reached there, he was told they had been sold to Georgia, but upon arriving in Georgia he found they had been sold, to a person who resided in Tennessee, and thither he went, but could get no further tidings of them, and after making diligent search and enquiry, he was obliged to return home without accomplishing the object of his journey.

As soon as he arrived at home he called and informed me that his children were not to be found--he appeared greatly dejected and remarked that he had deprived himself of every comfort that he might save money to buy his children, but now they were not to be found, his money could afford him no satisfaction, and all he had to console himself with, was a hope that they were dead. He was exceedingly affected and wept bitterly, and never afterwards seemed to take comfort in any thing, but sunk under his sorrow and affliction and in a short time died.

Robert Wharton, before mentioned, was Mayor of Philadelphia about twenty years and an Alderman about forty years, and although application was frequently made to him, he never surrendered a fugitive slave to his claimant. I have heard them say that he could not conscientiously do so, and that he would rather resign his office. He considered the declaration "that all men are created equal; that they are endowed by their Creator, with certain unalienable rights; that among these are life, liberty, and the pursuit of happiness;" of paramount authority to all law. He was of an ancient and highly respectable family, who were among the early settlers in Pennsylvania, and uncle to William Wharton, a well-known benevolent citizen, now living in Philadelphia.

NOTES

1. *N.A.S.*, January 7, 1841, 122. Samuel Curtis' account was reported in the *City Archives of Philadelphia Record Service* 20:2,*Common Pleas Court Appearances Pocket*, March 1810, Case No. 20.

2. Robert Wharton was born in Southwark Philadelphia in 1757, where he spent his early years working as an indentured servant. In 1796, he was an alderman, two years later the Mayor of Philadelphia between 1798 and 1824, he was elected Mayor on fifteen different occasions. He died in 1834. Simpson, *Eminent Philadelphians*, 949.

No. XII.
A Kidnapping Ring[1]

There were in the State of Delaware, a company of men who, during several years, combined together and carried on an extensive business in trading in slaves. They would frequently purchase colored people who were born free, and who were bound by indenture to serve till they were twenty-one years old, and when their time of service had nearly expired, some one of those persons would purchase them for a few dollars and clandestinely transport them to Georgia, and sell them for a high price, slaves for life. To prevent detection, they would advertise them as having run away, and they not unfrequently decoyed free people into their possession, and disposed of them in the same manner. In this way, it was believed, that in a few years, some hundreds of free men and women were reduced to slavery. The following narrative will give a pretty correct idea of the manner in which this nefarious business was conducted. In the year 1803, Thomas Hope,[2] of Philadelphia, published a pamphlet of forty pages, under the signature of "Humanitas," from memoranda which I furnished him. The following is mostly extracted from that work.

In the sixth month, 1801, four men, viz. Patrick and Samuel Conner, and Isaac and Abraham Truax, came from Duck Creek in the State of Delaware in a small vessel, and stopped near Almond-street wharf, in Philadelphia. They all resided in the neighborhood of that village, now called Smyrna. This is the place where Daniel Neal of Philadelphia was so grossly maltreated a few months ago, and it has been long known as a rendezvous for kidnappers. In the course of the day that they arrived, one of the Truax's, being previously acquainted, went to board with a man by the name of T. B. who resided in Southwark, and was constantly, during that and the next day, urging him to join in a plan of inveighing colored men from the city, and under such pretences as seemed most likely to succeed, carry them down to Duck Creek, where he, Truax, lived;--he said they could make a fortune by it in a short time, and had nothing to do, when they got them there, but to deliver them to one Wright, who lived about twelve miles from his, Truax's house, and where the Georgia speculators came to purchase them. It was concluded that Truax should go down the river first, in the vessel in which he came up, and take as many colored men with him as he could persuade to go; and T.B. was to follow him in the Lewistown packet two days after, with as many as he could induce to accompany him, by which time Truax expected he could have every thing prepared. In the course of the day, by stratagems of various kinds, such as chopping wood, &c, for which he would give a good price, Truax succeeded in prevailing on four men to accompany him, who engaged to cut wood, work on his farm, &c. One of them, however, a young man, before the time appointed for their sailing, became dissatisfied, apprehending there was some deception in the business, and made an excuse that he must go home for some clothes. This, Isaac Truax objected to, and offered to purchase some for him at a tailor's shop; saying, his wages were so generous that he could soon repay him. The young man, however, was determined to go home, and went accordingly, but did not return. After waiting a considerable time they sailed without him.

T. B., who was left behind, on pretence of having a vessel at Jones' Creek, employed three colored men to assist him in working her up, took passage in the packet for himself and them, and were landed at Bombay Hook, where they found Truax going up the creek with his three victims. They proceeded to Truax's house, where he soon joined them, leaving his three men on board the vessel, with directions to work her up to Robinson's landing. Shortly after arriving at Truax's house, he mounted his horse and went to Wright's, where, as has been observed, the purchase and sale of the colored people was effected. There was a man in the neighborhood by the name of Hawkins, who was said to be a man of property and *character,* and would not engage personally in the business of kidnapping; but for his services in screening others from the penalty of the law, by going bail for them, if detected, he received a proportional profit on the sale of the men.

A Kidnapping Ring

What Truax did at Wright's, is not certainly known. During his absence, the threw colored men were put in a small out house to lodge, and Truax returning in the night, three his saddle in at one of the windows that opened in the back part of the building. It fell upon one of the men and awakened him, and he roused his companions, and they heard Truax and B. disputing about the amount the latter should receive for his services. The whole plan was now developed and opened to the view of the colored men the imminent danger they were in--on the very verge of being separated from their families forever, and consigned to a bondage that would terminate only with their lives. Their situation was horrible indeed. Fortunately for the colored men, Truax and B. were at the back of the house, and the night was dark--they went away as quietly as possible, till they had gone some distance, when they ran at their utmost speed, until they had got some miles. The next morning they called at a house on the road to get some refreshment, when the master of the house enquired of them where they were from, and on being informed, he observed, you are lucky men, for you have been in the very hot-bed of kidnappers. The other men also escaped; one of them, whose name was Johnson, having gone to a house for a jug of water, was apprised by a woman of the fate that awaited them, and he communicated the information to his companions, when they all left the vessel and proceeded home to Philadelphia. After arriving in that city, they informed Thomas Harrison, the faithful and unwearied friend of the oppressed, of all that had occurred, and he brought them to me. We advised them not to communicate the circumstances to any body, but to keep a look out for the men who had attempted to kidnap them. In the course of a week or two, we were informed that T. B. had returned and was them on board of a vessel near Almond street wharf, when we appled to Ebenezer Ferguson, a justice of the peace in Southwark, who issued a warrant for his arrest, and we proceeded with an officer to the vessel. The captain denied all knowledge of T. B., and positively asserted that no such man was on board. After some time we insisted upon searching the vessel, and upon going into the hold, T. B. was found stowed away in one corner; he was ordered on deck, when it was discovered that he was hand-cuffed.

The captain now changed his story—said that T. B. had stolen a pair of oxen, and was placed under his care to be transported to the State of Delaware, to be tried for the offence. But we informed him that T. B. had been stealing something of more value than oxen, and that the matter must be settled before he went to Delaware, and we proceeded to the magistrate who had issued the warrant for his arrest. T. B. denied all knowledge of the matter whereof he was charged, but nevertheless, the proof being positive, he was committed to prison. I was, at the time, one of the inspectors of the prison, and I directed that he should be confined in a cell by himself, and informed him, that if he would disclose the names of his accomplices, his punishment should be mitigated. He was furnished with pen and ink, and I left him.

The next day, upon calling at the jail, he handed me a narrative, not only of what they had done, but of what they had in anticipation. At the next Court of Sessions, T. B. was arraigned, and pleadguilty to three indictments, which had been found by the Grand Jury against him. This being unusual, the Court inquired if any promise of favor had been made to the prisoner, and upon being informed that there had, the Court sentenced him to nine months imprisonment at hard labor, and a fine of one hundred pounds on each indictment; the extent of the penalty prescribed by the law being an imprisonment for one year and one hundred pounds, for each offence.

It was believed that the charge of stealing oxen was a mere pretence, as Hawkins, his accuser, was an accomplice, and got up under the expectation that he could not be wrested from them, and by that means take him to Delaware and then release him—but in this they were disappointed.

Patrick and Samuel Conner, and Isaac Truax were arrested and committed to prison at Georgetown, in the State of Maryland, but before their trial came on, they broke jail and escaped. T.B. served the term of two years and three months, agreeably to his sentence, when the fine was remitted. He was a mechanic, and after his release followed his trade respectable in the district of Southwark, and, on that account, I have given the initials only of his name, being unwilling to perpetuate to his disadvantage, offences of which I have good reason to believe he repented.

A Kidnapping Ring

Some time after the conviction of T. B., Wright, whose name has been mentioned in the forgoing narrative, went to Philadelphia in pursuit of a fugitive slave, where he was arrested under the following circumstances:--Two colored men, had been decoyed from Philadelphia to Dutch Creek, under the pretence of employment, and upon coming to at a landing, two white men came on board the vessel, and said that they had been bringing some calves down to that place to be sent to market in Philadelphia, and that they had escaped in the woods, and they solicited the colored men to assist in retaking them. Not at all apprehending any danger, they readily complied, but they had not proceeded far, when in a thick piece of woods, they were both seized, tied and put into a cart with a covered top, and taken to the house of Wright, where they were chained to the garret floor and kept until the next night, when they were taken to Georgetown to be shipped to the South.--From some cause they did not arrive at Georgetown till daylight, and as they were proceeding on their journey, a sister to one of the colored men, was going for a bucket of water when she saw her brother in irons. She immediately gave information of the circumstance, and the two colored men and their captors, were all committed to jail. The Acting Committee of the Abolitionist Society in Philadelphia were written to, and they procured evidence of the freedom of the two colored men, sent it to Georgetown and they were set at liberty. The kidnappers were detained in prison to take their trial; but before the Court came on, they broke jail and escaped.

Wright, as mentioned above, going to Philadelphia, was arrested and committed to prison, but he had remained there only five or six days, when he was taken before Chief Justice Tilghman on a writ of *habeas corpus,* and where also appeared one of the colored men who had been kidnapped and contained in Wrights house. He testified to the facts here stated, and said that Wright was covered with a loose garment that extended from the top of his head to his feet, with glasses to see through, so that he could not see his person, but that from the size and voice and statue of the prisoner, he had no doubt that he was the identical man. The Chief Justice, however, was of opinion that the testimony was insufficient, and he was discharged, after receiving from the Judge some salutary counsel.

NOTES

1. *N.A.S.*, February 1, 1841, 138.

2. Thomas Hope, a shipbuilder, was also the publisher of the *Philadelphia Price Current*; 1805 *P.D.* (No. 5), *N.P.*

No. XIII.
Samuel Clark[1]

SAMUEL CLARK, a free colored man, lived in West Nottingham, Chester County, Pennsylvania, near the line that separated that State from Maryland. He was orderly and industrious, and had a wife and several children, whom he supported comfortably. On the night of 25th of 10th mo. 1801, his house was suddenly broken open and five men rushed into it with great violence, and immediately seized several of the family and attempted to carry them off. Clark was at no loss to discover the object of his assailants, and resisted them to the utmost of his power, when one of the company fired a pistol, and wounded the old man in his hand and arm severely, and a daughter, about eighteen years old, received a shot in the neck, which, after a few days, caused her death. Clark and his wife were considerably advanced in life, and the child of whom they were thus bereft, was of much service to them in supporting the family. After a hard struggle, they succeeded in carrying away a brother to the girl they had thus deliberately murdered. He was a young man, and, at the time, confined to his bed with severe illness. They beat him on the head with an axe helve, until they had almost deprived him of life. They then conveyed him a few miles, to the house of a man by the name of Reynolds Hare; they ordered him to go into the meadow and get some horses, on which they intended to carry him away. He was bruised and wounded, and almost covered with blood, and they, no doubt, thought he was so crippled that he would be unable to make his escape. However, after getting out of their sight, he went into a barn and secreted himself under some chaff and straw. Not returning as soon as they expected, they went in search of him, and he said they literally walked over him, and he heard them swear they would kill him if they could find him. But they were disappointed; and after they were gone, he made an attempt to go home. When within about a mile of his father's house, and in the woods, he fainted and did not recover sufficient consciousness to find the way home for more than twenty-four hours, and when he arrived there, he found his sister languishing under the wound she had received from the ruffians who had kidnapped him, and the whole family overwhelmed with grief. His parents had given up the prospect of ever seeing him again, and when he made his appearance among them, it seemed, as the old man afterwards expressed himself to a friend, as though he had risen from the dead.

In a few days after the circumstances here related were perpetrated, I received a letter from Joseph Cheseman, who resided within a few miles of Clark's, detailing the particulars, with the names of the men who had so wantonly outraged this peaceable family. And in company with Gilbert Gaw[2], a respectable citizen of Philadelphia, I called upon Joseph B. McKean,[3] then Attorney General, and laid the matter before him, and requested that he would represent the facts of the case to his father, Thomas McKean,[4] who was at the time Governor of Pennsylvania, that such measures might be adopted as would bring the perpetrators of the murder to justice. But the matter there ended, and nothing was done. As the offence of which those men were guilty was punishable with death, in case of a conviction, I did not feel it among my duties to press the matter further.

If the victims of this lawless violence had been white people, there cannot be a doubt but the Executive of Pennsylvania would have issued his proclamation, offering a high reward for the apprehension of those aggressors upon defenceless humanity; but heart-rendering and affecting as the case was, the sufferers being colored people, the matter was permitted to sleep.

It will hardly be necessary to inform the reader that the object of those men was to kidnap the younger branches of the family, and sell them to the speculators, there being at the time several in the neighborhood, who would have taken them to the South and disposed of them as slaves.

NOTES

1. *N.A.S.*, February 11, 1841, 142.

2. Gilbert Gaw was listed as a Windsor chair maker in the *P.D. for 1800*, 53.

3. Joseph B. McKean (1764-1826) was the Attorney General during 1800-1808, associate judge for the city and county of Philadelphia during 1817-1825; *Who Was Who in America Historical Volume*, 348.

4. Thomas McKean (1735-1817) was Chief Justice of Pennsylvania during 1777-1799 and the governor of that state during 1799-1808. *Who Was Who in America Historical Volume 1607-1896*, 348.

No. XIV.
Reuben Moore[1]

REUBEN MOORE, and orderly respectable colored man, with whom I was well acquainted, and who had a family in Philadelphia, in the summer of 1799, during the prevalence of the yellow fever in that city, was walking down Market street, and saw two white men dragging a colored man along the street by the collar; when he approached them and inquired what the man had been doing. One of the white men replied, that he was a runaway slave. The prisoner denied that he was a slave, and said he had no knowledge of the persons who had arrested him. Reuben asked them to take their captive before a magistrate. This the strangers resented as an insult, and ordered him not to interfere. He, however, followed them some distance, and upon discovering that they were about to take the man away without giving him an opportunity of making his defence, he observed, addressing himself to the colored man, "I will go for some person who will see you righted." Almost as soon as the words were out of his mouth, James Frazier, one of the men who had the black man in custody, drew a pistol out of his pocket, and with an oath declared, that if he said another word, and did not immediately go about his business, he would "nail" him. Reuben's sympathy was excited, and he was determined to see justice done in the case; and not apprehending the fellow would have the audacity to murder him in the midst of a populous city, in open day, after a little hesitation, he said--"I will go for some one who will see the poor man righted." On saying this, Frazier fired at him. The ball entered his breast, and the shot was scattered about his body--for it was loaded with both--when he fell on the pavement, and, it was supposed, was killed. Surgical aid was immediately called, but little hopes were, for some time, entertained of his recovery. After some days, the ball was extracted, but the shot remained in him until the day of his death. Frazier was apprehended and committed to prison to await his trial, and the poor captive was set at liberty. He remained in jail about three months, when a compromise was made by paying Reuben a considerable sum of money, and the murderous fellow was discharged and returned to Maryland, where he belonged.

Reuben Moore recovered so as to be able to attend to some light business, but his health was never fully restored.

I had the foregoing narrative from Reuben himself, and from Peter Barker, who witnessed the transaction, it having taken place in Market street, a few doors below Fourth street, opposite to his store.

NOTES

1. *N.A.S.*, February 11, 1841, 142.

No. XV.
Phebe[1]

In the early part of the year 1810, a colored woman, about twenty-two years old, by the name of Phebe, held as a slave by Benjamin Donahue, of Newcastle County, in the state of Delaware, being tired of her bondage, left her master's service and went to Philadelphia; and there, meeting with a friend who resided about six or seven miles from that city, she engaged with him as a domestic servant, and accordingly went home with him. After remaining in his service a few months, she ventured to inform him of her situation, and solicited him to endeavor to procure her freedom. With this request he readily complied. Although poorly clad she had taken up none of her wages. Finding her an industrious, capable woman, he offered to lend her the amount necessary to purchase her manumission, and called upon me to negotiate the business; when I addressed the following letter to B. Donahue, viz:

"PHILADELPHIA, 7th mo. 26th, 1810
BENJAMIN DONAHUE:
  Application has been made to me on behalf of a black girl, who, I am informed, is thy slave. The person who has interfered on her behalf is willing to pay sixty, or at most, seventy dollars for her manumission. If thou art willing to set her free on these terms, please execute a manumission and forward it to James Wheelan of this city, and the money will be paid. I am, respectfully,
        ISAAC T. HOPPER."

The first intelligence I received from him, after sending this letter, was the following note from the Mayor.

"MAYOR'S OFFICE, Sept. 22nd, 1810.

MR. ISAAC T. HOPPER:
Sir--Benjamin Donahue having made application to me, and stated that he is the lawful owner of a negro girl named Phebe, his indented servant, (not a slave) and that she has absconded from his service; that from your letter directed to him, it appears that she is concealed in the city of Philadelphia; and by the same letter it appears that you are knowing, or have an agency in the said concealment; and it appearing to me, from a perusal of the act of Assembly, that any person concealing a runaway servant, is liable to forfeit twenty shillings for every twenty-four hours of such concealment, and that you have been induced to take an active part in favor of said girl under the impression that she is a slave; as a previous step, I have thought proper to address you a line on the subject, and to request that you will have the girl delivered to her proper master. A compliance with this will prevent the necessity of having recourse to measures prescribed by law.

Yours, respectfully,
J. Barker, MAYOR."[2]

This note was handed to me by Benjamin Donahue. After reading it, I returned, by the same individual, the following reply. "9th mo. 22nd, 1810.

RESPECTED FRIEND:
Benjamin Donahue has handed me a note, signed John Barker, Mayor. I presume thou put thy name to it, without reading it,* as it contains a statement not justified by my letter to him, upon which it appears to be predicated. He is, however, left at liberty to pursue such measures as he may deem advisable.

I am, respectfully,
ISAAC T. HOPPER
To John Barker, Mayor."

*The signature of the Mayor was in his handwriting but the

body of the note was written by his clerk.

A few days afterwards, as I was passing the Mayor's office, I stepped in, and found Benjamin Donahue in conversation with the Mayor. Soon after entering, the Mayor said, "Mr. Hopper, did you get a note from me?" I replied, "Didst thou get a reply to it?" He answered, "Yes." I then queried, "Why does thou ask me if I received it!" Turning to Donahue, he observed, "Mr. Donahue, we had better drop this business, like a hot potatoe, for Mr. Hopper knows more of the law in such cases as this, than you and I put together." I remarked, that I thought the Mayor had better let him adopt such a course as he thought most to his advantage.

After considerable conversation, I discovered that there was no indenture, and that the woman was really claimed as a slave. The story of her being an indented servant, was a mere pretence, fabricated in the hope that it would induce me to disclose the place where she had taken refuge.

The next day, Benjamin Donahue called upon me and manumitted Phebe, for the consideration of sixty-five dollars, which I received from her friend and benefactor, and paid to him.

NOTES

1. *N.A.S.*, March 4, 1841, 154.

2. John Barker (1736-1818), better known as General John Barker, a tailor, held the post of alderman in Philadelphia in 1800. During 1808, 1809, and 1810 he served as Mayor of that city. 1805 *P.D.*, 53.

No. XVI.
Thomas Hughes[1]

THOMAS HUGHES AND JOHN P. DARG. -- Thomas Hughes came with his master, John P. Darg, to this city, in the latter part of the 8th month, 1838, and soon afterwards left his service, taking with him seven or eight thousand dollars of the master's money. Six thousand, nine hundred and eight dollars, were recovered through my instrumentality and returned to Darg. Barney Corse negotiated the business, and previously to his having any knowledge that the lost money had been recovered, he agreed with Darg that Hughes should be manumitted forthwith, on condition that the whole, or the greater part of the money taken, as advertised in "The Sun," should be returned. Much the greater part of this money was returned, as above mentioned, and consequently Tom became legally entitled to his freedom. It is generally known, that he was sentenced to the State prison for the term of two years, that being the shortest term allowed by law for the offence of which he was convicted. It has been invidiously asserted, that he had been tampered with by abolitionists previously to leaving Darg's service; but all who have read the trial must see, that there is not the least ground even for suspicion of the kind. It has also been said, that, preferring slavery to freedom, he had voluntarily returned into bondage. This is equally false with the other. The facts of the case are these.

His sentence expired the 22nd of last month, and on that day I visited him in prison at Sing Sing. I stated to him, in the presence of one of the Inspectors, that I had come to inform him of the position in which he stood -- that he was a free man, and therefore at liberty to stay at the North or to go to the South -- that on this point there was no doubt, for I had advised with three of the most respectable lawyers in New-York, and they were clearly of opinion that he was free -- and that if he wished to remain at the North, I would do all I could to protect him. I told him, at the same time, that I had no advice to give him in relation to the matter -- that I wished him to exercise his own feelings and judgement in the case. He knew Darg, and the business he followed (gambling,) and that no confidence could be reposed in him--and that, if he went with him, I had no doubt he would very soon sell him, and that he would never see his wife. After a short pause, he informed me that he had considered the matter, and had come to the conclusion to remain at the North. I then observed to him, that I hoped he would remain firm in whatever conclusion he should then adopt.

Darg and his wife had been several times to see him -- They informed him that they should not attempt to take him unless he wished to go; but that, if he would accompany them to the South, he should live in freedom with his wife, for whom he manifested a warm affection whenever he spoke of her. The keeper agreed to discharge Tom the next morning at 9 o'clock. Immediately after I left the prison, Darg had another interview with him, and again on the morning of the day he was liberated, and, no doubt, held out such inducements as prevailed upon Tom to change his determination; and, I have reason to believe that some, at least, of the officers of the prison lent their aid to effect that object.

At 9 o'clock, Tom received his final discharge in the presence of Darg. I then asked him what he wished to do, when he spoke in substance as follows: "I am now a FREE MAN, and can stay at the North, or go to the South. I have been told (he did not say by whom) that Mr. Darg is insolvent, but he has shown me more money than I ever saw him have before, and also some of the notes which I removed. I have always found Mr. Darg true to me, and I wish to go with him." I then replied, "I am satisfied, but thou shouldst have told me so yesterday." He then stepped into a carriage with Darg, which was in waiting, and drove off, highly elated with the idea that he was about to enjoy his liberty and the society of his wife. But there is much reason to fear, that he will be disappointed in both, and that ?ere? this he has been sold to some of those wretches who speculate in human flesh. Darg knew Tom was free, and did not attempt to exercise any right of ownership over him; neither had Tom any suspicion that his liberty would be called in question. I have heard that it has been asserted, that he preferred slavery to liberty; but so far from this being true, he declared that he would take his own life rather than return to the South as a slave. It has been said, that while in prison at Sing Sing, he became a Christian. There is some ground to fear that his Christianity was rather superficial, or he would hardly have been willing to place himself in a situation where he must lend his aid to a business followed only be men who prey upon the community, and who are the most abandoned of mankind.

The following account of his life was taken from himself, while he was in prison in this city:

"I was born at Richmond, Virginia; my father was my first master; at the age of eleven months, myself, mother and twin sister, were sold to my father's brother; who, as well as my father, was a planter of great wealth, before my recollection. My mother and sister were resold, but to whom, or where taken I never could ascertain. At the age of thirteen years, I was sold, and my father's son became my owner, who then resided in the state of Kentucky; his orders were so severe I remonstrated with him, for treating a brother as he did me; for doing which I was sold, hand-cuffed, and my feet tied under a horse's belly; taken to Maysville, shipped on board a boat for Louisiana, together with about five hundred more slaves, and sold; fortunately for me, as I supposed, my master was a gambler, and resided at Louisville, Kentucky, with whom, as his body servant, I soon returned. I resided with him for three years, when fortune turned against him, and he informed me he should be obliged to sell me. During my residence at Louisville, I ascertained my father had moved to Kentucky; I told my master that my father was a white man and a planter of great wealth; that if I could see him I thought he would purchase me and set me free. Upon which he consented to let me go and see him; on arriving in the place where he resided, I found he was quite as wealthy as he was in Virginia; I called upon him, told him that my name was Thomas, the son of his slave Rachel,

and that from good information, I had no doubt he was
my father, which he did not deny. I told him of the
injustice of my relatives, in selling me; informed him that
I was to be again sold, and begged him to purchase and
manumit me. I told him of the miserable life I was
leading, subject to the will of any person who might
become my master; but to all my entreaties he turned a
deaf ear, and in public would not speak to me as he
passed me. I remained in the place two weeks, to ascertain
if possible, where my mother and sister were; but so
indifferent was he to their fate, he had not taken the
name of their purchaser, or the destination of the drove
of which the formed a part. I again returned to Louisville,
and soon found myself going to Louisiana to be sold; on
my arrival, Mr. John P. Darg became my purchaser, who
being of the same profession as my former master, that
is, a gambler, my life was spent in much the same manner
as before, the fact of Mr. Drag's being a gambler, I have
been compelled to contradict, but it is true. Two days
previous to my leaving New Orleans, I married one of my
master's slaves. It is painful for me to leave my wife, but
should I be taken to the South I am doomed never to see
her, as I shall no doubt be sold; or should I remain his
slave, his fortune may change and I be forever separated
from my wife, and perchance family; or raise children only
to augment his wealth, liable to be torn from each other
at any moment; the idea of which made my situation
doubly painful; -- under these considerations I resolved,
before I left New Orleans, never to return a slave. As I
had ever been a trusty slave my master allowed me to
carry the key to the trunk in which he carried him money.
I supposed by taking his money and leaving him, he would
be willing to give me my liberty, in case his money was
returned; but I found other difficulties; it was necessary to
have some person to return the money; this, two colored
men engaged to do, but as soon as my master advertised
the money, offering a large-reward, they became alarmed
and sought to secrete me. Had I informed the gentlemen

who came to inquire if I had taken my master's money of the facts, I have no doubt it would have been all returned; but I concealed the fact, in hopes the colored men would return it to my master, until my fears were awakened by one of the Friends, as to the safety of the money. I then told him to whom I had given it, and desired him to go and get the money, as I dare not do it, return it to my master and ask him to manumit me. To this he reluctantly assented, saying I had done very wrong, of which I am fully satisfied; but as my master could state, were he here, he has intrusted me with larger sums for a long time and I never defrauded him of a cent.

"I trust, when I say I never had any other design than to secure my freedom, that my statement will be believed, and that I intended to return every farthing of the money to its lawful owner; neither was any man who has been implicated in this unhappy affair, ever to be benefited in any way; They ever manifested their regret to think I had been so imprudent, and not withstanding officers Peck and Merritt have held out every inducement to get me to swear that they, the persons charged knew of my intentions, and advised me to the step, before I took the money; saying that I should not be tried, but used as a witness, and many other promises of like purport; I clear my conscience, and do justice to innocent men, when I say they knew nothing of me until after I had left my master, and if any man is guilty I am the one; if any man is to be punished let that punishment fall upon me, and let those gentlemen be credited for their honorable motives in trying to restore to my master the money I had wrongfully taken.

"I will also here express my regret for concealing many things, and for having made statements at variance with this; but they were not true; I was compelled to do so by the presence of my master or one of the police officers above alluded to, who have ever done all they could to prejudice me against those men and the principles they profess, so much so, that it has seemed to me, they not only wanted me to swear to the truth, but to a little more than the truth, to suit their purpose.

"I have here stated every circumstance as it has occurred, and to whom the guilt of the whole belongs.

His
"THOMAS HUGHES"
mark.
Aged about twenty-two years.

"Witness present,
HORACE DRESSER.[2]
"Halls of Justice, New-York, Nov. 22d, 1838."

NOTES

1. *N.A.S.*, March 25, 1841, 167. Thomas Hughes' story was reported in the *New York Sun*, September 2, 1838.

2. Horace Dresser (- 1877) was one of the "first lawyers who spoke in the New York Courts in behalf of the Negro race and his best energies were directed to defending and assisting fugitive slaves." *Appleton's Encyclopedia of American Biography*, ed., James G. Wilson (New York, 1888-1901), II: 231.

No. XVII.
Emery Sadler[1]

A farmer, whose name, I think, was --------- Lucas, and who resided in the State of Maryland, was possessed of several slaves; and owing to some circumstance, I do not now remember what, concluded to dispose of them. Among the number was one by the name of Emery Sadler, who, in consequence of his good conduct, was a favorite with his master, and he refused to dispose of him to the speculators, several of whom were anxious to buy him; and he remained in his possession after most of the others were sold. Arnold Jacobs, one of Lucas' neighbors, called upon him and proposed to purchase Emery. Lucas informed him that he was willing to take a moderate price for the man, provided he could find a purchaser who would treat him kindly, and not permit him to be removed from the neighborhood--alleging, that he was a faithful slave and had a wife, a free woman, for whim he also felt much regard. Jacobs said he was well acquainted with the character of Emery and his wife, and had long thought he was too clever to be a slave; and his only object in wishing to buy him was to make him free--that he thought Emery was so well known and respected in the neighborhood, that he could collect a considerable sum towards purchasing his freedom, and *he* would be willing to contribute something towards it himself.

Lucas now concluded he had met with the very man he wanted, and observed, that he should have the slave for the sum of three hundred and twenty dollars--said he could readily find a purchaser who would give four hundred and fifty dollars, but such was his regard for Emery, that he was willing to make a considerable sacrifice if he could be made free. The bargain was then closed, and Emery was transferred to his new master, little thinking of what was to follow. Jacobs took his slave home, and in a few days sent him to collect money to refund the amount paid by his *benevolent friend* and master. In a very little time, Emery returned, bringing with him eighty dollars, which he handed over to Arnold Jacobs, who now proposed that he should go to Philadelphia and try what he could do there. Accordingly, Emery packed up what few articles he possessed, and, with his wife, went immediately to that city.

He had been there but a few days, when he and his wife hired with William Pritchett,[2] leather dealer, for twenty dollars a month--the wife as a domestic in the family, and he to assist about the store. After living with W. P. three months, Emery proposed that Jacobs should be informed that sixty dollars were ready for him, and that it should be sent to him, unless he would prefer coming for it. Not many days elapsed before A. Jacobs made his appearance in Philadelphia, and sixty dollars was promptly paid to him.

He told Emery he was now satisfied that he would pay him the money he had advanced, and that he had come to the city in his chair to take him to Maryland and manumit him, which could only be done, legally, in open court.--Emery hesitated and wished to consult with some of his friends, and two members of the abolition society were sent for. A. Jacobs assured them that his whole conduct in this business was the result of pure benevolence, and that if Emery would go home with him, he would execute a deed of manumission, and that he should return to Philadelphia in a few days. Under these considerations, they advised him to go. Emery's mother was an ancient woman, and lived as a servant in the family of Samuel R. Fisher[3]; she and Emery's wife were very unwilling that he should go to Maryland, fearing it was only a scheme to entrap him.

Samuel R. Fisher also apprehended that Emery's liberty would be in danger by his going to Maryland, and he called upon me and communicated all the circumstances of the case, and requested that I would examine into the matter and advise the man how to act on the occasion. I accordingly went to see Jacobs, whom I found at the store of W. Pritchett, and inquired what object he had in view in taking Emery to Maryland. With great apparent frankness he told me that it was indispensable that he should go there, for by the laws of Maryland he could be manumitted only in open court. In reply to this, I told him he was now in Pennsylvania, and that I could write a manumission in ten minutes that would be as valid, to all intents and purposes, as any that could be made in Maryland, and that I could see no occasion for his going there. At this he appeared to be very much offended, and said, he had no object but that of kindness to Emery, and he thought it cruel that any unnecessary obstacles should be thrown in the way of his doing his own business in his own way. After much conversation on the subject, he told me, that he was unable to pay the cash for Emery, and had to give his note for the amount, and that unless Emery went to Maryland, so that Lucas could see him, he would push him for the money, which would put him to great inconvenience. He also said that it was very hard that he should be involved in difficulty, needlessly, when he had risked so much with no other motive whatever than that of kindness to the man.

Notwithstanding my advice to the contrary, Emery concluded to go with him, and said, he thought it would be ungrateful to refuse. When I found that matter was settled, I took Jacobs to the back part of the store; thinking he might express hismelf more freely if we were alone, and then asked him if he admitted that Emery was free. He replied, "I do, and I have no object in taking him home with me, but to secure his freedom according to law." I inquired if he was a slaveholder; he said he was. I remarked that I supposed there might be some honest slaveholders, but I had never trusted one who had not deceived me, and told him in plain terms that I had no confidence in what he had said, and wished him to understand, explicitly, that if he sold Emery, he would be prosecuted as a kidnapper.

Emery took leave of his wife and mother, who were much distressed, fearing that it would prove a final separation, and stepped into the chair with his master and drove off. In a few days, William Pritchett received a letter, written at the request of Emery, conveying the sad intelligence that he had been betrayed and was then in prison at Warwick, in Maryland, and would be taken to the South in a few days. Wm. Pritchett without delay went to Warwick, but he arrived there too late, for EMery was then a day or two on his journey to Alabama with a drove of slaves that were being taken there for sale.

It afterwards appeared that Jacobs had sold him to a slave-trader before he went to Philadelphia, who was in waiting at Warwick, and took possession of him and put him in irons as soon as he arrived. It is difficult to find language that would convey an idea of the anguish the news of this event inflicted on his wife and aged mother, and it is as difficult to portray in their true colors the turpitude and depravity of the hard-hearted monster that could perpetrate such a base act. Emery had lived long enough in Philadelphia to make many friends, and all who were acquainted with him, with one accord, seemed prepared to bear testimony to the excellency of his character—the circumstance produced much excitement, and was a subject that drew from several of the public prints severe animadversion. In the first instance A. Jacobs got an abatement in the price of Emery of one hundred and thirty dollars under an expectation that he would manumit him, and then received eighty dollars in Maryland, and sixty dollars in Philadelphia, and afterwards sold him for four hundred and fifty dollars--a pretty good speculation, if he had met with no reverses.

The treachery of Arnold Jacobs soon became known to the acting committee of the Abolition Society, who immediately instituted proceedings against him, and at the next Mayor's Court he was indicted by the Grand Jury for kidnapping; and application being made to the Governor of Pennsylvania, he demanded Jacobs of the Governor of Maryland, and he was by that magistrate ordered to be surrendered accordingly; and an officer was despatched duly authorized to arrest him and take him to Philadelphia for trial.

Upon arriving at the house of Arnold Jacobs, the officer made known his business and exhibited his warrant. Jacobs received him politely and invited him to stay with him and lodge, it being then evening, and in the morning said they would adjust the business. The officer retired to bed, and in the morning rose early, and upon going into the parlor found Arnold Jacobs there armed with two pistols. He then, addressing the officer, informed him that if he attempted to arrest him, or said one word in relation to the business that brought him there, he would shoot him dead upon the spot, and accompanied this murderous threat with such indications as convinced the officer that he would carry it into effect, unless he complied with the requisition just made; and he returned home without accomplishing the object of his journey.

These proceedings were laid before the Governor of Maryland, who ordered the posse comitatus to aid the officer, who again repaired to Maryland and called upon the people to assist him. A very few persons collected at the place designated for them to meet, and they all proceeded to the house of Arnold Jacobs. He was informed of their coming and had prepared himself for defense; and as soon as they approached his house, with awful imprecations he declared he would not be taken alive, and that he would kill the first man that attempted it. The officer and those that were with him being thus intimidated, he returned home without effecting the business he went upon. However, finding the storm gathering thicker and blacker, Jacobs became alarmed, and being afraid to put the laws at defiance any longer, sent to Alabama, purchased Emery at a heavy expense, and restored him to his afflicted wife in Philadelphia. The Committee had instituted a suit against the individual in Alabama who held Emery, but he having obtained his freedom, as above mentioned, it was never brought to issue. Emery returned home in the year 1827, after an absence of about eighteen months.

NOTES

1. N.A.S., April 15, 1841, 178. P.P.A.S. Acting Committee: Minutes, 1784-1802, Reel 4.

2. William Pritchett was a leather dealer. P.D. for 1806, 36.

3. Samuel R. Fisher was listed as a merchant. P.D. for 1806, 48.

No. XVIII.
Stephen Lamaire[1]

Etienne, alias Stephen Lamaire, was a slave to a person by the name of ---- Lamaire, in the island of Guadaloupe, who, in consideration of his faithful services, gave him his freedom; after which, as appeared by the testimony of several witnesses who were examined on his trial, he followed the business of a barber and kept a shop of his own in that island. After some time, he was appointed an officer in the French army, against Victor Hughes, and had the command of a fort, and he remained in the army until the close of the war.

He was a man of good talents, and had acquired considerable influence, particularly amongst the people of his own color. Some time after the close of the war above mentioned, there were some symptoms of an insurrection among the colored people in consequence of the revocation, by the French government, of the decree abolishing slavery in the West India Islands; and Stephen was instrumental in saving the lives of a number of white people, who had rendered themselves obnoxious to the resentment of the blacks by their efforts to reduce them to slavery.

In consequence of the unsettled state of affairs in Guadaloupe, Stephen determined to come to this country, and ---- Beoch, a particular friend of his old master, procured for him a passport. A person whose name was ---- Anslong, then at Guadaloupe, had two slaves whom he was about to send to the care of Dennis Cottineau,[2] of Philadelphia, with directions to send them to a farm he owned in New Jersey, near Princeton, and Beoch proposed to Anslong, that Stephen should take passage in the same vessel with them, to which the former agreed, and manifested much interest on Stephen's behalf. When the vessel was about to sail, Anslong persuaded Stephen to give up his passport to him, telling him that he would, give it to the Captain for safe keeping. Stephen had understood from Anslong, that he would not be charged for his passage in consequence of services he might perform on board the vessel. But when the vessel arrived at Philadelphia, in the 3d mo. 1803, Stephen was astonished on being informed that Anslong had paid his passage, as well as that of his two slaves, and had forwarded the receipt for it to Cottineau, and had written to him to send the three men to N. Jersey, calling them his slaves! Upon finding the situation in which he was placed, he applied to a colored man by the name of Ambrose, with whom he had been acquainted in Guadaloupe, and be brought him to me. He related his case very circumstantially, and the two men who were really the slaves of Anslong, confirmed his statement. I could hardly believe Stephen's story, it seemed so improbable that any man could be guilty of such bold and daring treachery. However, I questioned him very closely, and charged him not to deceive me, telling him, that if he was a slave there could be no doubt but it would be made to appear, and it would only be making his condition worse, and in addition to that, it would put us to considerable expense and trouble if we should be deceived.

After fully investigating the case, I became satisfied that he was free, and advised him not to leave the city, and requested him to inform me if Cottineau should attempt to use coercion. He then called upon Cottineau and informed him that he should not submit to his directions to go to Jersey, upon which the latter took possession of his trunk, containing his papers, clothes, &c. and had him arrested and committed to prison.

Application was made to John Inskeep, one of the judges of the Court of Common Pleas, and he allowed a habeas corpus, returnable 3d mo. 16th, 1803. The parties attended, but as Stephen's trunk, containing his papers, &c. had been sent to Princeton, the case was adjourned to 4th mo. 27th, at which time D. Cottineau engaged to produce the trunk. The parties met at the time adjourned to, and several witnesses were examined, some of whom knew Stephen in Guadaloupe, as a free man in business; and their testimony was reduced to writing. Cottineau produced a receipt for the passage money paid for three slaves, by Anslong, and urged that it was evidence that Stephen was his slave, he being one of the three mentioned in the receipt. This case presented considerable difficulty. Several witnesses testified that they had known Stephen as the slave of Anslong. It was therefore agreed, at the suggestion of Judge Inskeep, to refer the matter to the

Supreme Court. Accordingly, a habeas corpus was ordered by Judge Shippen,[3] returnable before the Supreme Court. About this time, Shippen and Smith, and, I believe, Yeates also, Judges of that Court, were impeached, and they were not willing to give Stephen a hearing until their case should be decided; and Stephen was kept in jail until the 2d of 11th month following, when he was brought before the Supreme Court. There were on the bench, Shippen, Chief Justice, and Smith and Yeates, Associate Justices. Jasper Moylan and Jared Ingersol[4] attended on behalf of the claimant, and Joseph Hopkinson[5] for the defendant.

The testimony taken before Judge Inskeep was by consent of the parties. A certificate was produced and read, of the municipalities of Guadaloupe, showing that Stephen had been an officer in the army for several years, and had conducted in a manner becoming the station he filled. The national decree, abolishing slavery in that island, was also read. J. Ingersol admitted the authenticity of the certificate of the municipality, and also the decree of the national Convention, but contended that the decree had been reversed, and that, therefore, Stephen again became a slave.

After argument of counsel, the Court said that the testimony in favor of Stephen's freedom and that against it was about equally balanced, and when that was the case, it became the duty of the jury to decide in favor of liberty; and accordingly, they unanimously decreed that Stephen was free, and he was accordingly discharged. The Court ordered him to pay $20, the sum Anslong had paid for his passage from Guadaloupe.

Stephen was a tall person, near six feet high, well proportioned, and had a remarkably fine open countenance. Soon after his liberation, he opened a shop in Market, near Tenth street, and soon got into good business as a barber. He was punctual in his business, courteous in his manners, and it may be said in truth the he was dignified in his deportment; so that he soon became respected by many of the most distinguished citizens.

I have said that Stephen Lamaire commenced business in Market street. He had two rooms, one front and the other back of it. One day, when he was out attending to his business, some men brought to his place several barrels on a dray. It was raining, and they asked permission of a lad, who was left in charge of the shop during Stephen's absence, to leave the barrels in the back room, saying they contained flour, and they promised to call for them when the rain should be over. The lad consented, and the barrels were stored in the back room accordingly. When Stephen came home, the boy told him what had taken place. Stephen immediately went to Alderman Abraham Shoemaker,[6] and informed of the circumstance, and asked his advice as to how he should act in the case. The magistrate advised him to let to matter rest for a few days, and if no body called for the barrels, to call and see him again and he would advise him further as to what it would be proper to do. The next day a constable came to the shop, in search of some sugar, which it was said had been stolen, and a drayman who was seen to take it from the premises where it belonged, said he had left it there. Stephen showed the officer the barrels, which were found to contain sugar, with a little flour on the top, and which proved to be the stolen article they were in search of. They took the sugar, and arrested Stephen for receiving stolen goods, and took him before Michael Freytag,[7] a Justice of the Peace in Moyamensing, who committed him to prison, not withstanding Alderman Shoemaker appeared and testified that Stephen had acted by his advice. I was sent for soon after he was committed, and became his bail, and he was discharged.

When the Mayor's Court came on, the Grand Jury found an indictment, and Stephen was arraigned for trial. The facts mentioned being established to the satisfaction of the Court, the Recorder remarked to the Jury, that he had not only acted as an honest, but as a prudent man, and recommended that they should find a verdict of acquital without leaving the box. This they did without hesitation. The Court animadverted severely on the conduct of Freytag.

In Philadelphia the colored people have numerous benevolent societies, for the relief of those, who through sickness or other causes, may need pecuniary assistance. Stephen filled the office of Treasurer to several of these societies, and, occasionally, had very considerable sums of money in his hands, and always discharged his trust with scrupulous integrity. He lived many years in Tenth street, between Walnut and Chesnut, and carried on his business reputably; and almost, if not quite, every new year's day, from the time he was discharged by the Supreme Court, as above mentioned, he called upon me and left some evidence of his gratitude -- sometimes a box of raisins or figs, or cakes -- and

never ceased to manifest his thankfulness for my attention to him as long as he lived. He has now been dead about three or four years.
4th mo., 1841

NOTES

1. *N.A.S.*, April 22, 1841; *P.P.A.S.* Acting Committee Minutes, Reel 2, 1803.

2. Dennis Cottineau was listed as a merchant in the *P.D. for 1800*, 35.

3. Edward Shippen (1729-1806) was the Associate Justice of the Pennsylvania Supreme Court from 1791-1799 and Chief Justice 1799-1805. He was impeached in 1804. *Who Was Who in America Historical Volume 1607-1896*, p. 553.

4. Jared Ingersol (1749-1822) was an Attorney General of Pennsylvania during 1790-1799, and District Attorney of the United States for Pennsylvania 1800-1801. Simpson, *Eminent Philadelphians*, p. 594.

5. Joseph Hopkinson was a member of the Common Council in Philadelphia, *P.D. for 1800*, 33.

6. Abraham Shoemaker was listed in the *P.D. for 1806*, 33.

7. Michael Freytag's name was in the *P.D. for 1806*, 33.

No. XIX.
Wagelma[1]

Wagelma, a colored lad about ten years old, was bound by his mother in Philadelphia to Peter de Boudee, a Frenchman, as apprentice, till he should be twenty-one years old. De Boudee being about to remove part of his family to Baltimore, from whence they were to take passage for France, in order to send the boy there with his wife in the 8th month 1801, put him on board the Newcastle packet. De Boudee had not obtained the consent of the boy, nor that of his mother, agreeably to the requisition of the act of 1780.

The mother of the boy was ignorant of his intentions until the boat was about to leave the wharf, when she communicated the circumstance to me. It was early in the morning, a little after sunrise. I hastened to the wharf where the Newcastle boat commonly lay; but, upon arriving there, I saw her in the stream, under way, with a gentle breeze.

I immediately mounted a fleet horse, and proceeded to Greenwich Point, about three miles below the city, and in about 20 minutes arrived there. A ferry was kept at this place by a widow, Elizabeth Marshall, a highly respectable woman with whom I had long been acquainted. I made known to her my business, and requested that she would order one of her ferrymen to put me on board the boat, to rescue the lad, with which she readily complied. The boat was in sight, and near turning the point, but as the wind was not quite fair, she was near the Jersey shore. No time was to be lost, and we set off for the packet. On reaching her, the hands supposed I wanted to go to Baltimore, and the captain ordered them to assist me in getting on board, upon which I made known to him my business, and inquired for the boy. He referred me to the cabin. Upon entering it, I found my visit anticipated by De Boudee, who was there with six or eight of his friends. I opened the business to him, and informed him that the lad must be restored to his mother -- that the laws of Pennsylvania did not permit him to be taken out of the State, without certain preliminaries which had not been complied with. He put the laws at defiance, as he expected soon to be out of their reach. The vessel was gliding gently down the river, and I began to think it was probable that I should be obliged to make a trip, though very unwillingly, to Newcastle. I called the captain into the cabin, and requested that he would order the boy to be put on board the ferry-boat, which was lying along-side of the packet ready to receive us; but he was not disposed to render me any assistance. I pulled a small volume out of my pocket containing the laws of Pennsylvania, and of some of the other States, as well as those of the United States, on the subject of slavery, the slave trade, &c. I read to him the clause in relation to removing colored people out of the State, circumstanced as this lad was. He became alarmed, and ordered the boy to be given up, upon which I directed him to go on deck, with which he promptly complied. The Frenchman became very clamorous, and threatened violence. the men in the small boat assisted the little fellow to get into it. As soon as this was observed by De Boudee and his friends, they attempted to throw me overboard, and as there were so many of them, I though it likely they would accomplish their object; but I was determined not to go alone, and I seized one of the company by the coat. They laid hold of my hand and compelled me to let go my grasp, when I would immediately lay hold of another, and in this way we spent some minutes--the man in the boat witnessing the conflict. They several times struck me on the hand with their canes. At length, the man in the small boat let her drop a little back, when I suddenly let go my hold of the Frenchman, and was thrown over the side of the packet and fell into the ferry-boat, after which we made the best of our way to the shore.

The animal I rode refused to carry us both, for upon the boy being put on his back behind me, the beast became perfectly unmanageable, and I was obliged to put him off, and he trotted along-side of me all the way to Philadelphia.

When I arrived at my house with the lad, I found his mother waiting for my return with the most intense anxiety. The meeting was mutually joyous to the mother and the son, and it was really amusing to hear the little fellow give his mother an account of my encounter with the Frenchmen. To witness the great joy those people manifest on such occasions I have often thought was an ample reward for all the difficulty, and sometimes bodily harm, that I encountered in rescuing them from their unrighteous oppressors.

Wagelma was a likely intelligent boy for one of his age. Slavery was not, at the time of the event I have related occurred, tolerated in France, but it was very uncertain whether he would not have been sold in Baltimore, or sent to the West Indies, where he would doubtless have been held in slavery all his life. One thing is certain, if De Boudee had succeeded in getting him away, he would have been for ever separated form his mother and friends, which must as a matter of course, have inflicted much suffering upon him and them, for no people possess stronger affection for their relatives than they.

NOTES

1. *N.A.S.*, April 29, 1841, 186; *P.P.A.S.*, Acting Committee Minute Book, vol. 3 (1798-1810), 142, 222, Reel 4.

No. XX.
William Bachelor[1]

In the 4th month, 1802, Joseph Ennells[2] and a Capt. Frazier, of Dorset County, Maryland, dealers in slaves, having purchased several running, (that is, those who had left their masters' service,) came to Philadelphia in pursuit of them. Those men brought with them a free mulatto man, who called himself David, alias Sam, to assist them in searching for the fugitives. In the course of their searches, they met with William Bachelor, a respectable colored man, about sixty years old, whom they claimed as the property of Ennells. They arrested him and took him before John Barker, an Alderman, where appeared David, alias Sam, who declared, on his oath, that he knew the man they had arrested, and who called himself Wm. Bachelor, perfectly well; that he (Sam) had at one time been overseer of a company of slaves, and that the man then before the magistrate was one of them, but that he had changed his name, and that his real name was not Wm. Bachelor.

David, alias Sam, was an intelligent, smart fellow, and told his tale with much confidence. He was so positive and circumstantial, and Ennells and Frazier appeared to be such respectable men, that the magistrate turned a deaf ear to Williams' earnest and pathetic declarations that he was a free man, and granted a certificate under the act of Congress, authorizing Ennells to take him to the state of Maryland, from whence it was said, he had eloped several years before; and they immediately set off on their way there. Ennells and his companion were on horseback, and William on foot. They had left the magistrate's office but a few minutes, when Doct. Kinley happened to see them, and after endeavoring, in vain, to prevail on them to return to the magistrate, and protesting to William's being a free man, he came running to me, almost out of breath, and upon entering my door, exclaimed, "They have got old William Bachelor, and are taking him to the South as a slave. I know he is free; he was, many years ago, a slave to my father, and he manumitted him; he carried me in his arms when I was an infant." He was exceedingly agitated and alarmed for the safety of the old man who, he said, had been a faithful servant to his father.

I inquired which way they had gone, and was informed that they went towards Gray's ferry. I immediately went in pursuit, and overtook them before they had reached the river Schnylkill, and about half a mile from it. I politely accosted Ennells, and told him that he had made a mistake in capturing William Bachelor, for he was a free man. Ennells immediately drew his pistol out of the holster and said, "We have had him before a magistrate, and have made proof, to his satisfaction, that the fellow is my slave, and have got his certificate, and that is all that is required to authorize me to take him home;" and added, "I will blow out your brains if you say another word on the subject, or make any attempt to molest me." I told him if he was not a coward, he would not attempt to intimidate me with his pistol, and observed, that I did not believe he had any intention of using it in any other way, but, as he was much agitated, he might fire it unintentionally, and I requested that he would put it up, or turn it another way, and not point it towards me, that it was in vain to think of taking the old man to Maryland; and if he would not voluntarily return to the city, I would certainly have him stopped at the bridge, where he would be handled much more roughly than I was disposed to deal with him.

While this controversy was going on, poor old William Bachelor's countenance bespoke the deepest anxiety, and addressing himself to me, he said, "O, master Hopper, don't let them take me, for I am not a slave, I am a free man, and all the people of Philadelphia know I am free; I never was in Maryland in my life." Ennells, upon the old man's mentioning my name, immediately remarked, "Your name is Hopper, is it?" I answered, "Yes, it is." He then observed, "I have heard of you; it is time the world was rid of you; you have done too much mischief already." I asked him what mischief I had done. He replied, "You have robbed many people of their slaves." I replied, that he was mistaken, I had only prevented Southern marauders from robbing free people of their liberty.

After much altercation, he agreed to return to the city with William, and took him to John Baker, the alderman who had but a short time before surrendered him to be taken to Maryland. Joshua B. Bond, a well known and highly respectable merchant of Philadelphia, Dr. Kinley, and many other respectable citizens, attended, and proved to the satisfaction of all, even of Ennells himself, that William was free, and he was accordingly set at liberty.

It was believed at the time that Ennells knew the man he arrested was not his slave; it was therefore concluded that he should be prosecuted. Thomas Harrison, a worthy citizen, long well known in Philadelphia as the friend of the oppressed, and who did more to relieve, assist and protect the colored people, than any other man in this country, and myself, called upon John Inskeep, an alderman, who issued a warrant for the arrest of Ennells. He was charged with attempting to take a free man out of the State by force, as a slave. Accompanied by two constables, we proceeded to the house of John Tomlinson, who kept a hotel in Market-street, where Ennells lodged, to execute the warrant. Upon making inquiry of the barkeeper, we were informed that he was in the dining room, up one pair of stairs, to which we went, and on entering the room, we saw him sitting at a table with his face towards the door, engaged in writing, and a pistol lying each side of him. As soon as we entered, he immediately raised himself up, and putting his hand on one of them, ordered us to withdraw, or he would give us the contents of it.

I informed him that those men, (pointing to the constables,) were officers, and had a warrant to arrest him for attempting to take forcibly out of the State a free man as a slave, and urged him strongly to put down his pistol and go with us. I told him, that if he refused, we would soon have a force that would compel him to submit. I would have him recollect, that he was in the heart of Philadelphia, and that it was the height of folly, as well as extremely imprudent, to try to evade or resist the law. I remarked to him, that his pistol was a very unnecessary article in Philadelphia, whatever it might be elsewhere, and it appeared he had not attempted to use it in any other way than to frighten people, and had not succeeded in doing that.

Finally, he agreed to accompany us to the magistrate's. On the way there, Ennells could not restrain himself within any thing like proper bounds; and upon some provocation being given him, (I did not notice what it was,) he gave one of the officers a severe blow in the face with his cane. The officer, in an instant, knocked him down and laid him sprawling in the gutter, and attempted to repeat his blow, for he was greatly enraged; but I laid hold of his stick and prevented it. I then observed to Ennells, that I thought he and I could agree better, and taking him by the arm, we walked on and the officers followed.

When we arrived at the magistrate's, I related the whole transaction, when he was bound over to appear at the next Mayor's Court, to answer the charge, and John Tomlinson, proprietor of the hotel where he lodged, became his bail.

Soon after the session of the next Court commenced, Jared Ingersol, a highly respectable lawyer, informed me by note, that he wished to see me at his office, and upon my calling upon him, he exhibited several letters from persons of great respectability in Maryland and Virginia, certifying to the good character of Ennells, and proposed that the prosecution should be abandoned. I told him that, as an individual, I possessed no authority to consent to the measure, but that the Committee of the Abolition Society should be immediately convened, and the matter laid before them; that I knew they had no vindictive feelings to gratify, and that I presumed his proposition would be acquiesced in. The committee met the same evening, and upon my representation, it was agreed that the prosecution should be dismissed, he paying the costs; to which he readily assented.

An effort was made at the time of William Bachelor's discharge to arrest David, alias Sam, for perjury; but he took care to keep out of the way, and left the city, and I never heard of his being there afterwards.

NOTES

1. *N.A.S.*, May 6, 1841, 190; *P.P.A.S.*, Acting Committee Minute Book, Vol. 3 (1798-1810), 172, Reel 4.

2. Joseph Ennells was listed in the Maryland 1790 Census as having twenty-one slaves, *Heads of Families at the First Census of the United States Taken in the Year 1790, Maryland* (Washington, 1917), 56.

No. XXI.
Prince Hopkins[1]

Prince Hopkins, a colored man, was sawing wood in the street, in Philadelphia, in the first month, 1802, when he was arrested by a constable, at the instance of a man by the name of ------ Kingsmore, son of John Kingsmore, of the city of Baltimore, as the slave of the latter, and taken before Alderman Michael Hillegas, who sent for me. Prince was a shrewd, sensible man, and put them upon the proof that he was a slave, and denied that he knew any thing about the parties claiming him. But young Kingsmore made oath that he knew him perfectly well, and that he was the slave of his father, and had eloped from him.

Upon my entering the magistrate's office, I found Prince in tears, and he appeared very much terrified. Young Kingsmore related so circumstantially the manner in which his father became possessed of him, that I began to conclude that the poor fellow's case was hopeless. I asked the Alderman's permission to take Prince into a private room, that I might have an opportunity of interrogating him alone. Permission was granted. I then took him into the parlor, and enjoined it upon him to tell me the truth, assuring him that what he communicated to me should not be used to his disadvantage. After some hesitation, he gave me the following account of himself.

He told me that he was originally the slave of Priscilla Gover, of Hartford county, Maryland; and that when he was about eighteen years old, Gideon Gover took him to Sunbury, in Pennsylvania, and that he resided at that place with Samuel Harris, who married Priscilla Gover's sister, about two years, and was then returned to his old mistress in Maryland. I enquired of him whether he went there with his mistress' consent. He replied, "She sent me there; and if you will write to Mr. Harris, he will tell you so, for he is *half a Quaker.*"

I then went into the office and told them that Prince admitted he was the man who had formerly resided with Kingsmore, and added, but he is a free man, having lived, with the consent of his former owner, more than six months in Pennsylvania. Young Kingsmore at this became much irritated, and charged me with giving him unnecessary trouble. I told him that I did not want to give him any trouble, and that it was not worth while to give himself any, in the present case, for that the man was free, and I would defend him in his just claim to liberty. He then requested that the man might by detained in custody till he could obtain legal advice. I was perfectly satisfied with the truth of Prince's story, and requested the magistrate to permit him to go and finish sawing his wood, and I would be responsible for his appearance when he should be wanted. My request was granted. I directed Prince, when he had finished sawing his wood, to call at my house, which he promised he would do.

He had not been gone long, before young Kingsmore returned, bringing with him a lawyer by the name of -------- Pollock. I expect he had been well feed, for he talked long and loud, and threw out some pretty hard threats as to what would be done with me for my most injudicious and impertinent interference, as he was pleased to call it. As the facts stated by Prince remained to be proved, I proposed that the magistrate should give me a commitment, and when Prince should call at my house, after he had finished sawing his wood, I would send him to jail with it. This proposition they took for an insult, and said the fellow was not to be trusted; and bore so hard upon me that I thought it was pretty near time to defend myself. I then told them that I would rather trust that negro, as they called him, than either of them; and I left the office, taking the magistrate's mittimus with me.

When Prince had finished sawing his wood, he called upon me, agreeably to his promise, and I gave him the commitment, and he took it to the jail and gave it to the keeper, who locked him up. I wrote immediately to Samuel Harris, at Sunbury, and he sent an affidavit made before Wm. Hepburn, fully confirming Prince's statement. Upon receiving this document, I took it to the magistrate, who thereupon granted a discharge for Prince, and he was never afterwards interrupted.

NOTES

1. *N.A.S.*, May 13, 1841, 194; *P.P.A.S.*, Acting Committee Minute Book, Vol.4 (1810-1822), 89, Reel 5.

No. XXII.
Germaine[1]

Germaine was a slave to John Pigot, of the city of Baltimore. Pigot entered into an agreement with Germaine to manumit him for the sum of $200. The latter procured a small blank book, in which his master wrote the contract, and which Germaine kept in his possession. It is dated May 5th, 1801. With his master's consent, he left his service and commenced the business of a barber in that city. He was honest and industrious, and whenever he could get a little money he would pay it to Pigot, and he entered it to the credit of Germaine in his little book. In this way, he, in a little time, paid his master $65. The little book is now in my possession.

But after some time had elapsed, Germaine was informed that Pigot had concluded to sell him to a speculator in slaves, and that it was probable he would soon be arrested and sent to the South. This information greatly alarmed him, and he ventured to give his master a hint of what had been suggested to him, but he could get no satisfaction, and was confirmed in the opinion that he was in great danger. At length he made up his mind to go to Philadelphia, where he hoped his master would not find him, until he could make up the balance of the $200. He accordingly went there and opened a barber's shop in Front, near Coates street, in the Northern Liberties.

But he had not been long there before Pigot was informed where he might be found, and he sent a power of attorney to a man in Philadelphia by the name of Charles Acue, who had him arrested in the 5th mo. 1802, and taken before Michael Hillegas, an alderman. Germaine stated his case to the magistrate, and pleaded with Acue to permit him to remain in Philadelphia, promising to pay his master every cent agreeable to his contract. But his entreaties were in vain, Acue insisted upon sending him to

Baltimore, and the alderman furnished him with the requisite certificate for that purpose, and Germaine was handed over to the custody of an officer to be transported to that place. It was then after 9 o'clock at night, and as the packet was to sail early the next morning, the officer took him to an inn in market street, near the wharf, where he proposed keeping him till the packet should sail.

Upon being informed that a colored man was in the custody of an officer at the inn above mentioned, I concluded all could not be right, or the man would have been committed to prison. I called upon Thomas Harrison and communicated to him my suspicions, and we went to the inn where we found the officer and the prisoner.

Germaine looked extremely dejected, and was so much so that he seemed hardly capable of explaining his case; but after some little time, he took his small book out of his pocket and gave us a circumstantial account of himself. We stated to the officer who had charge of him, that by the contract of Pigot with Germaine he had become free, and that he was a debtor, but not a slave. At our request the officer consented that he should be placed in prison till morning, when we could have an opportunity of inquiring further into the case, and between eleven and twelve o'clock at night he was safely lodged there. In the morning Germaine found himself before the Alderman again, instead of being on board the packet on his way to Baltimore, as he had expected.

When we appeared before the magistrate he seemed somewhat surprised, and exclaimed in rather an angry tone, "Well gentlemen what do you want! I have already heard and decided this case and do not want to be troubled with it again." I replied, "If thou wilt have a little patience, I will tell thee what we want in a very few words: we want justice. Thou hast given a certificate to send a free man into slavery, and we wish thee to recall it." I then explained the case to him and observed, that he certainly must be lawyer enough to know that Germaine was not a slave. He paused, and then asked the officer, who was present, for the certificate, which was handed to him. I referred him to several cases of a similar character, that had recently been decided by John D. Coxe, President of the Court of Common Pleas; and also to a case that had been decided by Edward Shippen, Chief Justice of the Supreme Court. After some consideration he said, "The man is a debtor and no slave." Upon saying this, he tore the certificate in pieces, and told Germaine that he might go where he pleased. The officer, fearing he might be brought into difficulty, requested that the man might be kept in custody till he could inform Acue, the agent of Pigot, of what was done. The Alderman replied, "The man is free, and I won't detain him a minute for any body; if Mr. Acue is not satisfied send him to me." Germaine took his departure, and never was any poor fellow better pleased. He subsequently paid Pigot the balance due him agreeably to his contract.

NOTES

1. N.A.S., May 20, 1841, 198; P.P.A.S., Acting Committee Minute Book, Vol. 3 (1798-1810), 176.

No. XXIII.
Joe[1]

In the summer of 1787, a vessel arrived in New-York, from the island of Bermuda. Among the hands was a slave name Joe, or Joseph. Joe had no idea of returning to Bermuda a slave, and, in order to secure his liberty, the natural right of all men, left the vessel and made the best of his way, on foot, to Philadelphia, where he hoped to find protection. But the day he arrived there, as he was passing down South Second street, and had proceeded as far as the corner of Norris' alley, opposite the house once occupied by the benevolent Wm. Penn, and which is still standing, he was accosted by a certain Captain Cox, as a fugitive slave, and ordered into the house. Joe did not appear to be at all alarmed, and readily complied. Captain Cox was a native and inhabitant of Bermuda, and was well acquainted with Joe and his owner. Joe feigned much pleasure in meeting with his *old friend*, as he called the captain--said he had come to New-York in a vessel that he named, and that permission had been given him to go a few miles into the country to visit his sister--that he had returned to the city at the time appointed, but the vessel had sailed. He also said that he had called upon the consignee and advised with him as to the best course he should pursue. The consignee informed Joe that his captain had left directions for him to go to Philadelphia and get a passage home, but if he should be unsuccessful, to return to New-York and wait till he should come again, which would be soon. This ingenious story satisfied Captain Cox, who informed Joe that there was a vessel then in Port that would sail for Bermuda in a few days. Joe was directed to the kitchen, while the captain went to make enquiry about the vessel, and engage a passage home for him. I was an apprentice with my uncle, in whose family Cox was a temporary resident, and I closely watched Joe's countenance, and soon became convinced that he was not so much gratified with meeting with his *old friend* as he pretended to be, for the tears were trickling down his cheeks.

My feelings soon became enlisted on behalf of the poor man, who could not altogether disguise the anguish of his mind. I had heard Algerine slavery spoken of, and I queried within myself whether, if Captain Cox had been captured by them and reduced to slavery. I should not be doing a meritorious act if I could be instrumental in assisting him to regain his liberty; and I soon came to the conclusion that it would not be less so to assist Joe in getting out of the grasp of Captain Cox. Accordingly I interrogated the poor captive as to his real situation and wishes. After telling him that I would be his friend, and promising to be true to him if he would open his mind freely to me, he gave me a look, that I shall always remember, as much as to say, will you betray me? he ventured to tell me that he was a slave, and did not want to return into bondage. I then set to work to devise some means for his escape. I was but a lad, and had but few acquaintances in the city, and was very much at a loss how to proceed; at length I called upon a friend who lived in the neighborhood and advised with him; he gave me the name of John Stapler, a friend in Bucks County, and said if the man could get there he thought he would be safe. I accordingly wrote a letter to the friend, explaining poor Joe's situation, and commending him to his protection, and gave it to Joe with instructions how to proceed. The captain soon returned and informed him that he had secured a passage for him to Bermuda, with which he professed to be much gratified, and forthwith went to the vessel. After a day or two he made an excuse to go to the house he had left to get his clothes. It was near sunset when he left the vessel, but instead of calling for his clothes, which were not worth five dollars, he make the best of his way to Bucks county. It was a pleasant moonlight night, and he reached the place of his destination about the break of day. He was received with all possible kindness and hospitality, and spent the remainder of his days in the neighborhood very comfortably, where there was none to make him afraid.

Joe told a falsehood, but it is said that necessity knows no law; his liberty was at stake, which was as dear to him as his life; and although I cannot justify falsehood under any circumstances, yet it is a question whether Joe was much more censurable than Abraham of old, when, in fear of his life, he said his wife was his sister. This was the first instance in which I was instrumental in effecting the escape of a fugitive slave.

NOTES

1. *N.A.S.*, May 27, 1841, 202.

No. XXIV.
Pegg[1]

Pegg, a colored woman, was originally a slave to Abraham Vandegriff, of Bucks County, in Pennsylvania, who, by his will, left her to John Harrison, of Point-no-Point, with directions that he should manumit her at the age of twenty years. He left John Harrison his executor, who bound Pegg to Christian Hess, of the city of Philadelphia, for the term of ten years. After she had remained some years in his service, he sold her to James Collins; he sold her to John Bishop, who took her to Virginia and sold her to David Welton, of Hardy County; he sold her to George Reynolds, of Berkley County, who sold her to Casper Rinker, of Frederick County, by whom she was held as a slave. After remaining some time with him he made an attempt to transport her to the south for sale, for which purpose he took her to Winchester; but Pegg becoming apprized of his intentions, refused to go, and as he was taking her through that town, about 9 o'clock at night, she laid hold of a post in the street, and cried murder as loud as she could. Fortunately for Pegg, this happened to be opposite the door of a respectable lawyer, by the name of Joseph Sexton, who, upon hearing the cry of murder, immediately went to the door to investigate the cause. Pegg stated her case and implored his assistance; at which Rinker became greatly enraged, and urged his right to take her where he pleased; alleging that she was his slave. But Pegg was so clear and circumstantial in her narrative, that Sexton had the woman committed to prison until the case could be enquired into. The next morning he sent for Jonathan Wright, who resided a short distance from town, and who was known to be a prominent and active friend of the colored people. Upon going to Winchester, he, accompanied by Joseph Sexton, called at the prison and conversed with Pegg, who soon satisfied them that she was a free woman. Jonathan Wright was a minister in the Society of Friends, and had been to Philadelphia not long before this event, on a religious visit, and had become acquainted with many friends in that city. He addressed a letter to James Pemberton,[2] detailing Pegg's history, as he received it from her own mouth. This letter was dated in the 11th month, 1798, and was handed to Thomas Harrison, Secretary to the Acting Committee of the Pennsylvania Society for the Abolition of Slavery &c.; who undertook to defend Pegg in her just claim to freedom. Christian Hess, her former master, had removed to the city of Burlington, New Jersey, and two of the committee were appointed to wait upon him--he exhibited her indenture, which had been duly executed before Lewis Wiess, Esq., a magistrate of Philadelphia, dated 12th of January, 1789, binding her to Hess for the term of ten years; but it did not appear that a manumission had been executed by John Harrison, agreeably to the will of Abraham Vandegriff; whereupon application was made to Harrison, and he accordingly executed a manumission dated 12th month 3d, 1798; and Frederic Beatez, a well known scriviner, and Thomas Harrison, both of the city of Philadelphia, subscribed their names to it as witnesses.

A particular and circumstantial narrative of Pegg's history was forwarded to Jonathan Wright, accompanied with a copy of the original indenture and of the manumission, duly authenticated. The narrative so exactly corroborated the statement previously made by Pegg, that no further difficulty was anticipated; but in this reasonable expectation the friends of Pegg were greatly disappointed; for by a letter from Jonathan Wright, dated 1st month, 16th, 1799, it appeared that Rinker, the claimant, was determined to dispute every inch of ground, and would admit nothing, no matter how clear, unless it was authenticated in legal form. J. Wright's letter informed the committee that it would be necessary to send two persons to Virginia to identify Pegg. Christian Hess was engaged to go to Winchester for that purpose, his expenses being paid; and after much delay, he was induced to go. Upon his return in the 9th month, 1800, he brought letters from Jonathan Wright and Goldsmith Chandler, which mentioned that Hess had testified so clearly to the freedom of Pegg, that no doubt was left in the minds of the judges; in consequence of which a suit was instituted for her freedom.

It was agreed that a commission should issue to take testimony in the case, in Philadelphia, and a letter was received requesting that the names of suitable persons for commissioners should be forwarded to Winchester. This request was complied with, but the court declined to accept them, observing, "perhaps they are Quakers." The commission was therefore issued, directed to any two aldermen of the city of Philadelphia. John Inskeep, Mayor, who was also an alderman, and Robert Wharton, and alderman, were called upon to act in the case, and they readily agreed to serve.

John Harrison, who was executor to the estate of Abraham Vandegriff, and also residuary legatee, testified that he bound Pegg to Christian Hess, and Hess testified that Pegg, whom he saw at Winchester, and whom Casper Rinker claimed as a slave, was the same person who was bound to him by John Harrison. Thomas Harrison and Frederick Beatez proved the execution of the deed of manumission. A copy of Vandegriff's will had been forwarded to Winchester, accompanied by a certificate of the Register of Bucks County; but a letter was received from Joseph Sexton dated 2d month 10th, 1802, informing that the certificate was informal, and that it would not be safe to go to trial until it was corrected. The committee addressed a letter to Robert Frazier, an attorney of Bucks County, who procured a certificate in due form--this certificate, with an official copy of Vandegriff's will, was forwarded to the Governor at Lancaster, and in a few days they were returned with his certificate, to which the state seal was affixed, certifying that James Hanna was register general for the Probate of Wills for Bucks County. Considerable delay occurred in executing the commission. When it was completed, except the signature of the commissioners, we discovered that in order to reach Winchester in season, it was necessary that the documents should be in the post office the next morning by seven o'clock, and it was eleven o'clock at night before we could procure the signature of Robert Wharton. Much anxiety was felt lest we should not procure the signature of John Inskeep in season. I retired to bed about 12 o'clock, but I could not compose myself to sleep; about 3 o'clock in the morning I rose and went to Thomas

Harrison's. I met him at his door upon the point of going to my house, for me to accompany him to John Inskeep's who was then at his country seat about three miles from the city. We arrived there a little before sunrise, and met a young woman just going out of the door, and requested her to inform the Mayor that we were there and wished to speak with him as soon as possible. In a very few minutes he made his appearance and affixed his signature to the documents which we had procured to be prepared. We had gone there on foot, but he would not permit us to return in the same way. He ordered a horse to be saddled and bridled, and I, without loss of time, mounted and made the best of my way to the city. I placed the papers in the post office, and they arrived at Winchester in season; but one hour later would have been fatal to Pegg's cause. T. Harrison staid and took breakfast with the Mayor, and went to the city with him in his carriage.

A letter was received from Goldsmith Chandler, dated 3d month 12th, informing that the documents sent by the committee so fully established the freedom of Pegg that the jury were but a few minutes in deciding in her favor; and she was accordingly decreed free, and set at liberty. Pegg, during the pendency of the suit, had been hired as a servant, and upon the case being decided she received her wages. Thus a case that was perfectly clear from the first, occupied the attention of the committee for a space of nearly four years, at the expense of considerable time and money; every possible obstacle was thrown in the way of her obtaining her just claim to freedom, and if the committee had not been as determined and persevering as her claimant, in all probability she would have remained all her life a slave.

NOTES

1. *N.A.S.*, June 3, 1841, 207; *P.P.A.S.*, Acting Acting Committee Minute Book, Vol. 3 (1798-1810), 44,54, 62, 69, 97, 130, 138, 165, Reel 24.

2. Joseph Ennells was listed in the Maryland 1790 Census as having twenty-one slaves, *Heads of Families at the First Census of the United States Taken in the Year 1790, Maryland* (Washington, 1917), 56.

No. XXV.
Sarah Roach and her Child.[1]

Sarah Roach, a light mulatto woman, was a slave in Maryland, and was sold by her master to a person residing in the State of Delaware. The laws of the latter State prohibit the introduction of slaves, unless brought in by persons who remove into it to settle and reside. All others, who may be taken there, under any other circumstances, become immediately free. Under this law, Sarah became entitled to her liberty; but she remained in bondage several years before she became acquainted with the position in which she was placed by being taken into Delaware. When she was made acquainted with her rights, she left her master, and went to Philadelphia, where she resided many years.

A few months after she was taken to Delaware, she became a mother. Her child, a daughter, remained with her claimant; but when she was about sixteen years old, she left him, and went to her mother in Philadelphia. Sarah had no idea that her daughter was free, and she called to consult me as to the best way of disposing of her, so that she might elude the vigilance of her master. Upon being made acquainted with all the circumstances of the case, I became satisfied that the daughter was legally entitled to her freedom, as she had been born in Delaware, after the mother had been removed there, contrary to the laws of that State; and I requested Sarah to inform me if any person should attempt to arrest her child.

The girl had been but a short time in Philadelphia, before her claimant discovered where she was. He went to that city in the summer of 1806, and arrested her; and without taking her before any magistrate, hurried her on board a sloop, that lay near Spruce street wharf, unloading staves. Knowing the girl was legally entitled to her liberty, and apprehending she would be wrested from him, if he remained with her in the city, he removed his vessel from the wharf, and anchored near the island, which is situated between Philadelphia and New Jersey, and commenced unloading the staves in a boat, placed by the side of the sloop, with the intention of transporting her cargo to the wharf which he had a short time before left.

Several colored people followed the master and the girl to the vessel. The mother came to me in the greatest distress, and informed me of the arrest of her daughter. I immediately made application to Abraham Shoemaker, an Alderman of Philadelphia; and upon the case being explained to him, he issued process to bring the girl before him. An officer was procured, and we proceeded to the wharf, where we hired a boat and two colored men to convey us to the vessel, on board of which was the object of our pursuit. The claimant of the girl saw us approaching, and being aware of our business, went into the cabin of the sloop, and immediately returned upon deck, with a gun in his hand. When we were within a few rods of the vessel, he, with an oath, ordered us to keep off, threatening us with instant death if we did not. I made no reply, but requested the men to go ahead, and take no notice of his threat. He became very violent and vociferous, until we moored our boat along-side of that into which they were unloading their staves. The man on board the sloop pointing his gun towards me, I informed him that the person with me was an officer, who was authorized to take the colored girl then on board his vessel before a magistrate, where I thought we should be prepared to show that she was free. He refused to permit us to go on board, and kept his gun pointed at my breast. He was in a violent passion, and very much agitated. I calmly reasoned with him, telling him he should recollect that he was a hundred and twenty miles from the Capes, and that if he should injure any person, it would be impossible to escape, for there were hundreds of people on the wharf, who would prevent it, and witness against him. While this conversation was going on, I kept gradually advancing towards him, until I came so near that I laid my hand on his gun, and pushed it aside; and at length, I laid hold of it, and turned the muzzle from my side. He gave a violent jerk to get it from me, and pulled me on board the vessel, but I still kept my hold of the gun. In the scuffle to get it from me, he trod upon a roller that lay on the deck, when he lost his balance, fell upon his back, and left me in sole possession of his weapon of death, which I immediately threw into the river. One of the hands, who was near the bow of the vessel, upon seeing his comrade sprawling upon his back, took up an axe, and ran towards me. I knew it would be in vain to attempt to retreat, for I could not get out of his reach; and if I could, I felt no disposition to do so. I advanced towards him, looking him full in the face, and said "Silly fellow, dost thou think to frighten me with that axe, when thy companion could not do it with his gun? Put it down. You are resisting the legal authority of the officer, (who all the time quietly kept his seat in the boat,) and are liable to suffer severely for your conduct." After some minutes, they became more moderate. We then inquired for the girl. They declared she was not on board. I then went into the gold--for the ship was nearly emptied of her cargo--and there I saw the girl, stowed away in a remote part of the vessel. I called her, and she came to me. I assisted her to get on deck. No person could discover, from her appearance, that she was in the least tinged with African blood. Her features were regular, her hair straight, and she was uncommonly handsome. I directed her to step into the boat that had taken us to the sloop, and I followed; the rest of our company not having left it. We proceeded without delay to Hollingsworth's wharf, a little below Spruce street, where we landed, and from thence went to Alderman Shoemaker's.

The claimant did not appear, and we obtained a warrant, charging the two men, who had conducted so violently, with resisting the officer. In company with another officer, I repaired to the sloop, captured the men, and in the course of a short time, had them before the magistrate. The Alderman read the charge against them, and they made no attempt to deny the truth of it; but, in mitigation of the offence, they alleged that we had come to take away their property. This apology availed them nothing, and they were ordered to enter into bonds with security for their appearance at court, to answer for the offence with which they were charged. This they could not do, being strangers in the city, and they began to anticipate a lodging in prison.

We knew that we should have some difficulty in proving the facts in relation to the birth of the alleged slave, and therefore proposed to the claimant, that if he would pay the officers five dollars each, and all other expenses, and manumit the girl, we would consent that the charge against them be dismissed. He readily agreed to this proposition, complied with the terms of it, and left the office. The girl went home with her mother.

NOTES

1. *N.A.S.*, June 10, 1841, 2.

No. XXVI.
George Cooper[1]

George Cooper, a light mulatto, went to Philadelphia in the spring of 1802, and in the 5th month of that year, he was arrested as the fugitive servant of Samuel Laird,[2] of Carlisle, one of the Judges of the Court of Common Pleas, and committed to prison. At the time, I was one of the inspectors of that institution, and as I was passing through it, George accosted me, and informed me how he was circumstanced. I addressed a letter to his claimant, and in a few days I received an answer, date May 9th, 1802, which mentioned, that he (Laird) had bought George Cooper of George Holmes, with whom his mother lived at the time of his birth. Upon investigation, it appeared, that the mother was a servant until she should be thirty-one years old, and was registered as such. Of course, her children were born free. George was about twenty-five years old, and was claimed by S. Laird as his property until he should arrive to the age of thirty-one, in consequence of his mother having been a servant until she was of that age.

Believing that Samuel Laird had no legal or equitable claim upon George, application was made to the Chief Justice, Edward Shippen, and a habeas corpus was issued, directing the keeper of the prison to bring George before him. A day was appointed for hearing the case, and the claimant was duly notified. Laird wrote to James Thompson, who was the master of Friends' Latin School in Philadelphia, to employ counsel to defend his claim to the service of George. At the time appointed, Edward Tilghman attended as counsel for Laird, and James Thompson also was present. Thompson was not a professor with Friends, but he did not appear to be a strenuous advocate for slavery, and was evidently embarrassed and ashamed of the business he had undertaken. I attended as George's friend, without an attorney. Thompson appealed to George, and told him, that he must know that his master was an honorable man, and would not take any undue advantage of him, and proposed that he should return home and let his case be tried at Carlisle; but George objected to this, saying, that his master was one of the Judges of the Court that must try him, and of course he would be judging in his own case. He was informed that Judge Laird could not sit on his case. In reply, he shrewdly remarked, that what had been said of his master was true: "He is an honorable man, and has great influence among the people; and although he may not sit as a Judge, his colleagues will and his influence is such that I would think myself as safe under his adjudication, as I would under that of his associates. I would therefore much rather be tried where I am. I have no wish to go to Carlisle."

After the case had been fully opened, Edward Tilghman admitted that George was free, and the Chief Justice discharged him accordingly.

George continues to reside in Philadelphia and conducts discreetly. I frequently see him when I go there, and he always looks respectable. Both master and servant mutually gave each other a good character.

NOTES

1. *N.A.S.*, July 1, 1841.

2. Samuel Laird was listed as having two slaves in the 1820 *Federal Census of Philadelphia*, 51

No. XXVII.
Maryland Slave[1]

In the autumn of 1828, Doctor Rich of Easton, in Maryland, went with his wife to her father's in Philadelphia, with the intention of remaining there until after her confinement, which was then near at hand. She took with her a female slave. They remained in Philadelphia several weeks, until she had fully recovered from her confinement. The slave was informed by some of her colored friends, that by being brought into Pennsylvania she had become free; and she called upon me to ascertain if that was the case. After hearing her story, I informed her that the laws of Pennsylvania permitted her master to take her away, unless he should retain her in that State six months; that no doubt he was aware of this circumstance, and would return home before the expiration of that time. She was very much disappointed, and manifested considerable anxiety. After a few minutes' reflection, she said, she would not go to Maryland, but would stay in Philadelphia. I asked her if she thought it would be right to leave her mistress in the situation she then was, without any one to attend upon her. She replied, that she had no scruples on that point, for her master was wealthy, and could readily get as many servants as he wanted.

Finding she was determined not to return to her master, I gave her such advice as I thought suited her case, and she left my house. She was not under my roof more than ten minutes. The next morning, the doctor and his father-in-law, Parson Wiltbank, an Episcopal clergyman, went in search of the fugitive. A colored woman, who resided in the parson's family, had an acquaintance living in the district of Southwark, and on going there, they found a band-box belonging to the slave. The people being ignorant of the law, the doctor took advantage of this circumstance, and greatly alarmed them by threating them with prosecution for harboring his fugitive slave. They assured him that his woman had been in their house but a few minutes, when she left her empty band-box, and, they believed, had gone to my house, where they supposed she then was.

About eleven o'clock, the same day, Parson Wiltbank called at my house, and after conversing a few minutes on familiar subjects, he related the circumstances of his daughter's visit to Philadelphia, and informing me that the female slave whom she had brought with her had absconded, he inquired if I had seen her. I told him I had, and gave him an account of the interview I had had with her. He said she had been treated with much kindness, and descanted, at some length, upon her ingratitude, as he termed it, in leaving her master's service. I replied, that *she* gave a very different account of her treatment; but, be that as it might, I could not censure her for trying to get her liberty. He asked if I knew where she was. I informed him that I did not. He then asked me if I could find her. I told him that I supposed I could; that I believed there were no colored persons in the city who would wish to secrete themselves from me; that they all knew I was their friend. He then said, if I would get her to come to my house that evening, at eight o'clock, he and her master would come there, when I would see that she would acknowledge she had a kind master, would beg his pardon, and gladly return home with him. This proposition excited in my mind indignation and contempt; and I replied, that I did not doubt but that fear would induce her to *profess* all he had said. "But what trait hast thou discovered in my character, that has led thee to suppose I am such a hypocrite as to betray the confidence this poor creature has in me, by placing her in the power of her master in the way thou hast proposed? No, I will never do it; I should never have a moment's peace after doing so." He then asked me to see the woman, and inform her that if she would return, she should not be punished for her offence, and should be treated as though nothing had happened. I informed him that I was perfectly satisfied she would not voluntarily return to her bondage; but if it would be any satisfaction to him, or her master, she should be informed of what he had mentioned. He then left me, saying, he would call again in the evening. He called, accordingly, bringing with him Doctor Rich.

Maryland Slave 151

I informed them that the message left in the morning had been communicated to the woman, and, as I expected, she refused to return. After some observations in relation to slavery, the doctor, addressing me, said, "She is now in your house, and I can prove it; and if you do not let me see her, I will commence a suit against you to-morrow for harboring my slave." In reply to this, I asked him, "Art thou acquainted with Solomon Law? he resides in thy neighborhood." He answered, "Yes." I proceeded. "He brought three such suits as thou now talkest of bringing, and was defeated in them all. The expense amounted to about seventeen hundred dollars; and he being unable to pay, it ruined him; but perhaps thou has seventeen hundred dollars to spare." He replied, "Yes, I can spare seventeen hundred dollars." "Well, thou canst find lawyers enough that need it; and those that do not will be glad to have it; so thou wilt have no difficulty in going to work." They then withdrew, and I saw no more of them until near 11 o'clock that evening; when one of my family informed me that a man was watching my house. Upon going to the front door, I saw a person walking very deliberately up and down the street opposite my house. I went over to him, and thus accosted him: "My friend, art thou watching my house?" He answered, "Yes." "Well," I replied, "it is very kind; but I am quite satisfied with the watchmen employed by the public. I do not think there is any occasion for thy services." He replied, "I have taken my stand, and I intend to keep it." I said, "I have no objection;" and returned into the house. Just as I was entering my door, the doctor came up to me, accompanied by two or three other persons. He was wrapped up in a large cloak, which so concealed his person, that, at first sight, I did not know him; but upon discovering who it was, I thus addressed him: "Why, doctor, is this thee parading the streets at this time of the night, and in this inclement weather?" [It was about the time called Christmas.] he replied, "It is." "Art thou watching my house?" "Yes." "Well, now, from motives of kindness, I do assure thee thy slave is not in my house; and that thou mayest not think thyself under the necessity of so exposing thyself, thou mayest search it." In reply to this, he said, that he would get a warrant in the morning, and search it with the proper officer. I then informed him, that if he would see that nothing should be taken from my front room, which I occupied as an office, they might make a watch-house of it; as I observed there were several of them, and it would not be necessary for them all to be out at the same time; but this he declined, and I left them. But just as I was about retiring to bed, I had occasion to go into the kitchen, and found the two colored girls, my domestics, in a very pleasant mood. I concluded I would watch their movements, to see what they would do, without letting them know that I noticed them. One of them put on an old bonnet and cloak, and went to the front door and opened it, looked up the street, and down the street, and saw nobody, for the watchers had secreted themselves; but they were closely observing her movements. At length she suddenly threw open the door, and run down the street at her utmost speed. The party pursued, and soon overtook her. She feigned great alarm, and called the watchman, who arrested the offenders and brought them to me. I told the watchman that those men were watching my house for a fugitive slave, and that they had mistook the individual whom they had so rudely seized, for the person they were seeking. I proposed that they should be set at liberty, and they accordingly were discharged.

The next morning I rose as soon as it was light, went out, and invited those men to come in and warm themselves: but they refused. About sunrise, they all disappeared, but two; and when breakfast was ready, I invited them to take breakfast with me; telling them that one could keep watch, while the other got his breakfast. They thanked me, but informed me that Doctor Rich had told them to hold no communication with me.

About eleven o'clock, the doctor came. I invited him to take a seat, and then asked him how his concerns progressed. He answered, "Not very satisfactorily," "Why, what's the matter? where is the search-warrant thou talked of getting?" He replied, "The magistrate refused to grant one." I then advised him to call upon Joseph Reed, the Recorder. He said he had been with him, and he also declined to interfere. I then proposed to him to take part of the seventeen hundred dollars, which he said he had to spare, and make application to a lawyer; perhaps *he* could help him out of his difficulty. He said he had been to Mr. Broome, who told him that I knew as much of the law in those cases as he did, and advised him to let the matter alone. I then told him to get an officer, and I would grant him the privilege of searching my house; for I had more authority in that case than all the magistrates, judges, and lawyers in the city. He observed, "That is very gentlemanly; but I infer from it that she is not in your house; or else she is where I can't find her." I again assured him that she was not in my house. He then said, "Suppose you were to come into my part of the country, and lose your horse, and you were to call on me and ask if I knew where he was, and I was to tell you I did, but would not inform you; would you not think I treated you very unkindly?" I replied, "that I should; but in this part of the world, we make a difference between men and horses. We think these people have souls; but we do not think so of horses." He said, "That makes no difference; you confess you could find my woman, if you had a mind to do so, and it is your duty to tell me where she is." I told him when I was of that opinion, I would; but, till then, he must excuse me.

A retail dry goods store was kept nearly opposite my house, and one of the slave-hunters obtained permission to stay in it all one afternoon to watch my premises, under the pretence of waiting for some person whom he said he expected to meet him there. His real object was not discovered until a day or two afterwards. So confident were they that the fugitive was secreted about my premises, that they kept sentry several days and nights. William Warrence occupied a house a few doors round the corner in another street from that in which I lived, and the back part of his yard very nearly joined mine; and fearing the slave might escape the back way, some of the company called upon W. Warrence and were trying to hire him to keep a look out and arrest her if she should attempt to do so. Warrence's wife happened to overhear their conversation, and upon discovering the object of the visit, ran to the kitchen and got a pitcher of hot water, and returning, said, "Do you ask my husband to watch neighbor Hopper's premises? Go about your business, immediately, or I will throw this in your face." The man decamped in a hurry.

J. Hill, a colored man, who had often given shelter to the weary fugitive, protected this stranger, and in a few days he removed her into the country, five or six miles from Philadelphia, where she was employed as a servant in a respectable, kind family. Here she appeared happy and contented; but thinking she would be safer, after some time, she came to this city, and in the course of a year or two she married. She and her husband were industrious and frugal, and lived happily together.

J.H., above mentioned, was of an irritable temper, and when his angry passions were excited, he was extremely vindictive. Taking offence at one of his neighbors, he charged him with criminal conduct, for which a suit was brought, and heavy damages recovered. From that time he missed no opportunity of wreaking his vengeance on every person of his own color that happened to fall in his way.

After the subject of this narrative and enjoyed her liberty nine or ten years, J.H. conceived the horrible and detestible idea of making a little money by betraying her into the hands of her master. He accordingly came to this city, in company with one of those wretches who make it a business of seeking out and capturing those defenceless men and women who have fled from worse than Egyptian bondage. J.H. left his companion in the street near the residence of the woman they were after while he went to see her. When he entered her peaceful and happy abode, she was busily engaged at the wash-tub; but upon the sight of the man who had rendered her such essential services in a time of need, her whole heart overflowed with gratitude and joy. She clasped him in her arms, and exclaimed, "Oh uncle Hill, (as she familiarly called him,) how glad I am to see you.' Having nothing in the house that she thought good enough to set before him, she left her work and ran to a cook shop in the neighborhood to procure something to gratify his palate and satiate his hunger. Hill accompanied her, and directed her to a shop where he told her she could get what she wanted, and whither she went. Upon entering it, she was pounced upon by the treacherous wretch who was in waiting, taken to the recorder and sent to prison, from whence, in a few days, she was removed to Baltimore; and the last I heard of her, she was in prison preparatory to being transported to New Orleans.

It is difficult to conceive of a character more entirely destitute of every principle of justice and honesty, or of one more deeply sunk in depravity and crime, than is here exhibited in the character of John Hill. And what estimate shall we form of the character of the individual--a man of education, a husband and a father--who could invoke the services of such a man in such a case?

NOTES

1. *N.A.S.*, July 18, 1841, 18.

No. XXVIII.
Solomon Clarkson[1]

Solomon Clarkson was a slave to John Hanson of New-Castle county, in the State of Delaware. At an early age he was sensible of the degradation consequent upon his condition, and determined to obtain his freedom in the best way he could. He was well aware that if he complained of hardship, or manifested much dissatisfaction with the condition of slavery, that his master would soon put it out of his power to seek his liberty in another part of the country, by disposing of him to some speculator, who would transport him to the South. As he increased in years his desire for freedom increased also; and in the year 1803, when he was about nineteen years old, he left his master and made the best of his way to Philadelphia. After being in that city a short time, he hired with Peter Barker; and in the course of a few months he opened his situation to that kind-hearted friend. Knowing he could not be long safe in Philadelphia, Peter applied to me to negotiate with his master for his freedom. Solomon was a fine-looking young man, healthy and well made, and every way calculated for making a valuable slave, and Hanson was by no means disposed to part with him without securing a good price. I addressed a letter to Hanson, informing him that I had been applied to on behalf of Solomon, and wished him to name the lowest terms upon which he would manumit him. After some time had been spent in corresponding on the subject, he agreed to take one hundred pounds, or two hundred and sixty-six dollars, sixty-seven cents. Peter Barker paid this sum, and Solomon agreed to live with him as a servant until the amount advanced should be refunded.

Solomon's condition was now changed, but he soon began to aspire to something higher than that of a servant and Peter consented to his making an effort to rise above it. He accordingly left his place, and hired with a doctor Reynolds. In the course of a few years, he managed to raise a sum of money sufficient to pay Peter Barker the balance due to him, and to defray the expenses of education in a respectable school in Allen Town, New Jersey. He went to that institution in the year 1812, and remained in it between one and two years. He had a remarkable capacity for learning, and in that time he made such advancement as qualified him to keep a school on his own account. He accordingly opened one in Philadelphia, and has ever since been employed in that line of business. He has been, and continues to be, very useful. Solomon Clarkson generally visits me, in New-York, once a year. The last time I saw him was in the eighth month, last year; he then informed me that he had thirty scholars. He possesses unusual intelligence for the opportunities he has had, and has conducted so as to conciliate the confidence and respect of all who are acquainted with him. By his own energies he had raised himself from the abject condition of a slave to that of a respectable, and useful citizen.

NOTES

1. *N.A.S.*, July 15, 1841, 22.

No. XXIX.
Levin Smith[1]

Levin Smith was a slave in Maryland. He had a wife and several children. In the year 1802, his master sold him to one of those speculators in human beings, who were in the practice of buying slaves for the Southern market. His purchaser lived in the State of Delaware, near to Smyrna, and had a small farm. He took Levin home with him, and set him to work until he could meet with an opportunity of selling him for a good price. Levin's wife and children were free, and remained a short time in Maryland, after he was removed to Delaware, when they went to Philadelphia. Levin became apprised of his master's intention of selling him, and made his case known to William Corbet, who lived in that neighborhood. He advised him to go to Philadelphia, and gave him a few lines to me, describing his case. In a few days, Levin called upon me, and handed me the letter from William Corbit, by which I learned that Levin's new master was a desperate fellow; and I was given to understand, that he might be expected to make a violent effort to regain possession of the fugitive. Levin went to live with his wife and children in the district of Southwark, and commenced the business of sawing wood to support his family. His wife took in washing. I instructed him to inform me if he should hear of his master being in the city. He had not been in Philadelphia more than a month, when his master, having discovered his place of residence, went there in pursuit of him. A small sloop that traded between Philadelphia and Smyrna, then called Appoquiniminque, lay at Gurling's wharf, in the lower part of Southwark, and Levin's master agreed with the captain to transport him home. It was high water about day-light in the morning, and they had planned to seize Levin in his bed, take him on board the vessel, and immediately start down the river. All this was to be done before Levin's family could have time to inform his friends: and if it had not been for an accident, occasioned by the captain's drinking rather too freely the previous evening, it is probable they would have succeeded. In the afternoon of the day before that on which the vessel was to sail, some goods were deposited in a store near where she lay, that were to be taken in her to Smyrna, but the captain neglected to take them on board.

Agreeably to previous arrangement, Levin was seized in his bed about break of day, his hands tied, and he conveyed to the vessel, where the captain informed them that he must wait until the store, in which the goods above mentioned were deposited should be opened. Levin's wife followed her husband to the vessel; and some of her friends, who lived near their residence, being informed of what was doing, ran to my house to solicit my assistance. I was in bed, when I heard a violent knocking at my door, and immediately got up, hoisted the window and inquired what it meant. Upon being informed, I dressed myself as quick as possible, put on an old coat and hat that I commonly kept near at hand, to wear when I went to fires, (being a member of a fire company,) and proceeded to the vessel. When I got there, I was informed that they had taken Levin to a small tavern near by; and upon getting there, I found a considerable crowd before the door. I inquired of the landlord where the persons were who had a colored man in custody, but he refused to give me any information; when one of the company about the door called out--"They are up stairs in the back room." The landlord stood in the door, and seemed disposed to prevent me from going in; but I pushed myself by him, and immediately went to the chamber, where I found Levin, with his hands tied together, guarded by five or six men. I inquired what they were going to do with the man. The words had scarcely escaped my lips, when as many as could get hold of me, seized me with great violence, hoisted the window and threw me out. I fell upon empty casks that lay in the yard, and at the time, did not feel at all hurt.

I knew perfectly well that if the man was not immediately rescued, they would force him on board the sloop and carry him off. I therefore determined to prevent it, if possible. As soon as I recovered from the fall, I went round to the front door that I had entered but a few minutes before, and proceeded up stairs to the door of the chamber from whence I had just been so unceremoniously ejected. I found it locked, so that I could not gain admittance. I then returned to the back-yard, got on the top of a high board fence, and from that upon the pent house, and in through the window, to a room adjoining that in which the party were. I took a small pen-knife out of my pocket, opened it, and holding it in my hand, threw open the door. Upon entering the room, among the kidnappers, I exclaimed, "I will see if you will get me out so soon again." I had no intention of using my knife, for any purpose but to cut the cord with which the poor captive was bound; and I did that before the company could recover from the consternation which my second appearance among them seemed to produce. Immediately upon cutting the cords that bound the man, I told him to follow me, and ran down stairs as fast as I could, with him after me. A wretched, motley company pursued us, calling "Stop thief!" until we arrived at the office of William Robinson,[2] a justice of the peace, who lived in Front below Almond street, in Southwark, near half a mile from the place whence we started.

The magistrate had not come down stairs, but in a few minutes made his appearance. I informed him of the circumstances of the case; how the man, Levin, was originally a slave in Maryland, and had been sold to a citizen of Delaware, who had removed him to that State, by means of which he became free. No person appeared to claim the man, and the magistrate drew up a statement of his case, to which he annexed his name, and the names and residences of the Acting Committee of the Abolition Society; with a request, that if any person should attempt to deprive Levin of his liberty, one of them should be informed of it. He was never after molested.

I returned home and took my breakfast, not being aware that I had received any injury by the fall. But upon attempting to rise from the table, I was suddenly seized with a violent pain in my back, which continued for several days, with such severity as to incapacitate me for attending to business. I have never entirely recovered from its effects.

NOTES

1. *N.A.S.*, July 22, 1841, 26.

2. William Robinson, a justice of the peace, was listed in the *P.D. for 1800.*

No. XXX.
Samuel Wilson[1]

Samuel Wilson was a slave to a person who resided upon the Eastern Shore of Maryland; and becoming weary of his condition as such, he adopted the following stratagem to obtain his freedom. He asked permission of his master to go a fishing, which was granted; and he left home, as his master supposed, for that purpose. As he did not return, his master, the next morning, fearing some accident might have happened to him, went to the place where Samuel usually fished, when to his astonishment and regret, he found the canoe anchored, a short distance from the land, bottom upward, and the man's hat on the shore near it. No doubt remained in the mind of his master that he was drowned.

Samuel went immediately, and as privately as he could, to Philadelphia, where he felt himself secure, as he had good reason to conclude that no efforts would be used to find him; and so it proved; for he was not even advertised. He let himself during several years in different families, and his faithfulness in whatever he undertook gained him many friends. All who knew him respected him.

Several years elapsed, I think seven or eight, when his master went to Philadelphia; and on a first-day morning, as he was passing down North Second street, and opposite the meeting-house commonly called Christ's Church, the congregation, having just been dismissed, were coming out in great numbers. Among them was Samuel, who being under no apprehension of danger, walked directly up against his master before he saw him! Master and man were mutually surprised; and the former immediately seized the latter by the collar and exclaimed, "Why, Sam, is this you?" Sam replied, "You are a stranger to me, sir." A smart controversy soon commenced, and was carried on with considerable spirit on both sides; so much so, as to attract the notice of those passing by. Sam retained his composure, and, with the fortitude of a philosopher, insisted that he was free, and was never a slave to any man. He said he could readily satisfy the gentleman that he was mistaken, and proposed the they should go to Charles Wharton's,[2] with whom he said he lived, and who would testify to the truth of all he said.

They accordingly went to Charles Wharton's, and when they arrived at his house, Sam ran up the high steps that led to the front door, opened it, invited the gentlemen into the parlor, and asked them to take a seat, while he called "Mr. Wharton." Sam had got his master, and the person who was with him, completely off their guard, and he concluded to turn it to his own advantage. Instead of calling "Mr. Wharton," he left the gentlemen quietly sitting in the parlor, decamped the back way, and made good his retreat.

After some minutes, Charles Wharton went into his parlor, and was surprised to find it occupied by strangers. He inquired what business brought them there--they apologized for the apparent intrusion, and stated to him the circumstances of the case. He informed them that the man had lived with him several months as a coachman, and had conducted himself to his satisfaction in that capacity; that he passed for a free man, and he always supposed he was so; and that was all he knew about him. The master then requested that Sam might be brought forward to answer for himself. C.W. replied, that if he was the man they alledged him to be, it was not probable he was then about the premises; but he said he would inquire. Search was made, but Sam was not to be found; and the master and his friend withdrew, grievously chagrined at the deception that had been practised upon him.

Sam knew that he would not be secure in Philadelphia, unless he could obtain a manumission. To accomplish that object, he made application to Jeremiah Warder, a respectable merchant, who undertook to negotiate with his master, and finally succeeded in securing the freedom of Sam for a moderate amount,--I think it was one hundred and fifty dollars,--which he paid, and Sam remunerated him by his faithful services.

Sam practised deception, it is true; but when we consider that he had lived the greater part of his life a slave, which is calculated to blunt the moral sense, and that his liberty was at stake, it would seem to palliate, though not to justify, the act. On every other occasion, those who knew him testified, that he was remarkable for his veracity and integrity. If professed ministers of the gospel can attempt to justify *slavery* from the Bible, or from the peculiar circumstances with which it is connected, surely *they* could find an apology for Sam in this case!

About the year 1805, Samuel Wilson lived, as a servant, next door but one to me in Philadelphia, and conducted with propriety, and used to relate the manner in which he got his freedom, with much pleasure.

NOTES

1. *N.A.S.*, August 5, 1841, 34.

2. Charles Wharton, a merchant, was noted in the *P.D. for 1800*, 134.

No. XXXI.
Philadelphia Apprentice[1]

Captain James Brown, who resided in Penn street, Philadelphia, had a colored boy bound to him as an apprentice. Brown was in the habit of staying out late at night, seldom returning to his family before twelve or one o'clock. The boy was obliged to sit up and let his master in. Being often fatigued with the labor of the day, he would frequently fall asleep; so that when his master came home, he would knock at the door several times before he could rouse the boy from his slumbers. On these occasions, the poor lad was certain of getting a severe beating with the captain's cane. His common treatment in the family was also very severe; so much so, as to attract the attention of the neighbors; several of whom frequently called upon me, and solicited my attention to the case. I made several attempts to see the captain, but could never find him at home.

After the course of conduct here described had been continued several months, a circumstance occurred, in the summer of 1799, that led to a legal investigation of the conduct of Captain Brown. Returning home one night very late, and knocking, as usual, several times before he could wake the boy, he became exceedingly enraged, and as soon as the door was opened, he seized the poor lad and bit off his ear. The boy screamed so as to wake several of the neighbors; and in the morning two women brought him to me. He was very much depressed and terrified, lest his master should punish him for leaving his home. I left the boy at my house, and went to the dwelling of Captain Brown, with the intention of endeavoring to prevail upon him to cancel the indenture amicably; as I knew a prosecution would involve him in considerable expense, in which case, not only he must suffer, but his family also; and I was informed that his wife was greatly afflicted already, in consequence of his conduct, and often remonstrated with him on account of his cruelty to the boy; but he was always denied, so that I could not get to see him. Failing in my efforts to obtain a personal interview, I addressed a note to him, asking for an opportunity to have a conversation with him in relation to a complaint that had been made to me, of his ill treatment of his boy; but he took no further notice of it, than to inform me, by a few lines, that, if his servant did not return home immediately, he would prosecute me for harboring him.

Upon the receipt of this note, I took the boy to Ebenezer Ferguson,[2] a justice of the peace, in Southwark. - The poor fellow gave a melancholy account of his sufferings, which moved with pity and compassion all who heard it. He pleaded with the magistrate, and with me, to let him return home, alledging that, if he did not, his master would almost kill him; and it was with difficulty that he could be brought to believe that he should never again be placed in his power, or under his control.

The magistrate issued his warrant to arrest Captain Brown, and gave it to an officer, with orders to take him and bring him forthwith before him. I waited at the office until the constable returned, who said he could not find him. After several ineffectual attempts to arrest him, I called upon Thomas Harrison, whose mind was ever alive to the sufferings of his fellow-creatures, and whose soul was dipped into sympathy for the oppressed; not that idle sympathy that can be satisfied with lamenting their condition, and use no exertions for their relief; but a sympathy like the apostle's faith, manifesting itself by works, and extending its influence to all within its reach. I shall always reverance the memory of this friend,--he was my precursor as the friend of the slave, and was my coadjutor in scores of cases for their relief. Thomas Harrison and Mordecai Churchman accompanying me, we called upon the officer who had the warrant to take Captain Brown. Before sunrise we proceeded to the neighborhood where he lived, and waited, perhaps half an hour, when we saw a woman come out of the house for a bucket of water. As soon as she had got a few yards from the door, we entered, and waited till she returned. We then inquired for Captain Brown, and were told he was not up. Upon being informed of the room in which he lodged, I proceeded to it; and after some time, he was induced to surrender himself to the officer, and was taken to the magistrate's, where he gave security to appear at Court, to answer the complaint of his boy; who was placed under my care till the captain should have his trial.

When the trial came on, a sense of cruelty was opened that was shocking to the feelings of all who heard it. A neighboring woman testified, that one evening she heard the boy scream as though he was in great agony, and upon going in, she saw a pair of snuffers sticking in his head, which required considerable force to pull out. There were numerous witnesses who testified to the cruelty with which he had been treated. On one occasion, the captain seized him by the hair on the back of his head, and held his face to the fire until his eyebrows were singed and his face burnt to a blister. The captain was convicted. The Court ordered the indenture cancelled, and fined him sixty dollars, ordered him to pay the costs, and stand committed till the sentence be complied with. He paid the money, and was discharged. The boy was afterwards bound to John Harrison,[3] until he should be twenty-one years old. He proved an orderly, good boy, and conducted to the satisfaction of his master.

NOTES

1. N.A.S., August 12, 1841, 38.

2. Ebenezer Ferguson, a justice of the peace, was listed in the *P.D. for 1800*, 49.

3. John Harrison was listed as a gentleman in the *P.D. for 1800*, 59.

No. XXXII.
Ben[1]

Ben was born a slave in the family of Frisby Lloyd,[2] of Hartford county, Maryland. When he was about twenty-five years old, he made application to his master, to put a moderate price upon him, and permit him to go to Philadelphia and try to find some person who would pay the amount. This proposition greatly offended Lloyd, who told him that, if he ever said another word about his freedom, he would sell him to Georgia. Ben appeared freely to acquiesce with his master's determination, and quietly resumed his labor in the field. But from that time, he was constantly looking out for an opportunity to make his escape. After a few weeks, Ben noticed a man who lived in the neighborhood, and who was known to be a speculator in slaves, having frequent interviews with his master. He became satisfied that he was endeavoring to bargain for *him*; and he concluded that then was the time for him to make his escape, if he ever expected to be free.

One evening, in the third month, 1805, Ben started for the North. It was a pleasant, moonlight night, and he walked as fast as he could, until daylight the next morning; when he concealed himself in a thicket, where he remained till the next night. He had provided himself with a pretty good stock of provisions previous to leaving home, so that he did not suffer for the want of food. In the course of a few days, he met a Friend early in the morning, as he was on his journey, and inquired of him the way to Philadelphia. The Friend soon discovered that he was "a fugitive from labor." He directed him to go to his house and get some refreshment; and told him that he would then advise him as to his future movements. Ben complied, and soon found that he had fallen into good hands. This Friend's name was Bellerby, who, with his family, had recently come from England, and settled on a farm in the State of Delaware. Here Ben remained some time, when Peter Barker of Philadelphia, went to visit the family. Ben, as he afterwards expressed himself, took a great fancy to him; and when he was about to return home, he ran and opened the gate for him. Having now an opportunity of private conversation, he informed Peter how he was circumstanced, and asked his advice as to what was best for him to do to secure his liberty. Peter took a piece of paper out of his pocket, wrote his name, the number of his house, and the street in which he lived, and gave it to Ben. In a few days, Ben made his appearance in Philadelphia, and Peter hired him as a servant in his family. He remained in this situation a year or two, when he left his place, and hired with Jacob Downing.[3] In Philadelphia, he called himself Jeremiah Waters.

After he had lived some years in that city, he made application to me to write his master, and endeavor to secure his freedom; for he was in constant fear of being discovered, and taken away. He had not the knack of saving money, and had nothing to pay for his liberty; but he made a contract with John Reed, who agreed to advance a sum of money for him, and Jerry, as he was called, agreed to serve him until the amount should be paid. I opened a correspondence with F. Lloyd, and he finally agreed to manumit his slave for the sum of two hundred and fifty dollars, which I agreed to pay; and a time was fixed when he should come to the city and conclude the business.

Frisby Lloyd came at the time appointed; and as he was going down Market street, near Sixth, he met his man, and immediately arrested him. Ben's appearance was very much changed since leaving Maryland. He was well dressed, and was much more fleshy. He did not appear at all alarmed and boldly accosted his master thus:

"What do you mean, good man, by seizing me by the collar, like a thief?"

Lloyd replied, "You are my slave; your name is Ben."

"My name is not Ben, sir; it is Jerry Waters. I can soon satisfy you that you are mistaken, if you will go with me to Mr. Downing's. He lives in Fourth street, a few doors above Market."

Lloyd began to think that, possibly, he might be mistaken; and fearing he might get into difficulty, he released his hold of Ben, and they set off for Jacob Downing's. As they were going along the street, Ben appeared perfectly at ease, and manifested the most entire willingness to have the matter investigated. But when they came opposite to a Court, that run out of Market street, by the side of an Inn, known as the Black Bear, he suddenly ran up it, sprung over a brick wall, and being well acquainted with the neighborhood, made his escape. He came immediately to me, and informed me what had occurred. I told him he must not remain under my roof, and directed him to a place of safety.

In the course of about a quarter of an hour, Frisby Lloyd called upon me. After asking me if my name was Hopper, he took a letter out of his pocket, and asked me if I wrote it. Being answered in the affirmative, he said that, since he had come to the city, he had apprehended his slave. I informed him that I thought he had acted very improperly; for that the two hundred and fifty dollars, the sum he had agreed to take, was ready for him. He said, to use his own language, "that was a force put;" that he did not consider himself bound by it, and would not take one cent less than five hundred dollars. I remonstrated with him, and endeavored to convince him the injustice of his conduct; but the more earnest I was in pleading with him to comply with his promise, the more determined he appeared to have five hundred dollars. I then asked him,

"Dost thou consider the bargain at an end?"

He replied, "I do."

I answered, "And so do I. Take thy man home with thee, and do the best thou canst with him."

"Is that your conclusion?" said he. "I thought you were a humane man, and would rather pay a little money than suffer a fellow creature to go into slavery. You can soon make up the amount among your friends."

I told him, his opinion of me was very different from my opinion of him; for I did not consider that he was either humane, or just.

After endeavoring to work upon my feelings, by telling me that he understood the man had a wife and several children, and how much it would grieve him to separate them, he said he would be willing to make some considerable sacrifice rather than do so. He would, therefore, consent to take three hundred and fifty dollars. I informed him that it was perfectly useless to multiply words on the occasion; I would give him one hundred and fifty dollars, and not one cent more.

After a pause, of perhaps a minute, he said, "I did arrest the fellow in the street, but he was so altered in his appearance, and denied so confidently that he knew me, that I concluded I might be mistaken, and get myself into difficulty. I therefore let go my hold of him, and he escaped."

I replied, "Yes, I understood so; he has been here, and told me all about it."

This astonished him; and he observed, "Well, I suppose you will comply with your contract?"

I replied, "There is no contract existing between us; it has been annulled by mutual consent. Thou has acted very treacherously."

Finding he was caught in his own trap, he finally concluded to accede to my proposition, and executed a manumission, upon John Reed's paying one hundred and fifty dollars. Jerry indented himself for a term of years to J.R. as a compensation for the amount advanced.

But he was still dissatisfied; and after remaining some months in the service of his new master, he proposed him to allow him to go to sea, to which he assented. Jerry, accordingly, set out to look for a birth as a steward. His master gave him a recommendation as an active, honest man, and he soon procured a situation on board of a vessel bound for Canton. Seamen's wages were then high, and upon his return home, he had an amount sufficient to pay John Reed the balance due him. For many years afterwards, he supported his family by sawing wood.

NOTES

1. *N.A.S.*, August 19, 1841, 42.

2. Frisby Lloyd was listed in the Maryland federal census of 1800 as having sixteen slaves. *United States: First Census*, Maryland, 1800, 51.

3. Jacob Downing, a merchant, was listed in the *P.D. for 1800*, 42.

No. XXXIII.--Supplement to No. XVI.
Tom Hughes and John P. Darg[1]

The following account was given a few weeks since, by Tom Hughes, to a respectable citizen of this place. By this it will be seen how much truth there was in the oft-repeated assertion, that he was anxious to return into slavery. I give it nearly in his own words.

"I know it was a disappointment to my friends that I went with Mr. Darg, after my release from prison at Sing Sing. I feel great gratitude for the offer they made, to protect me from slavery. I felt sorry that their feelings should have been hurt; knowing that they were unacquainted with my motives in doing so. I went with Mr. Darg, hoping to get my dear Mary, whom I now never expect to see again. Some time before my release from prison, Mr. Darg brought Mary, my wife to see me. He declared that we should both be free, and that we should enjoy each other's society as long as we lived. He said the abolitionists would do nothing for me; and that I should suffer here at the North. But I went with him solely with a hope of seeing Mary. I thought if I received bad treatment, or if he attempted to hold us as slaves, we should run away the first opportunity that offered. But I soon found that Mr. Darg had deceived me. Soon after I came out of prison, I went with him to Washington, where he said I should see Mary. When we got to Baltimore, he shut me up in prison, and then told me he had sold Mary, and that she had gone to the South. I can't tell you how I felt. He asked me if I consented to come with him on Mary's account, or on his account. I thought it would make it better for me to say on *his* account; and I said so. I hope the Lord will forgive me for telling a falsehood. After being in Baltimore jail sometime, he called to see me, and told me as I did not consent to come with him on account of my wife, he would not sell me;

and that I should be free, and he would buy Mary for me, if he could find her. After I came back to New-York, I was told by Mrs. Darg that some ladies, Mrs. Merritt and Mrs. Peck, had written to Mr. Darg not to sell me, because it was reported by the abolitionists that he carried me to the South on purpose to sell me; and I expect this is the only reason why I was not sold. I know Mrs. Darg did not want to have me sold; and I know that she did not want to have Mary sold; because I believe she loved her. Mrs. Darg was very good to me and Mary, and I feel very sorry that I could not live with her and be free. Mr. Darg always treated me pretty well, but I think he is a great villain, and I have thought so for some time. He don't treat Mrs. Darg very well, and I am very sorry for her, and I am very sorry for her; but I would rather live in the States' Prison all my life, than to be a slave. I always calculated on being free; and I only went with Mr. Darg that I might get my wife, and some money."

NOTES

1. *N.A.S.*, September 2, 1841, 50.

No. XXXIV.
Anne Garrison[1]

The following narrative I took from the mouth of the individual, as she related it, a few days ago, while the tears rolled down the furrows in her grief-worn cheeks--the circumstances, and her unaffected manner of relating them, deeply affected my heart with sympathy for the victims of a system which dooms its innocent objects to such complicated misery.

"I am now about fifty-one years old. I was born a slave in the family of Henry Halliday, of Easton, Talbot County, Maryland. He died before I was born, and I lived with the widow until her daughter, Margaret, was married to Littleton Gales, when I went to live with them. They resided about three miles from Haverdegrass. I was then about sixteen years old. After living some time with them, I was married to Levin Allen, also a slave to Gales; by whom I had five children, two sons and three daughters, one of the latter died, an infant. My husband died while my youngest child was a babe, and two or three years after his death, my master Gales, died. At the time of his decease, he was much in debt; and I became alarmed for fear my children and myself would be sold to pay his creditors; but my mistress assured me that she would never sell any of us out of the neighborhood. This afforded me some comfort, for I greatly dreaded being separated from my children. About three or four years after my master died, my mistress sold my daughter Nancy to Doctor Niblock, who lived at Charlestown, about three miles from Gales'. After she lived with him about two years, he moved to the West, and took her with him. I heard she was going away, and I wanted to go and see her, and take a last farewell. But I had married a man by the name of George Garrison, and being near my confinement, I was not in a situation to go. I never saw her afterward. I heard that he sold her on his way out; but I could never learn to whom.

As she was leaving the neighborhood, she saw her brother ploughing in the field, and called to him, to tell him she was going with the doctor, and to bid him farewell.

Some time before my daughter was taken away, I was sold to Samuel Hollingsworth, of Elkton. My young master, Gales, put one of my sons in prison, at Elkton, and sold him from there to the speculators. Another of my sons was hired to a tavern-keeper in the neighborhood. After he had been there some time, he was also sold to a speculator, and taken to Baltimore. There he saw a friend of his, by whom he sent his love to me; as did my oldest child, Levin, who had been sold some time before. One of my sons, when about six or seven years old, was drowned, having fallen from a rock into the river, while fishing.

When I was sold to Hollingsworth, I had a young child, and I took it with me, though Hollingsworth did not buy it--my husband soon after took it away, and sent it up the country where its owners never heard from it, and it is now free; but I have never seen him since he was taken away.

About nine or ten years ago, my son Robert left the service of the widow Gales and came to this city and hired with John H. Hicks, who was about leaving home. His brother Henry wrote to the widow Gales, on his behalf, and contracted for his freedom for a certain sum of money, which my son refunded by his services.

About two months ago, Hollingsworth put my three children and myself in Elkton jail, and advertised us for sale. We were bought on speculation by Isaac Purvis of Baltimore, and removed from the jail at Elkton, to the prison in that city.

While at the depot at Elkton, just as we were stepping into the cars to be transported to Baltimore, a young colored woman, with whom I was acquainted, came to me, to take leave, not expecting that we should ever see each other again. I requested her to get her father to write to my son Robert, and inform him how I was circumstanced; and she promised me she would. Her father wrote accordingly, and my son made application to John H. Hicks, who kindly advanced two hundred and fifty dollars to redeem me from slavery. When I received this information, my heart leaped for joy; but in a moment, when I began to reflect that I must leave my three dear children in jail, to be sold as slaves, separated one from the other, and taken where they would never see each other, or I see them again, I was filled with the utmost anguish. Parting with them seemed more than I could bear. The two oldest are girls, one about sixteen years old, and the other about fourteen; and the boy about twelve. When I was about leaving them, the little fellow clung to me and said, "Oh, mother, beg master to let me go with you!"

Ann Garrison on relating the above case, in the most pathetic and earnest manner, solicited me to endeavor to procure the release of her children; but, alas, I am powerless in the case. I however, addressed a letter to a friend residing in Baltimore, and he made application to I. Purvis to know his lowest terms. I received his answer, dated Baltimore, 8 month, 31st, 1841. He says, "I find his price is fourteen hundred dollars; say five hundred for each of the girls, and four hundred for the boy. He appears to set great store by them, and praises them as being very fine children."

Reader, canst thou peruse the foregoing narrative unmoved? Canst thou behold such complicated misery and not sympathize with the sufferers? If Jesus wept at the grave of his friend Lazarus, and if "Rachel was found weeping for her children, and would not be comforted, because they were no," what must be the anguish of a mother on beholding her children shut up like a company of brute animals, waiting to be sold to the highest bidder? separated and carried to a distant place to toil out their lives in worse than Egyptian bondage? My soul abhors the idea that any Christian can contemplate such horrible scenes unmoved.

Who can, for a moment, tolerate a system fraught with so much guilt and misery? Who can remain an idle spectator of it, and yet feel unrebuked by his own conscience?

This case brings to my recollection some remarks of General Eaton, when in Tunis, which may form a suitable appendix to the foregoing narrative.

The Tunisians had taken 920 Sardinians and sold them as slaves; of whom he thus speaks:

"Many of them have died of grief, and the others linger out a life less tolerable than death. Alas, remorse seizes my whole soul when I reflect that this is indeed but a copy of the very barbarity which my eyes have seen in my own native country. And yet we boast of liberty and justice. How frequently in the Southern States of my own country have I seen weeping mothers leading the guiltless infant to the sales, with as deep anguish as if they led them to the slaughter, and yet felt my bosom tranquil in the view of these aggressions upon defenceless humanity; but when I see the same enormities practised upon beings whose complexion and blood claim kindred with my own, I curse the perpetrators and weep over the wretched victims of their rapacity. Indeed truth and justice demand from me the confession that the Christian slaves, among the barbarians of Africa, are treated with more humanity than the African slaves among professing Christians of civilized America; and yet here sensibility bleeds at every pore for the wretches whom fate has doomed to slavery." -- *Life of General Eaton*

NOTES

1. *N.A.S.*, September 2, 1841, 50.

No. XXXV.
James Poovey[1]

James Poovey was a slave to ___ Coates, blacksmith, of the district of Southwark, Philadelphia. James had learned the trade, was a strong, athletic man, and very valuable. A number of young men, in that city, formed a society, called the "Young Men's Society for the Free Instruction of Colored People;" and for many years, kept a school, during the winter evenings, in Willing's alley, which was attended by fifty or sixty male scholars, mostly adults; some of whom made rapid progress in their studies. Many learned to read, and write quite a legible hand, and some made considerable advancement in arithmetic. James attended this school several winters; but, although very attentive to his book, he made slow progress in learning. At length, however, by dint of application and industry, he learned so as to read with considerable facility, in the New-Testament; which seemed a great gratification. He now felt his bondage increasingly galling; and finally came to the determination to submit to it no longer. In the year 1802, when about thirty-three years old, he ventured to open his mind to his master, of which he gave me the following account:

He informed him that he could read; at which his master expressed much satisfaction. James added that he could read in the Testament. His master said he was glad of it. He then informed him that he had discovered it would be a great sin in him to serve him as a slave, any longer. "Aye," says his master, "how did you make that discovery?" "Why," answered Jim, "the New-Testament says, we must do as we would be done by; and if I submit to let you do by me as you would not be willing that I should do by you, I am as bad as you. If you will give me a paper that will secure to me my liberty, at the end of seven years, I will serve you that long; but I cannot be a slave any longer." His master refused to comply with this proposition. Jim then proposed that he should be permitted to go to sea, and earn money to buy his freedom; this was also peremptorily refused. James then informed him, that if he would not accede to one of the above propositions, he would never get any thing; for he would not make him another offer. He said he was determined to be free, and walked off.

His master made application to a magistrate, who issued a warrant, and James was arrested and committed to prison, as a disobedient, refractory slave. After he had been confined in jail nearly a month, his master went to see him, and asked him if he was ready to return home and go to work. Jim replied that he *was* at home; and that he expected to spend his days there; for he never would serve him again as a slave, or pay him one cent-- "What do you come here for?" said he, "you have no business here." This greatly provoked his master, who forthwith made application to the inspectors to have him confined in the cells, on short allowance, until he should submit. I was at that time a member of the board, and as the subject was a colored man, they referred him to me. At length, as a last resort, he called upon me. "Jim has, till quite lately, been a faithful, industrious fellow," said he; "but of late, he has got the notion into his head that he ought to be free, and refuses to serve me any longer; in consequence of which, I have placed him in prison. When I called at the jail to see him, he grossly insulted me, and still refuses to return to his business. I have been referred to you, to get an order to have him confined in a cell, on short allowance, until he submits."

I told him that I had been long acquainted with Jim; that I had been instrumental in teaching him to read; that I had often admired his punctuality in attending school, and his industry and attention when there. He remarked that learning to read had done him no good, but had, on the contrary, made him worse. I replied, that I thought it had not made him worse, but had made him wiser. "I have some scruples," said I, "about ordering him to be punished; for he professes to be *conscientious* about submitting to serve as a slave; and I cannot be active in persecuting him, or say other man, on account of his *conscientious scruples*. I have myself suffered because I could not conscientiously comply with military requisitions; and the Friends have suffered much in England on account of ecclesiastical demands. I therefore, have cause to know, in some degree, how hateful are persecutors, in the Divine sight, and in the sight of man." He inquired if I would not comply with his request; urging it as a duty upon me. I told him I must be the judge of that, and peremptorily refused. This irritated him exceedingly; and he left me, saying, "I hope to mercy your daughter will marry a negro."

At the expiration of the thirty days, that being the longest term allowed by law, for the offence for which he was committed, James still refusing to return to service, was committed for another thirty days. When that term was nearly expired, the master called again at the prison, when I happened to be there. He told Jim, if he would go home and behave well, he would give him a new suit of clothes, and a Methodist hat; for Jim was a Methodist. "I don't want your new clothes, nor your Methodist hat," replied he, "keep them yourself; I never will serve you or any other man, as a slave again. I would rather end my days in jail, where I now am." His master left him, and never afterwards molested him.

At the expiration of the second term for which he was committed, he was turned out of prison, and enjoyed the liberty of a free man. I frequently saw him afterwards, and he always looked respectable and happy. He let his beard grow under his chin, and never shaved it. One day, when I met him in the street, I said to him, "Jim why dost thou wear that long beard? it looks very ugly." He replied, "I suppose it does; but I wear it as a memorial of the Lord's goodness in setting me free; for it was Him, that done it."

NOTES

1. N.A.S., September 9, 1841, 55.

No. XXXVI
Virginia Fugitive[1]

In the winter of 1808-9, several Virginia Planters went to Philadelphia in search of colored people, slaves, who had taken refuge in that city. Most of them had been there several years; and some of them, by industry and frugality; had acquired some property. These men had been informed where they might be found, and in the evening, after they had returned from their labor, they were arrested, to the number of eleven, and placed in prison until the next morning; when they were taken before Alderman John Douglass[2] to have a hearing. As it was late when they were arrested, I heard nothing of it till the next morning. I generally rose early, and upon opening my front door I found a letter, that had been, during the night, put under it, addressed to me. This letter stated that several slaves had been arrested, and were to appear before Alderman Douglass that morning; that the owners were men of great respectability and wealth, and had the most satisfactory proof of the persons arrested being their slaves; so that my attendance there could be of no possible benefit to them. But, if I had no more regard for justice, and the rights of those *gentlemen*, than to endeavor to wrest their property from them, by attending at the magistrate's, who knew his business, and would do justice in the case, without my aid, that my life would certainly be taken; and that my house would be burnt, while myself and my family were asleep in it. The writer invoked the most awful imprecations on himself, if he did not carry into effect these threats. As nearly as I can now recollect, these were the very words of the letter. I put it in my pocket, without saying anything about it to my family; as my wife's fears were often alarmed for my safety, and I did not wish to increase them. I had received this letter but a few minutes, when several colored persons came to inform me of the arrest of the slaves.

The time appointed for the hearing was 9 o'clock in the morning; at which time I attended. Richard Rush[3] also attended, as counsel for the claimants. They produced testimonials of character, signed by a considerable number of highly respectable individuals in Virginia, among whom I remember the name of Bushrod Washington,[4] one of the judges of the United States Court.

The examination was carried on with much earnestness, and some warmth. I think but two of the party were the real owners; and one of these failed in his proof as to the identity of the person he claimed; in the case of several others, the power of attorney was informal, and pronounced by the magistrate to be insufficient. After a protracted controversy, which lasted more than two hours, he decided that four of the persons in custody were slaves, and surrendered them, to be removed to Virginia; and the other seven he discharged. This decision exasperated those men to a great degree; and they gave vent to their anger in very severe and threatening language. The constables employed on this occasion were men destitute of principle, and one of them, particularly, was truly a "lewd fellow of the baser sort;" it was he who had sent me the anonymous letter above mentioned. When he found his game had fled, he raved like a madman. It afterwards appeared that those slave hunters had agreed to give the constables fifty dollars for each of the persons arrested, provided they got them away; but if any of them were discharged, the officers were to have nothing. Hence, their great anxiety to prevent me from interfering in the case.

Three men and one woman were decreed slaves; all of whom were married to free persons. When the magistrate gave his decision, their lamentations at the prospect of being torn asunder and separated forever, were affecting in the highest degree. the hardest hearts seemed softened. Even the slave holders were moved with compassion, and finally agreed to manumit them for seven hundred dollars. This sum was advanced by Thomas Phipps, and they returned to their homes rejoicing. The colored people, I have said, had acquired a little property; upon this they borrowed some money, and honestly refunded the amount that had been advanced.

After the business was settled, and their anger had cooled down, I invited the strangers to call and see me. They did so, and we spent the evening pleasantly together. We had much conversation on the subject of slavery, and parted with feelings of mutual respect. Before they left my house, they expressed regret at having given latitude to their resentment, and said that if they held the same opinions respecting slavery that I did, they supposed they should have done the same. The colored people had no attorney.

One of these Virginians was named Thomas Hinton. I have forgotten the names of the others. Those colored people ever afterwards manifested the mostlively gratitude for the assistance rendered.

I have in the course of my life received many letters of the like character with the one above mentioned; but they never had the effect to intimidate me, neither did I ever experience any inconvenience from their foolish threats.

NOTES

1. *N.A.S.*, September 23, 1841, 62.

2. John Douglass was listed as an alderman in the *P.D. for 1808*, 53.

3. Richard Rush was listed as an attorney in the *P.D. for 1805*, 127.

4. Bushrod Washington (1762-1829), the nephew of President George Washington, was the Associate Justice of the Supreme Court during 1798-1827. *Who Was Who in America*, 564.

No. XXXVII.
James Davis[1]

James Davis was a slave in Maryland. About the year 1795, he left his master's service, and went to Philadelphia, where he, soon after, married. He resided in Mead alley, in the district of Southwark, and supported himself and family, comfortably, by sawing wood. In the summer of 1805, as I was going down Front street, early in the morning, when nearly opposite the alley above mentioned, all of a sudden my ears were saluted with the sound of several voices, which seemed to denote great distress. I immediately hastened to the place whence the noise proceeded. Opening the door of the house occupied by Davis, I saw four or five men, among whom were two city constables; the others were strangers; one of them was Davis' master. Upon going into the house, I was informed by his wife, they had spoken kindly to him, made many inquiries as to how he was getting along and expressed much interest for him. At length, his master told him that he thought, when he was able, he ought to make him some compensation for his time. He asked Davis if he could not make him a small payment during the ensuing autumn, as the busy season was near at hand. By these insidious means, he threw Davis completely off his guard; for he naturally concluded from his conversation, that he did not intend to wrest him from his family. As soon as he had got concessions from the poor fellow, sufficient to establish his claim to him as his slave, he threw off the mask, and appeared in his true colors, that of a cruel, hard-hearted slave holder. He ordered the officers to secure him, and they immediately hand-cuffed him. On seeing this, his wife and children uttered the shrieks that drew my attention to the house. My feelings were deeply affected, and I used all the entreaty of which I was capable, to induce the unfeeling sinner to release the man. But it was all to no purpose; he disregarded the cries and entreaties of the wife and children, and treated them and me with ridicule. The children hung round me, clasping my knees, and begging me not to let those men take away their father. The scene was distressing beyond description.

He was hurried off to a magistrate, and from there to prison. His admission that he was the slave of the claimant was proved against him, so that resistance was useless. The next day they called for him, and I saw him fettered, put into a carriage, and taken away. When he was about leaving the jail, with a countenance that indicated a heart oppressed with the deepest anguish, he requested to speak with me in private. I took him into an adjoining room, and he asked me if I could not give him some advice. I was at a loss what to say. After some hesitation, I told him not to attempt to escape till he got a good opportunity.

He was taken to Maryland and lodged in prison, where he remained several weeks; when he was sold to a speculator, who started with him to join a cottle about to be taken to a southern market. After crossing the Susquehanna, they stopped at a miserable grog-shop, called a tavern; and after partaking pretty freely of stimulants, they commenced shooting at a mark. During this time, Davis was sitting by the tavern-door, reflecting upon his miserable and forlorn condition. At length he saw a man, who had been fishing, come with a small batteau to the shore. When he stepped out, he took with him a stone, attached by rope to the batteau, and which supplied the place of an anchor and threw it on the ground. It now occurred to him, that if he could rid himself of his irons, he could get into the boat and make his escape. He said the advice I had given him, not to make his escape till he got a good opportunity, instantly rushed upon his mind. Hard fare, scanty meals, if meals they might be called, and above all, the anguish of mind he endured, had very much reduced him in flesh, and he found that by some exertion, he could slip his hands out of his fetters. He watched his opportunity, and when they discharged their pistols, by a violent effort he got his irons off, ran to the river, picked up the stone anchor, threw it into the batteau, pushed off, and made for the opposite shore. The men threatened him with instant death, if he did not immediately return; but regardless of their menaces he pursued his course. They loaded their pistols as quickly as they could, and discharged them after him; but without effect. Upon reaching the other side of the river, he set the boat adrift, fearing some one would take it back, which would enable them to pursue, and perhaps overtake him.

After leaving the boat, he bent his course towards Philadelphia, and came directly to my house. His haggard appearance, and emaciated form, had so changed his looks, that I could hardly persuaded myself that it was really James Davis who stood before me. But he soon satisfied me on that point. He knew it would not be safe to return to his old home; and a place was procured where he could safely have an interview with his family. The next day, I obtained a passage for him, in a market-wagon, to Bucks county, Pennsylvania. In a short time, he procured a small house, and sent for his family to go to him. They did so, and he was never molested; his pursuers being unable to discover the place of his retreat.

No people are more ardent in their affections than the descendants of Africa. This was verified at the meeting of Davis and his family. It was enough to melt the stoutest heart, to hear his wife and children, some of whom were small, ask with most intense interest, "Where have you been?" "How did they treat you?" "How did you get away?" &c. &c.

It was an interview that excited the keenest sympathy in all who witnessed it.

NOTES

1. *N.A.S.*, October 7, 1841, 70.

No. XXXVIII.
Mrs. Morris[1]

A colored woman, who was a slave to a person residing in Lancaster county, Pennsylvania, left his service and went to Philadelphia, where she married a free man by the name of Abraham Morris. She lived in that city several years with her husband. They had things comfortable about them, and appeared to enjoy life as much as their more wealthy neighbors. But this happy state was not of long duration. Her master by some means discovered where she was, and in the year 1810, sent a man duly authorized to arrest, and either sell her or take her home. He proceeded to Philadelphia and apprehended the woman. Abraham Morris was an intelligent, industrious man, and had by him some money. He applied one hundred and fifty dollars of it to redeem his wife from bondage. The parties applied to Daniel Bussier,[2] a magistrate in the district of Southwark, Philadelphia, to draw up a manumission. The money was paid, the manumission duly executed, and the business settled satisfactorily to all parties. But the man entrusted to arrest and sell the woman, put the amount he received for her into his own pocket, and absconded.

About six or eight months afterwards, the master of the woman not hearing from his agent, went to Philadelphia, and had her again arrested. She was taken to the magistrate who had, a few months before, witnessed the deed of manumission, and he committed her to prison as a fugitive slave. Abraham Morris now called upon me, for the first time, and related what had occurred. I concluded there must be some mistake in the account he gave. I could not believe that any magistrate would conduct so arbitrarily, as to commit a person to prison under such circumstances. I went with the man to inquire into the matter. On arriving at the office of the magistrate, I found him under the hands of a barber, who was dressing his hair. I politely accosted him, and told him I had called to make inquiry respecting the woman he had committed to prison the previous evening, as a slave. He replied that he wanted nothing to do with me, and ordered me out of his office. I informed him that I had come there at the request of her husband, and as his friend and adviser; and I hoped he would not refuse to grant my reasonable request. He again ordered me to leave his office. I then took half a dollar from my pocket and offered it to him, telling him that I wanted an extract from his docket. By this time, he had become a good deal irritated, and informed me that if I would not leave his office, as soon as he took the seat of justice, he would put me out. I replied, I wished he would take the seat of justice, for then I should get what I wanted; but if he did so, I thought it likely it would be for the first time. He sprang from his chair and fixed himself on a stool by his desk, which was raised about a foot above the floor, and surrounded by a railing; and in an authoritative tone of voice, said, "Mr. Hopper, I order you to leave my office." I again offered him the half dollar: saying, "I want an extract from thy docket, in the case of this man's wife;" pointing to Abraham Morris. "Please give it to me; here is the money to pay for it." He then stepped down, took me by the shoulders, pushed me into the street, and shut the door.

I made application to Richard Renshaw,[3] also a magistrate in the district of Southwark, and procured a warrant for assault and battery. The officer sent to serve it soon returned to Justice Renshaw's, bringing with him 'Squire Bussier, exceedingly enraged. He charged Renshaw with a want of courtesy, and conducted himself so rudely that Renshaw threatened to commit him for contempt. After he had moderated a little, he entered into recognizance to appear at court to answer for his conduct.

This being done, I made application to Jacob Rush,[4] President of the Court of Common Pleas, for a habeas corpus. The woman being brought before him, the case explained, and the documents relating to it exhibited, she was discharged, to the great joy of herself and husband.

Bussier was an illiterate, vain man, and I thought it might be of service to him and the community to convince him that limits were set to his authority, which he could not safely pass. When the grand jury met at the succeeding sessions, I appeared before them, and notwithstanding the barber also appeared as a witness, and testified for Bussier, he was indicted. The next day, after the bill was found, the attorney for the commonwealth sent for me to come to his office. He informed me that he had investigated the business in relation to my charge against Bussier, and had come to the conclusion that I had better not prosecute it any further. I asked him if he had any other business with me. He replied he had not. I informed him that when I wanted his advice I would ask him for it, and turned to come away. As I was about leaving his office, he told me it would not be necessary for me to attend court, as he would let me know when the trial would come on. The sessions, however, passed over, and I was not sent for. Upon inquiring of the attorney, how this happened, he informed me that the case was not reached. At the commencement of the next term, I attended, and reminded the court that Daniel Bussier had been indicted at the preceding term, for gross misconduct in the exercise of his office as a magistrate; and that the attorney for the commonwealth had promised to let me know when the trial would come on, but I had not heard from him; that since the court had adjourned, I had inquired the reason why I had not been sent for, and was informed the case was not reached. I wished to know when it would be proper for me to attend. The court was surprised at this information, and said they had no knowledge of any business being continued from the preceding term. They inquired of the attorney how the matter stood. He said that he was then much engaged, but he would explain the business presently. They requested that I would attend the next day.

The next morning, I received a note from the attorney, saying he wished to see me at his office; but as I had been deceived by him, I declined going there. I informed him, by the bearer of his note, that if he had business with me, I could be seen at home; accordingly, he very soon called upon me, in company with 'Squire Bussier, who apologized for his conduct, and assured me that he deeply regretted it. Upon his doing so, I consented that the case should be dismissed, he paying the costs.

When a fugitive slave was taken before a magistrate, and discharged for want of proof, or other cause, he received no pay;

but if the person was adjudged a slave, and surrendered to his claimant, the magistrate usually charged no less than five dollars, and in divers instances I have known them to receive ten, and sometimes more; for this reason, some of them, who were not over conscientious, were glad of the opportunity of delivering them to the claimant.

NOTES

1. *N.A.S.*, October 14, 1841, 74.

2. Daniel Bussier was listed as a justice of the peace in the *P.D. for 1806*, 136.

3. Richard Renshaw, a justice of the peace, was noted in the *P.D. for 1806*, 34.

4. Jacob Rush (1746-1820) was the Judge of the Court of Errors and Appeals from 1784 to 1806 and the President of the County Court of Common Pleas, 1806. *Who Was Who in America*, 529.

No. XXXIX.
New Jersey Slave[1]

A man who lived in East New Jersey, went to the city of Philadelphia, in the year 1809, and took with him a young man about eighteen years old, a slave, to wait upon him. He remained in that city four or five months, when the slave called upon me, and asked me if he was not free. I informed him that he was not; that the law allowed his master to keep him there any time short of six months; but if he retained him longer term in the State of Pennsylvania, he would then be free. His master it seems was not aware of this fact until that time had expired; when he was apprised of it, he became alarmed lest he might lose his *property*. To avoid this, he engaged a constable, who came with a carriage to the door of the house where the parties lodged, in Walnut, a few doors east of Second-street. The coachman left his carriage in the street, and accompanied the constable into the house. The boy had just been in the cellar for an armload of wood; and upon entering the parlor, saw the officer and the coachman ready to seize him, and take him away. The officer told the boy to put down his wood and go with him. The lad was frightened and immediately threw the wood against the shins of the officer, and ran down cellar, slamming the door to with much violence. As soon as the officer recovered himself, he went in search of the boy, but he had gone out at the front door, and went directly to my house. When he got there, his black, wooly head was covered with snow; and had it not been for the distress and alarm depicted in his countenance, his appearance was enough to excite a smile. I endeavored to console him, by telling him that he was now out of danger; that he was free, and I would protect him. After some time he became composed, and when relating the circumstance of throwing the wood against the officer laughed heartily.

After he had been in my house about half an hour, the master and the constable came to inquire for him.

The master asked me if I had seen such a boy, describing him, and saying that he had no upper garment on, but was in his shirt sleeves, though it was snowing very fast. I told him I had. He then inquired if I knew where he was. I replied that I should decline answering that question. After some pretty severe remarks in relation to my harboring runaway servants, he left me. In the course of half an hour, he returned with the officer, and said that Alderman Keppelle[2] desired his respects and wished to see me at his office. I replied, that I thought it likely Alderman Keppelle had not much more respect for me than I had for him; but if he had more *business* with me than I had with him, I was at home, and might there be spoken with. He again withdrew; but returned in the course of an hour or too, bringing with him two constables and a stranger. The latter was very vociferous and impudent, telling me he was a lawyer, and making use of many threats of the consequences, if I did not surrender to the *gentleman* his slave; and said they had a warrant, and would search my house. I asked his name, he informed me it was Crane. I told him I was not in the habit of having my house overrun with Cranes, or Storks, or any such animals; and requested that they would leave my premise.

One of the officers then said, "Mr. Hopper, I have a warrant to search your house." I replied, "Very well, execute it." He said he should not like to search my house by virtue of the warrant, but hoped I would consent to his doing so without; saying he had great respect for me. I told him that he need feel no delicacy on the occasion, and had better proceed to the extent of his authority. He then observed, "You consent do you?" I replied, "No, I do not; but if thou hast a warrant, my consent is not necessary -- proceed to the full extent of thy authority; but if thou goest one inch beyond it, I will punish thee." I afterwards learned that application had been made for a search-warrant, but that it had been refused.

After those people had left my house, I inquired of the lad, particularly, what proof could be procured to establish the fact that he had resided, with his master's consent, six months in Philadelphia; and he referred me to the landlord where he had been staying. I accordingly called upon him; but he, being unwilling to offend his guest, declined answering any questions in relation to the subject. I then questioned the servants, and soon ascertained that the facts of the case could be established beyond the possibility of doubt.

I returned home, and wrote a note to the Alderman, informing him that I would be at his office with the boy the next morning, at nine o'clock; and requested he would inform the claimant. In the mean time, I procured a writ of habeas corpus; and when we appeared before the magistrate, the claimant, being present, stated that he was a citizen of New-Jersey, had come to spend some time in Philadelphia, and had brought the boy with him; alledging that the laws of the State where he resided allowed him to do so. He descanted at some length upon the courtesy due from the citizen of one State to those of another.

I attempted to reply, but was stopped by the magistrate, who said he would not interfere with the citizens of other States; that he should surrender the boy to his master; and if he thought he had a legal claim to his freedom he might prosecute it in New-Jersey. I then gave the officer who was in waiting a hint to serve the writ of habeas corpus; and he did so. The magistrate was highly offended, and did not hesitate to manifest it. He asked what was my object in procuring the habeas corpus. I informed him that I had anticipated the result which had occurred, and had determined to remove the case to a tribunal where I had confidence justice would be done in the premises.

The next day the boy appeared before the Court of Common Pleas, which was then sitting. The claimant also appeared, with his counsel; and after two or three witnesses were examined, it appearing that the boy had resided in Philadelphia six months, he was discharged free.

NOTES

1. *N.A.S.*, October 21, 1841, 78.

2. Michael Keppelle, an alderman, was noted in the *P.D. for 1808*, 33.

No. XL.
Maryland Slave[1]

About the year 1826, Samuel Low went from Easton, in Maryland, to Philadelphia, in search of a fugitive slave. After arriving there, and procuring the requisite authority, he arrested a man and took him to the office of Abraham Shoemaker, one of the Aldermen of that city. The magistrate had gone to his dinner, and had left the front door of his office open, but both the inner doors were shut and locked. They put the man in the entry, and S. Low and his company were on the step guarding him.

I was soon informed, of the circumstance, and hastened to the office. Upon arriving there, and seeing the position in which the parties stood, I concluded it would be no difficult matter to give the man an opportunity to make his escape. I stepped up to the men at the door, and in a peremptory tone and manner, demanded of them by what authority they kept the man in duress. Low replied, "he is my slave." I asked, "how does that appear? this is strange conduct, indeed,--dost thou think the laws of Pennsylvania tolerate such procedure--how do I know but you are a company of kidnappers?" This engaged the attention of Low, and his company, who turned from the man to me, and stood with their backs toward him. He suddenly rushed by them, and had run two or three rods before they discovered he was gone. They immediately raised the cry of "stop thief," and set off in pursuit of him. He got to the head of Dock-street, where he was arrested, and again given into the custody of his master.

The man who arrested him was a Hibernian, and appeared to be a candid, honest-hearted fellow. I remonstrated with him, telling him that the man was not a thief, but a fugitive slave. He replied, "then they lied, for they said he was a thief." I am sorry I stopped him; however, I will put him in as good a case as I found him." By this time a considerable crowd had collected. The Hibernian followed them some distance, close to the man who had hold of the slave, when he suddenly seized the collar of his coat and drew it down, pulling his arms behind him, and while in that condition, put his foot before him, and threw him upon his face on the pavement. The slave immediately started and ran at his utmost speed followed by his master and others, again calling, "stop thief." After running some distance he entered the shop of Samuel Mason, Jr.[2] watchmaker, who immediately closed the door, and the fugitive passing through, went out the back way, and made good his escape, and was never after recaptured.

The master being thus disappointed of his booty, made application to Charles J. Gersol, and his brother Joseph, who commenced a suit under the act of Congress, in the Circuit Court of the United States, against Samuel Mason, Jr. for rescuing the slave. This case created much interest and was productive of great excitement. The trial was conducted by those accomplished lawyers, on behalf of the plaintiff, with great skill, industry, and ingenuity--I thought worthy of a better cause. I was examined as a witness. In the course of my examination, I was asked what was the course adopted by members of the Society of Friends, when a fugitive slave came to them. I replied, I was unwilling to answer for any body but myself--if they wished, I would inform them how I would act in such a case. One of the lawyers then said, "well what would *you* do? would you deliver him up to the master?" I replied, "no I would not--in me it would be a great crime to do so. I never should expect to enjoy peace afterwards. But, on the contrary, if a fugitive was to ask my protection I would extend it to him, to the utmost of my ability. If he was hungry, I would feed him, if he was naked, I would according to the best of my ability, clothe him; and if he needed my advice, I would give him such as I thought would be most beneficial to him."

This case was tried before Bushrod Washington, nephew to our late President, and Richard Peters; and although the former was an inveterate slave holder, I did not hear him charged with manifesting partiality on the trial, which lasted several days. It was contended by the counsel for the plaintiff, that Mason obstructed him, and thereby prevented the arrest of the slave, by shutting the door. The counsel for the defence, replied that there was much valuable property in the shop, such as jewelry, watches, &c. and that they would be exposed to great danger of loss by permitting a promiscuous mob, composed of all classes of people, to enter it.

This cause, after able argument on both sides, and a lucid charge from Judge Washington, was submitted to the jury, who retired to their chamber, to deliberate on it. After being out a considerable time, they came into court and stated that they could not agree. The court ordered them out again, and they were kept together several days, until the court adjourned, when they were dismissed. The case was tried again. It came on at the succeeding term, and was conducted with renewed energy and zeal, by the counsel on both sides of the question, and was submitted to the jury, who retired to their chamber. After being out long enough to become satisfied that they could not agree, they came into court and said there was no probability of agreeing upon a verdict, and asked to be discharged. But the court refused to grant their request, and sent them out again, and they were kept together a long while, I think about ten days. When they first went out, I was informed there were a large majority in favor of finding a verdict for the defendant. But becoming weary of their confinement, and absence from their business, several went over, and they all consented to find for the plaintiff, with the exception of one, Benjamin Thaw. He told them that he "had eaten one Christmas dinner in a jury room, and he would eat another there, before he would be guilty of such a flagrant act of injustice as he conceived it would be, to unite with them in finding for the plaintiff." This jury, like the other were kept confined to their room till the court got through their business and were ready to adjourn, when they also were discharged. The case was continued for another trial.

On the third trial, the jury, without much hesitation, found a verdict for the defendant. Two suits were instituted on the same occasion; one was against Richard Allan, Jr. but neither of them were ever brought to trial. I was informed that the expenses of those suits amounted to seventeen hundred dollars, and Solomon Low, being in limited circumstances, it caused his failure; having spent the money which justly belonged to his creditors, in relentlessly pursuing an innocent man.

I fully expected that a suit would have been instituted against me, for I certainly was much more the cause of the escape of the slave, than Samuel Mason; but they never made any attempt of the kind that came to my knowledge.

The man who escaped, was a hearty, firm-looking person; I suppose, from his appearance, about thirty years old.

NOTES

1. *N.A.S.*, October 28, 1841, 82.

2. Samuel Mason, a watchmaker, was noted in the *P.D. for 1806*, 139.

No. XLI.
East Jersey Slave[1]

A colored woman, who was a slave in East Jersey, about the year 1827 left the service of her master, and went with her son, who was also a slave to the same person as herself, to Philadelphia. She had two sons in that city who were free, and had lived there several years, with one of whom she took refuge. The man who owned the mother was a stranger to both these sons, having purchased her of her former master after they left the neighborhood, and he lived some miles from it. A few weeks after the woman had escaped from bondage, the master went to Philadelphia in search for her; and concluding as a matter of course, that the fugitives were under the protection of one of her sons, he disguised himself by procuring a suit of plain clothes, such as are commonly worn by Friends, and calling upon one of the sons, passed himself off as one of that denomination, pretending great friendship for the mother and expressed a strong desire to see her. And so completely was the man deceived by this insidious stratagem, that he informed him that she and her fugitive son were at his brother's, whose residence was not far from where he lived. The master now concluded that he had succeeded in accomplishing his object. He procured an officer and immediately proceeded to the place of her retreat. She happened to be in an upper chamber, and looking out of the window, saw her master and the officer coming after her, and notwithstanding he had changed his costume she knew him. Fortunately, her son was at home, and she communicated the information to him. He immediately closed the door, which before was open, it being warm weather, and fastened it. The master and the officer arrived at the house but were refused admittance. They then placed a man at the door to watch, while they went to get a search warrant. By this time it was dusk. A crowd of colored people had gathered about the house, and the master had not left it many minutes, when some of them seized the watchman, and held him, while the woman and her son rushed out of the house--ran about a quarter of a mile, and took refuge in a house occupied by colored people in Locust street.

The man who had been stationed at the door of the house, as soon as he was released, followed to the place she had entered and took his stand on the footway, in the street, opposite the door. Soon after she had taken refuge here, her master arrived with his search warrant, at the house she had just left. Finding his slaves had gone and being informed of the place where they were, he returned to the magistrate to procure another warrant, when several colored people called upon me and informed me of the circumstance. I immediately went to the place where the fugitives had taken shelter, and took one of my sons with me, a lad about fourteen years old, whom I left in the street, while I went into the house; here I found the woman and her son stowed away in a closet, exceedingly terrified. I requested them to come out, telling them they would be quite as safe on the mantle-piece--that their pursuers would want no better evidence of their being the persons they were in search of, than to find them hid.

I knew it would not be safe for them to remain long there, and after giving them instructions how to proceed, I directed the door to be opened when the crowd immediately rushed in. I affected to be much displeased and ordered the men in the house to put all the intruders out of it; and among the number thus turned out, were the two fugitives. It was now dark; and in the confusion that ensued they were not distinguished by the man placed at the door, from the rest of the crowd, and I gave them in charge of my son, who took the mother to my house. I soon returned into the house and inquired for the two strangers, but they could not be found. The watchman, seeing I remained about the premises, concluded the fugitives had not escaped. In a short time I returned home, where I found the poor woman in the utmost trepidation and alarm. Without delay, I sent her to a place of safety. The son, on leaving the last mentioned house, went directly to the river Schuylkill. Being afraid to cross on the bridge, lest some person had been placed there to arrest him, he continued up the margin of the river until he found a small boat which he used to cross it, and then made it fast on the opposite shore. He proceeded, agreeably to the directions I had given him, about thirty miles up the country, and there he was kindly received and employed by a farmer.

How often have such events as these brought to my remembrance the expressions of David, when he said he was "hunted as a partridge upon the mountains," and I have exclaimed, how hard, how cruel and how relentless is man--his heart seems as impenetrable as adamant. Happy would it be for those enemies of the human family, if they could say in sincerity with the king of Israel, "I have played the fool and have erred exceedingly." Although they, no doubt, are often convicted in the secret of their own souls for the cruelty and oppression they inflict on their fellow-men, for infinite goodness "will suffer no man to be at ease in his sins," yet, by rejecting those visitations of divine grace they become "like the heath in the desert and shall not see when good cometh." I have frequently thought that of all men slave holders are the most insensible to human suffering.

Those two slaves being once more at liberty, and the master finding all his efforts to recapture them, prove abortive, he called upon me and inquired if I could give him any account of them. I informed him that I had understood they were in a fair way of doing well, and that it would not be necessary for him to give himself any further trouble on their account. He said it was in vain to attempt to capture a runaway slave in Philadelphia, for he believed the devil himself could not catch them. I replied, I thought that was probable, but I did not think he would have so much difficulty in catching their masters as he was much more familiar with them.

I had much conversation with him on the subject of slavery, and he manifested, I thought, some remorse of conscience, and at length gave an account of the measures he had adopted to ensnare the poor fugitives into his possession, and said it had cost him upwards of sixty dollars. Having abandoned the prospect of finding them, he finally agreed to manumit them--the mother for fifty dollars, which was advanced by a man in Market street, by the name of Vail, and her son for seventy-five dollars--this sum was advanced by _____ George, in Chester county, and they were faithfully remunerated by the services of these colored people, respectively. They conducted well and afterwards enjoyed the sweets of liberty without any to make them afraid.

NOTES

1. *N.A.S.*, November 4, 1841, 86.

No. XLII.
Maryland Slaves[1]

A colored woman and three of her children, (two sons and a daughter,) were slaves to Joshua Purnell, of Dorchester county, Maryland, and about the year eighteen hundred and six, left his service, and went to Philadelphia. The mother was near forty years old, and all the children were between the ages of twelve and eighteen. They had resided in Philadelphia about a year, when Purnell was informed where they live, which was in the Northern Liberties. He went to that city, and after procuring the requisite authority, had them all arrested and committed to prison as his slaves. They had but recently left him, and when taken, readily confessed that they were his slaves. The magistrate before whom they were taken, Frederic Wolbert, told me he very much regretted that he was under the necessity of sending them to prison, but as they acknowledged they were the slaves of Purnell, and had run away, he could not avoid doing so.

They had not been in jail but a few minutes, before I called to see them. When I arrived at the prison, I found the man who claimed them, on the steps, about going away. From his appearance, I concluded he was their owner, and upon making inquiry of him, he told me he was. I invited him to walk in, as I would like to have some conversation with him--he complied with my request, went in, and took a seat in the office. I asked him to excuse me for a few minutes, that I had a little business but would soon return.

I then went to see the woman, and found her in great distress--she implored my assistance--said she had confessed that she was the slave of Purnell, because she saw several persons with him, by whom he could prove his ownership, and she feared her punishment would be severe if she denied it. Her agonized countenance is as vivid in my memory at this remote period as if the circumstance had occurred yesterday. She stood before me wiping the tears from her face with her apron, exclaiming, "my children, oh! my children. I can suffer myself, but can't bear the thought that my children must go again into slavery." My very soul was moved with sympathy, and after telling her I would do what I could, left her, saying I would call again. I returned to the office, where I found Purnell waiting for me. I told him, as he was a stranger, I should like him to go home with me and take tea; after some hesitation, he consented to do so. A few minutes after we had taken tea, he proposed returning to his lodgings, I informed him that I wished to have some conversation with him in relation to the colored people whom we had just left in confinement; and I exerted all the power I could command, to work upon his feelings, and excite his sympathy. For a considerable time he appeared inexorable. I proposed that he should manumit the mother and place the children with some persons who would pay him a reasonable price for their services, for a term of years. He was not the worst of men, though he was hard enough. I kept him in conversation till near eleven o'clock, when he proposed calling upon me again in the morning. However, I prevailed upon him to consent to my proposition, and I committed it to writing, and after much entreaty, prevailed upon him to put his name to it.

Among the reasons he urged against complying with my proposition, were, that it would be rewarding the slaves for running away, and that it would offend his family and neighbors, who, would severely censure him. In the morning he called upon me again, and we agreed upon the sum he should receive, and I set out to look for situations for the children. After much exertion, in which I was assisted by my old, indefatigable friend, Thomas Harrison, places were procured. Edmund Hollingshead, a very respectable farmer, who lived near Moorestown, New-Jersey, agreed to take the oldest boy, and paid, I think, one hundred and fifty dollars for his services till he should be twenty-five years old. E.H. was a kind-hearted, benevolent man, and covenanted to give the lad a reasonable portion of schooling and the customary freedom dues. The contract was faithfully fulfilled by both the parties, and, I was informed, that they were mutually satisfied with each other. I have forgotten what became of the other two children, but I recollect at the time, it was believed they were equally well disposed of.

The next morning after I had concluded the contract with Purnell, I rose early, went to the prison, and informed the captives of what I had done, which was a great relief to them.

After the business was all settled and Purnell counted the cost--what he had paid for taking them up, and other expenses, he said he had but little left.

A few years after these circumstances occurred, Purnell died, when it appeared that he had not acquainted his family with what he had done; and his executors ascertaining where the woman could be found, one of them had her arrested, as belonging to the estate. At the time she was arrested, she lived in the neighborhood of Darby, about seven miles from Philadelphia. She alledged that she was free, and referred to me as having been a witness to the manumission; and some respectable persons in the neighborhood, appeared on her behalf, and insisted upon her being taken to Philadelphia, that the case might be investigated; and thither they went. It was on the fourth day of the week, and I was at meeting. A person came there and called me out. I immediately went to William Moulders, in the Northern Liberties--he was a magistrate, and there I found the woman, and the person at whose instance she had been apprehended. I related the circumstances of her manumission, and stated that the document was on file among the papers of the Abolition Society, and proposed going for it; but the magistrate said it was unnecessary--that he was fully satisfied. She was again set at liberty, and never again molested.

NOTES

1. *N.A.S.*, November 11, 1841, 95.

No. XLIII.
Phebe Numbers[1]

Phebe Numbers was a slave to Charles Buckmaster, of the State of Maryland, whose daughter married Charles Hamm, of the same place. At the time of their marriage, he gave Phebe to his daughter, with the understanding that she was to be free at his death, which took place a few years after their marriage, when she was set at liberty, agreeably with the request of her old master. Phebe married, and lived with her husband in a small house near the residence of Charles Hamm. In the course of a few years, (in 1826,) Phebe went to Philadelphia, to make a visit to her sister, who resided in that city, taking her two children with her. Both the children being born after the decease of her old master, were free. They had been in Philadelphia but a few days, when she concluded to return home, and went to Pine-st. wharf to look for a vessel, in which she might get a passage, where she met Charles Hamm. As soon as he saw her, he arrested her as his slave; but knowing that he had no legal claim upon her, she refused to go with him; in consequence of which, he fell upon and beat and shamefully abused her in the public streets, insisting upon his right to compel her to go with him. A considerable crowd had collected, and they followed Hamm and Phebe, her children being with her, until they had proceeded as far as Second-street, a few doors below Pine-street, when Phebe seeing a cellar door open, ran down the cellar with her two children. They were small--the oldest not being more than six years of age. Hamm had become alarmed, from an apprehension that the people, who had collected on the occasion, would wrest his *property* from him. As soon as Phebe and her children entered the cellar, Hamm shut the door and stood upon it.

While matters were thus circumstanced, several colored people called upon me, and I immediately hastened to the place where Phebe and her children were prisoners, and found Hamm standing on the cellar door, as was above mentioned. I inquired of him by what authority he kept the woman and her children confined in that cellar. He informed me that they were his slaves. I asked his permission to speak to them, but he peremptorily refused. I then took hold of his arm and led him off the cellar door, and went down into it, when he immediately shut the door, and again took his stand upon it. This cellar was opposite the market; and as soon as the butchers, of whom there were many there, heard that I was shut up in the cellar, they came running out of the market, and unceremoniously removed Hamm from it, and Phebe and her two children, with myself, soon made our appearance in the street. I then told Hamm where I lived, and that I should take the woman and her children home with me, and if he had any claim upon them, he would find them there; and directing the woman to follow me, went home with them, followed by the crowd.

After I had taken her home, and had heard her story, I applied to John Binns,[2] an alderman, and procured a warrant, and when Hamm came to look after his slaves, as he termed them, I had him arrested, taken to the magistrate, and after considerable difficulty, he procured bail to appear at Court to answer to a charge of assault and battery committed upon the woman. Reuben Gilder, a saddler, who had a few years before come from his neighborhood, became his security.

Charles Buckmaster, the younger, and brother to Hamm's wife, called upon me, and confirmed Phebe's statement. A habeas corpus was obtained, and Phebe and her children were taken before the Mayor's court, which was then in session. David Paul Brown appeared as counsel for Phebe and her children, and _____ _____ on behalf of the claimant, who now abandoned his claims to the mother, but contended that the children were his property, as she had not been manumitted in the usual way, by a written instrument. He also contended, that he had a right to her, if he chose to enforce it; for although his father-in-law might at one time have intended to manumit her, yet he had not done so in legal form.

Charles Buckmaster, junior, was examined as a witness in the case, and he stated that he knew that it was his father's intention that Phebe should be free at his death, and that Charles Hamm was cognizant of that fact, and had acted accordingly, by permitting her to leave his service and live with her husband. After this case had occupied the attention of the court several hours, Hamm became alarmed on account of his treatment of Phebe, and by the advice of his attorney proposed a compromise. This was agreed to; and upon his offering to abandon his claim to the children, it was stipulated that the suit against him for assault and battery, should be dismissed.

The matter being thus adjusted, the court, by the consent of the parties, decided that the children were free, and they, with their mother, were accordingly set at liberty.

Phebe not thinking herself safe in Delaware, remained in Philadelphia, where she continued to reside, and having experienced much kindness from George Robinson and his family, as well as from many others, she called the next child of which she was the mother, Isaac George Tobias Numbers, as a mark of respect for her benefactors.

NOTES

1. *N.A.S.*, November 18, 1841, 94.

2. John Binns, an alderman, was listed in the *P.D. for 1810*, 35.

No. XLIV.
Red Betsey[1]

Jacob Read,[2] of Charleston, South Carolina, was a member of the Senate of the United States; and as Congress then sat in Philadelphia, he went there in the latter part of the year 1797, to discharge the duties of his station, and took his family with him, and several slaves to wait upon them. Among the number was a bright mulatto, who assumed the name of Betsey. Although her situation was much more tolerable than many others, she felt the galling chains of slavery too grievous to be patiently borne; and she determined to make an effort to be free. She was aware of the difficulty attending the enterprise; but after full deliberation, she resolved to make the attempt.

She accordingly left her master, and procured a situation as a domestic in another family; but being under the necessity of going into the street for water, and on other occasions, she suffered much from fear that she might be discovered and again reduced to slavery; though she was not advertised, and it did not appear that her master took any measures to recover her.

After she had remained in this situation some months, she called upon me for advice. She was very much depressed, and said that she could take no comfort in anything; that she could not sleep; for the dread of being apprehended was constantly pressing upon her. She solicited me to take her into my family, saying that she thought she would be safer there, than she was in the place where she then lived. I referred her to my wife, who agreed to employ her; and accordingly she came to reside with us. She was now under no necessity of going into the street on any occasion; but still, frequent and deep sighs indicated that her sufferings were but little abated.

In the year 1799, the yellow fever prevailed in Philadelphia; and in the early part of the season my brother was attacked with it.

The family where he boarded informed me, early the next morning after he was taken sick, that they were unwilling to keep him, fearing that he might communicate the disorder. There remained no alternative but to take him into my family, or send him to the hospital. After consulting with my wife, we chose the former, and I took him home. Just as I entered my door with him, she was assisting an indented colored girl, who was a member of my family, to go up stairs. She had been suddenly seized with the same complaint, and they both appeared very ill. We had several small children, one of them an infant, and several apprentices. It was proposed that the boys should go to their parents in the country, and that my wife should take the children to Peter Barker's, who resided in a part of the city that the infection had not reached, and who, with his wife, had kindly offered them a temporary asylum. She went with much reluctance, and left the sick in charge of Betsey and myself. Betsey proved an excellent, skillful nurse, having had much experience in that line, as the yellow fever frequently prevailed in her native place. My brother recovered, but the girl died; when I retired with my family to the country, and took Betsey with us.

After the fever had subsided, we returned to the city. Betsey had been a family-servant, and was an excellent cook; but having always lived amidst great affluence, she was rather too extravagant to suit my circumstances. Moreover, I thought her qualifications ought to command higher wages than was proper for me to give; and I concluded to seek a more suitable situation for her. Accordingly, I made application to G.W. a wealthy citizen, and inquired of him if he did not want an excellent cook. He replied in the affirmative. I recommended Betsey, and he agreed to take her into his service. After she had been with him some time, he called upon me, and expressed his entire satisfaction with her, except the great reluctance she manifested to go in the street on any occasion; and especially to market. Being satisfied that he would not betray my confidence, I explained to him her situation, and told him, that if he would become responsible for five hundred dollars, I would guarantee that she should not be taken from him, to which he readily agreed. I then sent for Betsey and informed her she might go where she pleased, without any risk; for I had made such arrangements as would render her situation entirely safe. This was joyful intelligence, but it seemed difficult for her to divest herself of the dread of being again reduced to bondage, that had so long distressed her. However, after this time she freely attended to any orders she received from her employers; and from that hour to this, she has mostly done their marketing, always accompanied with a servant to carry it home. She is now seventy-five years old, and has resided forty years in this same family, who place unbounded confidence in her intelligence, integrity, and good management. If a large dinner party is to be given, the money is placed in Betsey's hands, and she is left to make such purchases, and hire such aid, as she thinks proper.

Betsey was much attached to a man and his wife, who were her fellow servants, and who left the service of their master about the same time that she did, but were not quite so fortunate in procuring a comfortable subsistance. The wife was a dress-maker; but in consequence of their situation, she was often without work, and besides, her health was so delicate that she was frequently unable to pursue her business; so that Betsey, whose heart was always alive to the wants of her fellow sufferers, divided with them the fruits of her own industry. They have been dead some years, and she has had since then none to provide for but herself; and few people are more comfortable and happy than she is. She is generally called Aunt Betsey, in the neighborhood; though some called her Red Betsey, from the reddish brown of her complexion.

Betsey is uncommonly intelligent and discreet; possessed of much sensibility, and faithful in whatever given her in charge.

The plan I had devised to secure her freedom in case of her arrest, was this. I would have obtained a homini replegiando, and in this way she must have had a trial in the Supreme Court. When the case terminated, she would have been put safely out of the way, and I would have paid her master what a court and jury decided to be her value.

NOTES

1. *N.A.S.*, November 25, 1841, 98-99.

2. Jacob Read (1752-1816), a planter from South Carolina, was a member of the United States Senate during 1795-1801. *Who Was Who in America*, 434.

No. XLV.
James Hall[1]

John Tatum was a respectable farmer, near the village of Woodbury, Gloucester county, N.J. He was remarkable for his love of peace. About the year 1814, he had in his employ two colored men, who, preferring liberty to slavery, had left the service of their master in Maryland. By some means he became acquainted with the place of their residence, and went in pursuit of them. About twelve o'clock at night, the family were awakened from slumber by a violent knocking at the door. John Tatum rose and inquired what was wanted. In reply he was informed that they were in search of two runaway slaves, known to be in that house. He assured them that there were no such persons in the house; and expressed his surprise at their calling upon him at such an unseasonable hour. They turned a deaf ear to this declaration, and insisted upon searching the house; promising to conduct civilly, if he would permit them to do so. He opened the door, and four men made a thorough search, but found no slaves. They then withdrew, and went to a small house on the premises, occupied by a colored man by the name of Joseph, and his wife. The two slaves they were in search of, were in the house. When they knocked at the door, Joseph inquired who was there. They told him that they wished to find a person who resided about a mile distant, and they would give him twenty dollars if he would conduct them there.

Joseph was a shrewd old man, and suspecting they had something in view besides finding the person they inquired for, he declined the offer, but told them they were near the village of Woodbury, and could find the way without difficulty; and there they would find people enough to go with them to the place they inquired after, for much less than they had offered him. While Joseph and the strangers were thus parleying, his wife could not restrain her curiosity, and opened the door to peep out; which being perceived by those outside, two of them immediately rushed in; but they were soon laid sprawling on the floor. Joseph struck the first that entered, on the head with his gun, and gave him a severe wound; some of the inmates knocked the other down, and before they could recover, took their pistols from them.

The light was so faint, and there was such confusion, that the slaves were not discovered by their pursuers. Joseph now had the two intruders completely in his power, and charged them with an attempt to rob him. He ordered them to take their stand in one corner of the room, threatening them with instant death if they refused; and as the old man appeared determined to carry into effect his threat, they complied; though I have no idea that he had the most distant intention of hurting them. He then told them they must take their hats off. One of them readily complied, but the other refused: declaring he had rather suffer death than take his hat off to a negro. He said he was Judge of the County Court where he resided, and that he could not submit to such indignity. Upon his representation, he was permitted to remain covered.

The men who remained outside, hearing a scuffle in the house, which ceased soon after their companions entered, concluded they were killed; and fearing they might suffer the same fate, if they remained about the premises, they withdrew. The slaves could watch them from the window; and as soon as they were gone, they escaped to the house of John Tatum, and knocked at the window of the room where he lodged, which was on the lower floor. At their request he handed them the amount due to them out of the window; a thing he could easily do, as he was in the habit, at the end of each month, of putting up the amount due to those he employed, and writing their names on it. Having received their wages, they made their way to a distant part of the State. One of them, I think, had about seventy dollars, the other not so much.

The next morning, Joseph drove his two captives to Woodbury, and related the whole affair to a magistrate. They also told their story; the judge showed the deep cut in his head, and complained bitterly of Joseph's treatment. After investigating the matter, poor Joseph was most unrighteously committed to prison, and the two marauders discharged. However, he was not long detained there.

The court being in session soon after, the grand jury returned the bill of indictment ignoramus, and he was set at liberty.

A few days after those circumstances occurred, the same men went to Philadelphia, and arrested a man by the name of James Hall, whom they committed to prison as the slave of Judge Gibson. This was the individual who had been so roughly treated by Joseph, in New-Jersey. Hall was sent to prison about nine o'clock in the evening. One of the keepers came and informed me of the circumstance. I immediately made application to Alderman Abraham Shoemaker, procured a warrant against Hall for a debt of one hundred dollars, and lodged it at the prison. I did this merely to detain him till his case could be inquired into.

The next morning, I rose about break of day, and went to the prison to see Hall, and inquire into his case. Just as I arrived, I saw several men coming down the steps, who seemed greatly excited. Among them was a person, whom I well knew, by the name of Brady. It was said he had been imprisoned several years previous on charge of killing his wife; and had broke jail. He had lived several years in Philadelphia, taught school, and conducted reputably while there. He informed those men who I was. They gathered clamorously around me, and he was as noisy as any of them. I looked him full in the face, and giving him a significant nod, I said, "Will thou kill me, as thou didst the Egyptian, yesterday?" He immediately disappeared; but his companions continued their vociferations, and threatened violence, with many oaths. After a little time, I observed, "When you first made the attack upon me, I thought I might, perhaps, be in some danger; but now I am inclined to think you are the same fellows whose courage has lately been put to the test in Jersey. If you are, I don't think I have much to fear." Gibson said a negro man had struck him on the head with his gun and had cut it. - After considerable altercation, I informed them that I could meet them at Alderman Shoemaker's, at 9 o'clock, and went into the prison to see James Hall. Upon questioning him, he told me, confidentially, that he was a slave; but that he did not belong to any of the persons who had been the cause of his arrest and imprisonment.

At the time appointed, we appeared before the magistrate, who had no partiality for slaveholders. In the investigation, the claimant fixed the time when he said Hall had run away. But Hall proved, by several respectable witnesses, that he had been employed as a hod-carrier three years before that time. The magistrate came to the conclusion that they must be mistaken in the person, and accordingly set him at liberty. Judge Gibson and his friends having failed in their enterprise, returned home, chagrined at their disappointment. James Hall being at liberty, I strongly urged him to leave the city; but having resided several years there without molestation, he declined taking my advice. It was not long before his real master had him arrested, and produced such proof of his being his slave, as satisfied the magistrate before whom he was taken. He gave the customary certificate, upon the authority whereof he was taken to Maryland. I went to see him in prison, the day he was taken away; and after a gentle rebuke for his imprudence in not following my advice, I bid him farewell, not expecting ever to see him again. In this I was disappointed; for in two or three weeks from that time, he came, laughing, into my house.

Upon arriving in Maryland, Hall adopted the following cunning stratagem to effect his escape. He told his master that it was his intention to purchase his freedom; and in order to accomplish that object, he had been laying up money, and then had in my hands three hundred dollars; that he would give him an order upon me for that sum, and, moreover, would bind himself to serve him seven years. To these terms his master agreed. A manumission and an indenture were duly executed, and an order given upon me for three hundred dollars, witnessed by a justice of the peace in the neighborhood. The master mounted his horse, proceeded to Philadelphia, called upon me, and exhibited his order. But what was his disappointment, when I informed him that my acquaintance with his slave was of very recent date, and that I had never seen one cent of his money. To satisfy him that what I said was true, I went with him to the prison, and showed him the docket, by which it appeared that Jim had been several times convicted of petit larceny. The master set off for home declaring, as he left me, that he would sell him as soon as he returned.

But he was again doomed to disappointment; for soon after he had left home, James also left for the same place; taking care to travel on a road where he had good reason to think he was in no danger of meeting his master. Soon after his master had returned home, Jim, as he was commonly called, made his appearance at my house. I questioned him in relation to the order he had given upon me, and charged him with falsehood. He admitted the charge was correct; and said, that he thought any man who was a slave, had a right to deceive his master, if he could get his liberty by it. I gave him such advice as I thought suitable; and after getting some refreshment, he pursued his journey towards the East. I never saw him afterwards, but I have good reason to believe he was never again disturbed.

NOTES

1. *N.A.S.*, December 2, 1841, 102.

No. XLVI.
Mary Holliday[1]

Fanny, a likely mulatto woman, was a slave to John Sears, of Hartford county, Maryland. When she was about twenty-four years old, she escaped from his service, went to Philadelphia, and hired as a domestic in the family of Isaac W. Morris. After her arrival in that city, she called her name Mary Holliday. Being a prudent, industrious woman, and worthy of confidence, the family became much attached to her. She had remained but a few months in that situation, before her mistress (her master being dead) became informed of her location, and went to Philadelphia, in company with a man by the name of Dutton. She had her arrested on the 7th of 6th mo. 1805, and taken before Matthew Lawler, who was then Mayor. Isaac W. Morris informed me of the circumstance, and solicited my assistance, and I accompanied him to the office. It was not a difficult matter to discover that Mary could not conceal her alarm and distress, though she made an effort to do so.

Dutton was examined as a witness, and testified that he knew a mulatto, who lived with Mary Sears, by the name of Fanny; and he believed the woman then present, who called herself Mary Holliday, was that person. I insisted that the testimony was insufficient, as the witness could not say that he *knew* she was the same person, but merely that he believed so: that the case required as strong testimony as if she was on trial for her life, which was of less value than her liberty. I asked the Mayor if he would consider such testimony satisfactory in the case of a white person, he replied he would not, but he would in the case of a colored person. I asked how dark the person must be to justify him in receiving such testimony as was offered in this case; for Mary was a light mulatto. He answered as dark as that woman, pointing to her. I then asked him what he would think if such testimony was to be offered in the case of his daughter; adding, "there is very little difference in the color of her and the person now standing before thee." He made no reply. However he overruled my objections to the evidence, but consented to postpone the case three days, to allow time to procure testimony in her favor. I.W. Morris became security for her appearance on the 10th of the month. mary Holliday denied being the slave of the claimant, or that her name was Fanny. But in a short time after leaving the Mayor's office, Isaac W. Morris called upon me, and said that the woman had confessed that her name was Fanny, and that she was a slave. He also said that she had lived with them a long time, and his family had become much attached to her, and they could not bear the idea of her being taken away a slave; he added "I will be accountable for three hundred dollars, if thou wilt get her free." I replied, that I thought I could accomplish that object.

I then called upon Mary Sears, and offered to compromise the matter. After mutually agreeing that nothing which might be said by either of us on that occasion should be used on the trial, I made her an offer of two hundred dollars; which she promptly refused to accept. I was very anxious that we might settle the business without resorting to the law, and I finally offered her three hundred and fifty dollars. At length she informed me that it was in vain to treat on the subject; for she had come to the determination not to sell her on any terms; that she would take her home, and make an example of her. I replied, "I think thou wilt find thyself disappointed." Hearing this, she grinned upon me with an expression of fiend-like malice.

Finding my endeavors prove abortive, I obtained a homini replegiando, and at the time appointed, I attended with the woman at the Mayor's office, accompanied by a deputy sheriff with the writ.

I again urged the insufficiency of the proof that had been offered in the case. The Mayor observed, in rather a peremptory tone, "I have decided that matter, and shall surrender the slave to her mistress." Upon his saying this, I gave the officer a signal to serve the writ. He was a novice in the business, knew little about it, but was faithful to the instructions I had previously given him.

He laid his hand upon Mary's shoulder, and said, "By virtue of this writ," holding it in his hand, "I replevin this woman, and deliver her to Mr. Hopper." The Mayor looked suprised, and asked, "How do you say?" He then repeated the same words, and I directed Mary to go to my house. As she was turning to leave the office, her mistress laid hold of her by the arm, and said, she should *not* go. The Mayor asked me what writ is was. I replied " a homini replegiando." He said he did not understand what that meant. I told him that it was none the less powerful on that account. He then told the officer he must leave the writ with him; but the officer replied that he must return it to the sheriff's office. The Mayor then told him that he must give him a copy. He replied, it was too long to give a copy; that if he wanted one, he must send to the sheriff's office for it. All this time, the mistress kept her grasp upon Mary. I appealed to the Mayor to compel her to release the girl, as the matter was now referred to another tribunal. He accordingly ordered the mistress to let her go. Mary Sears was completely nonplused, and asked him what she could do. He replied "I don't know. You must ask Mr. Hopper; his laws are above mine. I thought I knew something about the business; but it seems I do not." Mary being released, went home with me.

Mary Sears, and her friend Dutton, employed Alexander J. Dallas, as her counsel; and William Lewis[2] undertook to manage the suit for Mary Holliday. This case was kept pending in the Supreme Court a long time; and the claimant frequently attended, bringing her witnesses from Maryland with her. This was attended with much trouble and expense. After several years, the case was brought on; but she had left some of her principal witnesses at home. The most of the forenoon was occupied in fruitless altercation between lawyers, on the admissibility of certain evidence, and on points of law. About one o'clock, the Court adjourned till three in the afternoon. During this recess lawyer Lewis sent for me, and said that the claimant had proposed a compromise. This was effected in consequence of her being informed that I had determined, even if Mary should be adjudged a slave, not to surrender her; but that they would have to go through another process of law, to recover the penalty of the bond. She had become completely tired of law; the trouble and expense had far exceeded her expectations, and she appeared glad of the opportunity of settling the business without further litigation. She agreed to accept two hundred and fifty dollars, and pay the costs. When the court met in the afternoon, they were informed that the matter was settled, and the jury, with the consent of the parties, found a verdict that Fanny, alias Mary Holliday, was free.

Soon after the suit was commenced, Mary left the service of J.W. Morris, and went out to day's work. She also collected money among her friends, and paid to him in small sums, of ten and fifteen dollars at a time, about three hundred dollars.

Matthew Lawler,[3] the Mayor, was much better acquainted with belligerent operations, than he was with law. During the revolutionary war, he had been an officer on board a privateer, and had part of his face carried away by a grape-shot. This may in some measure account for his ignorance of the homini replegiando. He was not friendly to the colored people; and although I believe he generally wished to discharge the duties of his office correctly, he often erred for want of knowing better.

NOTES

1. *N.A.S.*, December 9, 1841, 106.

2. William Lewis (1752-1819) was a member of the Pennsylvania legislature in 1787 and 1789. He was also the United States District Attorney in Pennsylvania in 1789 and a judge in the United States District Court for the Eastern District of Pennsylvania during 1790-1791. *Who Was Who in America*, 389.

3. Mathew Lawler, a mayor of Philadelphia in the early 1800's, was listed in the *P.D. for 1800*, 144.

No. XLVII.
A Slave Hunter Defeated[1]

About the year 1810, a slave, having left the service of his master, in Virginia, went to Philadelphia; where he remained but a few months, before his master became informed of the place of his residence, and sent a man in pursuit of him. This fellow had been in the city but a few hours when he arrested the slave and took him before Abraham Shoemaker. He was a fine-looking young man. I suppose, from his appearance, about thirty years old. The magistrate being desirous that the poor fellow should have justice done him, refused to hear the case until some person should be present to defend him; and I was sent for. Upon entering the office, the Alderman informed me that the individual arrested was claimed as the slave of a gentleman in Virginia, who had authorized the person making the arrest, by his power of Attorney, to apprehend his "fugitive from labor," and convey him home to Virginia.

I asked the man to let me see his power of attorney. He refused, and told me I had no right to interfere in the matter; that he had shown it to the magistrate, and he was satisfied. I then appealed to the Alderman, and requested that he would order the man to show me his authority. The Alderman asked him to let him see his power of attorney again, and he handed it to him. After examining it, he observed, "Mr. Hopper is a member of the abolition society, and has a right to be satisfied;" and handed me the document. It had been acknowledged in the city of Washington, before Bushrod Washington, one of the Judges of the United States Court, and appeared to be correctly drawn and executed. After the preliminaries were settled, the Alderman administered the usual oath, to make true answers to such questions as should be asked him touching the matter then before him. I then asked him if the man had been advertised. He replied, that he had. I asked him to let me see the advertisement; and he handed it to me. It was headed, "Sixty Dollars Reward." I asked him if he was to receive sixty dollars for apprehending the man mentioned in it. He answered that he was, provided that he took him home. I then asked what proof he could produce that the man he had arrested was the same person mentioned in the advertisement. He said that he could swear to that fact. I gave him to understand that in Philadelphia we did not permit any person, particularly a stranger, to swear sixty dollars into his pocket; and that unless he had better evidence than that, the man must be set at liberty. This startled and irritated him. He asked him if I thought he would swear to a lie. I told him I did not know whether he would or not; but there was one thing I did know-- and that was I would not be willing to *trust* him. He said that he was perfectly sure he was the man; that he knew him as well as he did any man living; that he was overseer for the gentleman that owned him; and that if we would examine his back, we would find it scarrified with the whip. I observed, "And perhaps thou art the man who scarrified him; if he is scarrified." He then ordered the man to strip, that we might examine him. I observed that no evidence had yet been produced that the man he had arrested was a slave; therefore they both stood on precisely the same footing; and that we had as good a right to examine *his* back, as we had that of the colored man; adding, significantly, "They whip for kidnapping in some places." This put him in a great rage.

The magistrate having refused to permit him to testify, on account of his being interested, he said there were two men on board of a vessel from Virginia, then at the wharf, who could testify that the man was a slave; and proposed going for them. I informed him that he was at liberty to go for his witnesses, but the man could not be detained, under present circumstances, one minute. I appealed to the magistrate to discharge him, and he did so. But as soon as he left the office, the slaveholder's agent seized the man, and swore he would keep him in custody till he could get his witnesses. I immediately stepped up to him, and with a manner that soon convinced him I was not to be trifled with, ordered to let go his hold, or I would take such measures as would make him repent of his temerity. I asked him how he dare lay a finger upon the man after the magistrate had discharged him. He reluctantly relinquished his grasp, and went to seek for his witnesses; swearing vengeance against me. The man went home with me; and after advising him how to conduct himself, I gave him a few lines to William Reeve, of Upper Evesham, in New Jersey. In the short letter I wrote on this occasion, I referred the friend to whom it was addressed, to the 25th chapter of Matthew, from the 34th to the 40th verse; and concluded with--"Verily I say unto you, inasmuch as ye have done it unto one of the least of my brethren, ye have done it unto me." I accompanied the man to the ferry, saw him safely over the river, and returned home.

In the course of an hour or two, the slave hunter called upon me, accompanied by a constable, and two other men, who I suppose were the witnesses he had spoken of. He inquired for the man, saying he had seen him go into my house. I informed him he had been there, but was now gone. He was exasperated to the highest degree, and said he had a search-warrant, and would search my house from garret to cellar. I answered, mildly, that he might proceed according to law; but that, if he stepped over the boundary line, it must be at his peril. After he had vented his fury in much abusive language for some time, the officer asked me to step into the parlor; saying he wished to speak to me. Under high professions of friendship, he told me they had no search-warrant; that the "gentleman" was about to apply to the Mayor for one, but he, the constable, wishing to save my feelings, had told him that he was acquainted with me, and had offered to accompany him to see me; and he had no doubt but I would permit them to search my house without legal process. I immediately stepped to the door, and opening it, observed, "You are at liberty to go about your business." They withdrew, and I saw no more of them; though I was informed they spent several days searching for the fugitive.

NOTES

1. *N.A.S.*, December 16, 1841, 110.

No. XLVIII.
An Aged Bondman[1]

A short time before the Yearly meeting of Friends, held in Philadelphia, made a rule of discipline to disown such members as held slaves and refused to manumit them, a committee was appointed, by the Western Quarterly meeting, to visit all their members, who continued in the practice. This committee consisted of men and women. In pursuance of the directions of the meeting, they called upon all such, and in a friendly manner laid before them the iniquity of the antichristian custom of holding their fellow-men in bondage, except one case. This Friend had but one slave, who was far advanced in years; and it was thought, by most of the committee, that it was imprudent to interfere in the case, as the slave was too old and infirm to support himself by his own labor; and as he was treated kindly, they were of opinion that his situation could not be made more comfortable than it was, and that he probably had no desire for his freedom.

But Isaac Jackson, one of the committee, a man of unbounded benevolence and kindness of heart, concluded that a conscientious discharge of his duty forbade him to omit this case; and he went alone to visit the individual, who still continued to resist the advice of his friends. He was courteously received, when he opened his mind on the subject. The Friend offered many reasons for keeping the old man in slavery; but Isaac Jackson refuted all his arguments so fully, that he not only consented to manumit the old servant, but gave a bond obligating himself and his heirs to maintain him the remainder of his life. The papers being duly executed, the slave was called into the parlor, and Isaac asked him if he would like to be free. He said, "yes." Isaac Jackson then reminded him that he was too old to procure subsistence by his labor; and asked him how he expected to get a living. The old man replied, "Providence has been kind to me thus far; and I am willing to trust to him for the rest of my life."

Isaac Jackson held up the manumission, and the bond that had been executed, and said, "Thou art a free man! Thy master has manumitted thee, and has secured to thee a maintenance, as long as thou mayst live."

The intelligence was so unexpected, that the old man was completely overwhelmed with gratitude. After sitting in profound silence a few minutes, he fell upon his knees and most devoutly thanked his Heavenly Father for prolonging his life till he had the happiness to become a free man. The scene was deeply affecting. The old man rejoiced in his liberty, and the master realized in his own bosom the truth of the Scripture de____ "The work of righteousness is peace, and the end thereof quietness and assurance forever."

NOTES

1. *N.A.S.*, December 30, 1841, 118.

NO. XLIX.
James[1]

James ____ was a slave to David McCalmont, of Newcastle county, State of Delaware. Preferring liberty to slavery, about the year 1805, he took the liberty to walk off. He went to the neighborhood of Pilesgrove, Salem county, New Jersey, and lived with a farmer. He was then about thirty years old. After remaining in that situation some months, and finding that his employer was friendly to the colored people, and was of course opposed to slavery, James ventured to open his heart to him. About this time, several persons, similarly circumstanced with himself, were arrested and taken to the South, whence they had fled. This greatly increased his fears; and he resolved to endeavor to get some person to advance a sum of money sufficient to redeem him from bondage, promising to remunerate him by a temporary servitude. The individual to whom he had made known his situation, proposed that application should be made to me, to negotiate the matter between him and his master. James approved of the plan; and the person, at his request, called upon me. He stated that he had full confidence in the man, and said he believed he would faithfully adhere to any agreement he might make.

I addressed a letter to David McCalmont, stating that application had been made to me on behalf of a colored man, by the name of James, who, I understood, was claimed by him as a slave; and I wished to know the lowest terms upon which he would manumit him. In the course of a few weeks, McCalmont called upon me, in company with Levi Hollingsworth,[2] a respectable merchant of Philadelphia. Hollingsworth informed me that his friend McCalmont was a highly respectable man, and treated his slaves with great humanity, and even kindness; that James would be much happier in his service, than he could be in any other situation; and strongly urged me to inform them where he might be found. In reply, I observed that it did not appear that *James* thought so, or he would not have left his service. I also informed him that, even if I had no objections to slavery, I was still bound, by every principle of honor, not to betray the confidence placed in me; but feeling as he knew I did on the subject, I was much surprised that he should make such a proposition. They then called upon Thomas Harrison, (of whose name I have had frequent occasion to make honorable mention,) and endeavored to enlist him in their favor, so far as to use his influence with me to tell where James might be found; representing to him, as they had to me, how well he was treated, and how happy he was in slavery. T. Harrison replied, ironically, that he knew very well that the slaves in that neighborhood slept on feather-beds, and their masters' children on straw; that the slaves eat white bread, and their children eat brown. "But," says he, "inclose ten acres with a high wall, plant it with Lombardy poplars, and the most beautiful shrubbery, build a castle in the middle of it, and give thee a coach and four, and every thing else thy heart can desire, and pen, ink and paper, to write about the Governor, (L.H. was a politician, and had written much in relation to the candidates for Governor, whose election was then near at hand,) and yet, after all, thou wilt want to get out." Not being able to obtain their object, they left Thomas Harrison, and McCalmont returned home.

In the course of a week or two, L. Hollingsworth called and informed me that James' master had agreed to accept one hundred and fifty dollars, and manumit him. Not many days elapsed, before I found a person willing to advance that sum; his name was John Hart, a druggist, of Philadelphia. James was accordingly manumitted, the money paid, and he bound for the term of five years. When the contract was about being concluded, it was remarked, "Perhaps he will run away." J. Hart replied, "I am not afraid of that; I will tie him by the *teeth*;" (meaning that he would feed him well.) James now appeared quite satisfied. His new master and mistress were kind to him, and he was faithful and diligent.

After he had been with J.H. a year or two, he asked permission to visit his old master and fellow-servants. J.H. kept a carriage, which he seldom had occasion to use during the winter, and he proposed to James to take one of his horses. This suited his taste exactly. He mounted a fine, noble-looking animal, handsomely caparisoned, and went to Delaware. On arriving at the residence of his old master, he tied his horse, and went into the kitchen. D. McCalmont was from home at the time, but soon returned; and seeing the horse standing in his yard, supposed he had some distinguished visiter. Entering his parlor and seeing no stranger, he inquired who that horse belonged to? He was informed that Jim was in the kitchen and had rode the horse there. D. McCalmont spoke pleasantly to his former servant, and in answer to his inquiries, James informed him that the horse belonged to his master, J. Hart, who had kindly permitted him to use it. His old master expressed himself pleased to see him, and told him to put the horse in the stable, and give him oats and hay. James was kindly received by all the family, and spent a day or two with them very agreeably. When he was about to return, he went to take leave of D. McCalmont, who thus addressed him: "Well, Jim, I am glad to see you, and I am pleased to find you have a good master, and are happy; but I would rather you would not come here again, in the way you have now; it will make my people dissatisfied." James returned home, much pleased with his trip, called upon me, and gave me an account of it.

He served the time he had agreed, and conducted to the satisfaction of the man who had so kindly advanced the money to redeem him from bondage. He remained with him a considerable time as a hired servant, after he was free.

NOTES

1. *N.A.S.*, January 13, 1842, 126.

2. Levi Hollingsworth was listed as a merchant in the *P.D. for 1800*, 21.

No. L.
Uncle Beck[1]

Ignatius Beck, a free colored man, residing with his family in Philadelphia, was engaged about the year 1810, by a respectable-looking man, (I do not remember his name,) to accompany him to the South as his body servant; for which he agreed to pay good wages. He was provided with a good horse, and also one for his servant. Ignatius took leave of his family, and set off with his master. Nothing material occurred, till they got to North Carolina, near the line that separates that State from Virginia. Here they arrived at a tavern, on Seventh Day evening. Early the next morning, the man informed Beck that, it being the Sabbath, he should not travel on that day; and as several of the slaves belonging to the landlord were going to attend a Baptist meeting, which was to be held about seven miles off, he might accompany them, if he had an inclination to do so; provided he would be sure to return with them in the evening. Beck was much pleased with the *kind* proposition of his master, and went accordingly.

In the evening, Ignatius returned, agreeably to his promise; but to his astonishment his master was gone, and had taken both the horses with him. He made inquiry how he was to get home. The landlord told him that he was at home; adding, "You are my property; I have bought you of your master." Ignatius now saw the snare into which he had fallen. He assured the man that he was free, and had a family living in Philadelphia; but this had no effect upon the monster who now claimed him as his slave; and he requested that he might hear no more on the subject of his freedom. Ignatius was a shrewd, sensible man, and feigned to submit to his new situation without further complaint. He endeavored to discover, in his intercourse among the white neighbors, if he could find any one to whom he could open his case, and who would advise him how to act in his deplorable situation. There was a man in the neighborhood, a justice of the peace, who appeared quite friendly. To him he ventured to give a history of his case; and to his great joy, he found he was willing to render all the assistance in his power. He inquired what evidence he could produce, that would prove him free. Ignatius referred him to Richard Allen, a colored Methodist preacher, well known in Philadelphia. The magistrate wrote to Richard, giving a full account of Ignatius, as he received it from himself. Richard called upon me, and left the letter; by which it appeared that Ignatius had been a slave, and had been duly manumitted in the city of Washington. A letter was addressed to Samuel Brooks, who resided there, and in a few days a copy of the manumission, duly authenticated, came to hand. This document, which contained a description of the person of Ignatius, I inclosed to the gentleman in Virginia, who had so kindly interested himself on his behalf; accompanied with a letter, in which I endeavored to excite his sympathy in behalf of the poor captive. These documents arrived safe. The benevolent individual sought a private interview with Ignatius, and told him that he was now fully satisfied his statement was true; and that he would consider of the matter, and advise him how to proceed. But still the case was involved in difficulty; for if a suit was instituted for his freedom, it would be necessary for some person to go there to identify him; and it might be difficult to find any person willing to go; moreover, it would be attended with delay, and considerable expense. He instructed Ignatius to go home, and call upon him again in a few days. In a short time he called, and his benefactor secreted him in his house about three weeks. The master, becoming alarmed, at the loss of his *property,* advertised the fugitive, and scoured the country many miles round; but could get no tidings of his man. After the excitement had subsided, Ignatius was taken from the cellar, where he had been most of the time, put on horseback, and started for home; accompanied by the son of his benefactor, who escorted him one hundred miles on his way. Upon parting, he gave Ignatius such instructions as enabled him to prosecute the remainder of his journey with safety. Such disinterested kindness is worthy of all commendation.

Soon after he returned home, he called and gave me an account of the whole affair. I requested him to keep the matter to himself, and if he should hear of the wretch, who had endeavored to entrap him, being in the city, to inform me. Not many weeks had passed, before Ignatius informed me that he had seen the fellow in the street, and had followed him until he went into a house in Lombard-street. I forthwith procured a warrant for his arrest, and taking an officer, went to the house. I was informed he had left the city, but could not ascertain where he had gone; and I never heard of him afterwards. Ignatius Beck is now living in Philadelphia, and is generally called by the colored people "Uncle Beck."

NOTES

1. *N.A.S.*, January 20, 1842, 130.

No. LI.
Tobias Boudinot[1]

In the year 1835, Judge Thomas Chinn, of Mississippi, came to this city, and brought with him a slave, for whom it was said he had given fifteen hundred dollars while on his way here. The Judge had been in this city but a few days, before the slave eloped, and was advertised in the papers, with a reward of five hundred dollars offered for his apprehension. Soon after the advertisement appeared, some mischievous person addressed an anonymous note to the Judge, informing him that his slave was concealed by me some where about the store which I then kept, in Pearl street. A warrant was procured, and put in the hands of a well-known slave hunter, by the name of Tobias Boudinot who had rendered himself notorious in that kind of business. Highly elated with the prospect of receiving five hundred dollars, as the reward of his iniquity in capturing the fugitive, he, accompanied by the judge, and a considerable number of southerners, who were here on business, came to the vicinity of my store, and distributed themselves at short distances from one another, in order to arrest him, in case he should attempt to escape. I was in my office, back of the store, unconscious of what was going on. It seems they waited for near an hour, expecting I would go out; preferring to make the assault in my absence. At length, some business called me to a house, a few doors down the street. I had been gone but a few minutes, leaving my son in the store, when four or five persons rushed in; and after looking round and not seeing their victim, sprang out of the back window, from which they jumped into the yard, a distance of about ten feet. Some of them were very near falling into the cistern, which was under the window. My son came immediately to inform me, and I returned without delay. Before I got there, they left my premises, and were searching a book-bindry in the rear, and some other houses in the neighborhood. When the inhabitants complained of such unceremonious intrusion, Boudinot informed them that he was looking for a felon; but my son soon undeceived them on that point; which highly enraged him, and one of the party gave him a blow in the face.

After I returned, I observed a respectable-looking man in the street frequently peeping into my office; and as soon as he would catch my eye, step back, as though he wished to escape observation. After he had repeated this manoeuvre several times, I went to the door, and said to him, "My friend, if thou hast business with me, come in, and let me know what it is; do not be peeping about my premises." He went directly away, and turning the corner, which was a few doors above my store, proceeded down Oak street. I followed him a few rods, where I saw a group of people, who appeared much agitated. Upon going to them, I soon discovered that they were the persons, who had, a few minutes before, so rudely trespassed upon my premises. Among the company, I saw a man whom I supposed was Boudinot; for I did not then know him personally, though I was no stranger to his character and calling. I asked his name, which he refused to give. I then thus addressed him, "Art thou the impertinent fellow, who had the assurance to trespass upon my premises in my absence." He replied, "I have a warrant, and I am determined to execute it." Upon his saying so, I observed, "Judas betrayed his master for thirty pieces of silver; and I suppose for a like sum thou wouldst seize they brother by the throat, and drag him into interminable bondage. If thy conscience was as susceptible of conviction and compunction as his was, thou wouldst probably do as he did, and thus rid the community of an intollerable nuisance." One of the southerners, with a most contemptuous sneer, said, "Brother!" I added, "Yes, *brother*." I returned to my store, but in a few minutes was informed that they were in Pearl street, a few doors above, abusing a colored man. I went there, and found them railing at a decent-looking colored man, whom Boudinot was holding by the collar, and upon whom they were heaping the most approbrious epithets, and the most violent and profane langauge. I inquired what all this meant? what had the man done to offend them? Boudinot said had he no business there, and refused to go away. I told him that the man had as much right in the street as he had;

and that if he (Boudinot) had business there, it would be well to attend to it; and if he had not, he had better go home, and not be collecting a crowd and raising a tumult in the street. Several of the company had dirks, and some of them pistols. One or two exhibited those deadly weapons, and menaced my son and myself with death, if we interfered. I called upon Boudinot to arrest them; and told him that, as an officer, (for he was a constable,) it was his duty to do so; and if he refused, I would complain of him and have him displaced. Seeing I was not to be trifled with, and fearing the consequences, he made the arrest; but when we got to the police office, the culprits were not to be found, and Boudinot alledged that they had made their escape.

A few days after, my son, who had offended those marauders by his interference in this case, was peaceably walking up Chatham street on his way home, about nine o'clock in the evening, when some person behind him knocked him down, and beat him in a most cruel and savage manner; so that he was obliged to keep his chamber a considerable time. Not a doubt can be reasonably entertained that it was some of the persons who had been engaged in the nefarious transactions above-mentioned.

Judge Chinn, I was informed, never recovered his *property;* and I have been told the *chattel* located himself in Victoria's dominions; though the Judge expressed his full belief that he would return to his service; and would never have left it, if he had not been persuaded to do so by some abolitionists. For my own part, I can say I never saw the fugitive. If any human being is to be despised, above all others, as an enemy to the human race, it is a slave hunter regardless of the sighs, groans, and tears of his fellow-men.

NOTES

1. *N.A.S.*, February 10, 1842, 142.

No. LII.
Ben Jackson[1]

Benjamin Johnson was born a slave, in Virginia. He informed me that when he was about sixteen years old, he became awakened to a sense of his situation as a slave; he could not reconcile it with the justice and goodness of his Creator, that one man should be born to serve another, without compensation; to be driven about, and treated as the beast of the field. As he grew in years, these considerations pressed more heavily upon him. When about twenty-five years old, he resolved to make an effort to effect his liberty. Accordingly, he left his master; and after encountering many difficulties, arrived in Philadelphia. In order more effectually to secure his liberty, he entered on board a vessel, and went several voyages to sea. When about thirty years old, he married, and soon after let himself to the late Dr. Benjamin Rush,[2] one of the signers of the Declaration of Independence, as a coachman. He continued in that situation about two years. Upon leaving the service of the doctor, he gave him a certificate of honesty, sobriety, and capability as a coachman; it likewise stated that he was a *free man.*

Some time after, about 1799, his master came to that city, and had him arrested as his fugitive slave. He was taken before Joseph Bird,[3] a justice of the peace, residing in Cedar street, in the township of Moyamensing. Benjamin Jackson was a man of extraordinary intelligence and tact, considering the opportunities he had had. The master demanded the usual certificate to authorize him to take the man to Virginia. Benjamin neither denied nor admitted that he was a slave; but produced the certificate given him by Dr. Rush, and requested that I might be informed of the circumstance. It was then evening, and the magistrate committed him to prison till the next morning. At nine o'clock, he sent me a note, asking my attendance at his office; requesting that, in the mean time, I would see Dr. Rush. I immediately called upon the doctor, who informed me that he knew but little about the man, further than that he had lived with him about two years, and was *then* a free man. I called at the prison, and had an interview with Jackson. The poor fellow was in great distress. I endeavored to impress upon him the necessity of telling me the real state of his case; and he opened his situation fully. He acknowledged that he was a slave, and belonged to the person who claimed him. I told him not to be discouraged, and I would see what could be done for him. I went from the prison to see the officer who had made the arrest. His name was Thomas Durnell. He seemed to sympathise with the captive, and said he would do what he could to assist him. Finding him friendly, I charged him to have the man at the magistrate's a short time *before* the time appointed. This he promised he would do. The next morning, about a quarter before nine o'clock, I was there, and also the officer and Jackson.

As soon as nine o'clock arrived, I demanded the discharge of the prisoner; alledging that no legal proof of his being a slave had been produced; but on the contrary, strong presumptive evidence of his being a free man; that Dr. Rush would not have given such a certificate as he had done, without some reason for doing so. I also urged that the claimant was apprised of the *time* to which the case was adjourned. Joseph Bird was a sincere friend to the colored people, and abhorred slavery. He told Jackson he was at liberty. But just as we were leaving the door, we saw the claimant coming with a quick step. It was not more than one or two minutes after nine o'clock. Benjamin saw his master, and ran for his life. He went down Cedar street to Fourth, and turning down Fourth street, he entered a house occupied by colored people, ran through it, and out the back way, and so came safely under my roof. When I got home, I was rejoiced to find him there. He remained under my protection about a week, and then returned to his own house. I advised him to proceed to New-York, and go to sea; but his wife was unwilling that he should leave her. I used my best endeavors to impress upon them the great danger he would be in, as long as he remained in Philadelphia.

They lived in a house between Vine and Callowhill, and Third and Fourth streets, up two flights of stairs. In the west end there was a window, and under it a shed. Jackson placed a ladder under it, to be ready for escape; but it was so short that it did not reach to the shed, by five or six feet. Here they lived, happier than the king upon his throne; except the dread, which continually attended them, lest the man-hunters should surprise Benjamin in an unguarded moment, and separate them forever. His wife was an industrious, tidy woman, and kept their room as neat and clean as a palace.

About two weeks after his arrest, as they were sitting together, after dark in the evening, enjoying themselves, the door was suddenly burst open, and his master, with a constable, rushed in. Benjamin was sitting by the window. He immediately sprang out, went down the ladder, and landing upon the shed, made his escape, and came to my house. The constable and the master followed; but as soon as they got out of the window, Jackson's wife cut the rope that held the ladder, and they both fell upon the shed; which hurt them considerably, and frightened them much more. This trick made them swear at a round rate.

Jackson was now satisfied that he could not safely remain in Philadelphia, and went to New-York to go to sea. His first voyage was to the East Indies. While he was gone, I negotiated with his master, and bought his freedom, for one hundred and fifty dollars. Upon his return, he immediately came to Philadelphia and gave me an order to receive his wages. Having business in New-york, I called at the counting-house of Preserved Fish, on the wharf, near Peck Slip, and received the money. I reimbursed myself, and gave a small balance to Jackson. The mental suffering his wife had endured, was too much to bear; she had sunk into a state of melancholy, from which she never fully recovered.

NOTES

1. *N.A.S.*, February 24, 1842, 150; *P.P.A.S.*, Acting Committee Minute Book, Vol. 4 (1810-1822), 28, 43, Reel 5.

2. Benjamin Rush (1746-1813) was a founder and organizer of the anti-slavery organization called The Pennsylvania Abolition Society. He assumed the presidency of this organization in 1774. He was a member of the Continental Congress during 1776-1777 and a signer of the Declaration of Independence. He was also the Surgeon General of the Middle Department in the Continental Army and a noted staff member of the Pennsylvania Hospital. He established the first dispensary in the United States. *Who Was Who in America*, 457-458.

3. Joseph Bird was listed as a justice of the peace in the *P.D. for 1800*, 21.

No. LIII.
The Self-emancipated Couple[1]

The following narrative was related to me by the individual who is the subject of it:

"I was born about the year 1790, a slave, in the family of James Caulker, who resided in Talbot county, State of Maryland. My master was in good circumstances and treated me kindly. I was well fed and clothed, but compelled to labor hard. Before I was twenty-one years old, I had a great desire to be free, and was sensible of the injustice of being deprived of my liberty. My master lived expensively, and about the year 1812, became embarrassed in his circumstances. Being unable to pay his debts, I was seized by the sheriff, placed in prison at Easton, and advertised for sale. During my imprisonment, several Georgia speculators called to see me, to ascertain what I was worth. Nothing could be more horrible than the sight of those men. After being in confinement near a week, my master made out to raise the money, paid the debt, and took me home. There I remained about four months, when he let me to William Moore, who lived in the same neighborhood, for fifty dollars a year. I continued in that situation about four years. He then took me home, and made me overseer of his farm. I continued in that situation about three years. I knew my master was much in debt, and I was in continual dread of being again attached and sold at auction, with the rest of his property.

"During this period, a circumstance occurred that sorely afflicted the family. My master took a young man by the name of Samuel Mauldin, into partnership, who resided with him. After some time, this young man and my master's daughter, his only child, became mutually attached, and determined to marry. This they carefully concealed from her parents, who, they knew, would oppose the connection. The young woman, then about twenty years old, made an excuse to visit her cousin, about fifteen miles off, at a small village called the Nine Bridges. After she had been there two or three days, some person informed her father that she had left home with the intention of being married. This information alarmed him, and he ordered me to accompany him to her cousin's. We proceeded with all possible speed, and arrived at the Nine Bridges about ten o'clock at night. We accidentally met Mauldin in the street, and my master immediately dismounted, and seized him by the collar; but he soon discouraged himself, and made off. We were at a loss to find the house where the girl was; but seeing a light, and hearing music, we made the best of our way to the place whence it proceeded. We entered without ceremony, and my master, being desperate, ordered me to seize the first woman I saw. I obeyed, and laid hold of one, and he of another. The lights were immediately extinguished. The women screamed. After a short time the lights came again. He threatened them with death, unless they produced his daughter. She soon made her appearance. Her father now thought he had accomplished his object; and being very much fatigued, he concluded to remain there till morning; but he determined not to let his daughter leave him till they reached home. He directed a bed to be placed for her in one corner of the parlor, and she laid herself upon it. Her father and myself undertook to watch her till morning; but we were both extremely weary, and soon fell asleep. About one o'clock, I discovered the girl had escaped. I immediately awoke my master, and we again set off in pursuit of the fugitive. Suspecting the road they would take, we soon overtook them; but hearing us coming, they turned aside into the woods, and we passed them, without knowing it. We then took another road, which led to Easton, where we expected they would go. On the way, we overtook a Methodist minister, and finding that he was going to the same place that we were, we rode in company to the house of Samuel Watts, who was uncle to the young woman. We were introduced into the parlor, and the clergyman went up stairs. After remaining a few minutes, my master inquired for his daughter, and was informed that she was married by the clergyman who had accompanied us. He was overwhelmed with grief; but as the marriage was now accomplished, we returned home, leaving her and her husband at her uncle's. They remained there about a week, when my master sent a gig to bring them home; and the parties became reconciled.

About eighteen months afterwards, Mauldin had been trading with a certain Daniel Hagens and Thos. Leonard. The latter charged Mauldin with taking the advantage of him in the way of trade, and fell upon him, and gave him a severe beating. Mauldin was determined on revenge. In about a week, he met with Leonard, at Hyman's landing; and saying to me, 'Ned, you must stand by me,' he immediately made an attack upon him. Several friends of Leonard, who were standing by, came to his assistance. Seeing they were likely to overcome Mauldin, I flew in among them, and wounded one of the party severely. Leonard was paid off, both principal and interest. A constable, with four other persons, soon after came to my master's house with a warrant, to arrest me for this offense. My master directed me to saddle a horse and go with them. I well knew that I should get a severe whipping; and was determined, at the risk of my life, not to submit to it. I went into the stable, under pretense of saddling the horse. There I laid hold of a club, which I had secreted, with which I knocked down the officer, and made my escape. In the evening, I returned home, but kept myself hid for about two weeks. I knew well the fate that awaited me, and was determined to avoid it by flight. This determination I communicated to my wife, who was a slave to _____, on the opposite side of the river Wye. I told her that I would certainly return, and take her with me. She consented to my project with much reluctance; representing the danger that would attend it, as we should probably be taken, and severely punished; but I resolved to make the attempt. Accordingly, about the year 1821, I left my master, and turned my face toward Philadelphia. After traveling about four miles, a man passed me on horseback. Oh, how I wished for that horse, to assist me on my journey! About dark, I saw the same horse feeding in a lot, on the road side. I was acquainted with a colored man near by, who furnished me with a bag of straw for a saddle, and a rope bridle. With these I caparisoned the horse, mounted him, and rode about sixty miles. I then turned him loose, and went three miles further on foot, to Smyrna. Thence I went on board a sloop, which took me to Philadelphia. Here I saw so many people, that I thought, surely some of these people, that I thought, surely some of these people will know me, and I shall be arrested and returned to slavery.

"The next day, I went to Burlington, N.J. Here I was an entire stranger, and did not know where to get a night's lodging. Fortunately, I met with a man from the neighborhood I came from, who was similarly circumstanced with myself. At first, we were mutually afraid of each other; but after some conversation, our fears were removed, and we became firm friends. He took me to a place to lodge. In the morning I rose, went to Rancocas, and let myself to John Stokes, where I continued about nine months. Having now got a little money, I went for my wife, agreeable to the promise I had made her. I proceeded to the neighborhood of her master, and secreted myself till night. After the family had retired to bed, and got comfortably asleep, a colored man, who lived in a small house on my master's farm, went over the river and brought my wife to me. It was a joyful meeting. I told her she must fly for her life. With fear and trembling, she complied. We travelled all night, and laid by in the day. In two nights, we travelled upwards of sixty miles, to Smyrna. Here we went on board a vessel, about to sail for Philadelphia. This was in the month of March. The weather became suddenly cold, and the ice prevented the vessel getting out of the creek, for three days. We were informed that a reward of fifty dollars was offered for apprehending us, and that several men were in pursuit. The captain of the vessel was an entire stranger to us, but to his kindness we are indebted for our escape. He hid us in his vessel, and as soon as the circumstances permitted, we left Smyrna; the next day we arrived in Philadelphia. My money was all spent; and I gave my watch to two boys, one white, and the other colored, who put us over the Delaware. We entered Camden about seven o'clock in the evening, and immediately set off for Rancocas, a distance of about seventeen miles; where we arrived about twelve o'clock. After staying there about a month, we went to New-York. At the end of five years, we went to Port au Prince, and remained there about eighteen months. I was satisfied to stay, but my wife was unhappy, and disliked the hot climate; therefore, we returned to the United States.

The Self-emancipated Couple

"I left a sister, a slave to James Caulker. Soon after I escaped from the house of bondage, she had a son, who, her master proposed, should be called by my name; but she objected saying that when he grew up, he would be reproached as having taken the name from a *runaway*. Such are the ideas instilled into slaves.

"I have already said my master was in debt. Soon after the birth of her son, my sister was seized by the sheriff, as his property, and with her infant, lodged in jail for safe keeping, till the day of sale. In consequence of hard usage, close confinement, and scanty fare, the infant died in prison. The mother was sold at public auction, and I have never since heard what became of her.

"When I first ran away, I met some who seemed to be afraid I couldn't take care of myself; but think, says I, I took care of myself and my master too, for a long spell; and I guess I can make out. I don't look as if I was suffering for a master, *do I* ?"

He asked the question with a roughish expression; well knowing that it needed no answer. In fact, he and his wife are very industrious and respectable people, and the last I knew, were living most comfortably.

NOTES

1. *N.A.S.*, March 10, 1842, 158.

No. LIV.
Samuel Johnson[1]

In the 12th month, 1804, about seven o'clock, P.M. I was called upon by several colored persons, who informed me that a free colored man, by the name of Samuel Johnson, had just been arrested as a slave. Without delay, I called upon Thomas Harrison, who accompanied me to the house where the arrest had been made. Here we learned that they had taken him to a tavern kept by Peter Fritz, in Sassafras street. We found him guarded by the landlord and two or three other persons. Upon inquiring, we discovered that Johnson was not claimed as a slave; but that they held him as a hostage, till he should produce his wife and children, who were slaves; and who had got information that they were pursued, barely in time to make their escape before the party in quest of them arrived at their dwelling. Finding the fugitives had fled, they became greatly exasperated, captured the husband, and conveyed him to the place above-mentioned; and because he refused to go with them voluntarily, they had severely beaten and forced him to accompany them; telling him if he would not inform them where they could find his wife and children, they would take him to the South and sell him. He informed them that they might make a slave of him, or murder him, if they pleased, but that no suffering they could inflict should ever induce him to betray his family. His hands were tied behind his back, and he placed in one corner of a back room, which was pointed out to us by a colored man, who had watched their movements.

We attempted to enter the room, but found the door fast; and Fritz declared we should not go in. We inquired his authority for making his grog-shop a prison. He replied that the man was placed in his custody by two of the city constables, and swore he should not be released till they arrived. We told him to open the door, or we would soon have it opened, and in a way that possibly might cost him something to restore it to its present condition. He was further informed, that he had already made himself liable to an action for false imprisonment. Seeing we were determined to have access to the man, the door was opened, and we walked in. When Johnson had given us a narrative of his case, I took my penknife out of my pocket, and cut the cord with which he was bound, amidst the threats and curses of his guard, and ordered him to follow us. One of the fellows having him in charge immediately sprang from his seat, laid hold of Johnson, and swore by his Maker that he should not leave that room, till the constables came, who had placed him in their custody. I stepped up to him, and peremptorily ordered him to release the man immediately, or he would be made to repent his temerity. After some altercation he let go his grasp. We then withdrew, and Johnson followed us. He was exceedingly alarmed for the safety of his wife and children; but happily they went out of harm's way. After a few days they retired to the country, and the place of their retreat was never afterwards discovered by those enemies of the human family.

Samuel Johnson was a free man, and lived in the State of Delaware. Whether he was born free, or had obtained his freedom by purchase, I do not now recollect; but his wife was a slave to George Black. They had several children, and as the oldest were pretty well grown, and as Black was deeply involved in debt, Johnson was in continual fear that their master would sell them to the Georgia speculators, to raise money to relieve himself from embarrassment; a custom that prevailed to a great extent in that part of the country. Johnson lived a short distance from George Black's, and was in the habit of visiting his wife once a week; sometimes oftener. They frequently conversed about their condition, and at length he proposed to her to make their escape; but many difficulties presented. At last, they made the attempt, and succeeded. They went to Philadelphia, and rented a small house. Samuel followed the business of sawing wood, and his wife took in washing, and went out to day's work. Here they lived as comfortably as they could desire; by industry and frugality they had acquired everything that was necessary to make them so. But the dread of being discovered was a bitter alloy to their happiness.

I think it was about two years, before Black discovered that they were in Philadelphia. He immediately went in pursuit of them. Fortunately, they were seen by an acquaintance of Johnson's, who apprised him that Black was in the city; and he immediately put his wife and children in the care of a friend until they could be removed to a place of greater safety. He remained in his own house, not suspecting that they would disturb him. Black engaged Frederic Burkhart, and Jacob Zebly, two of the city constables, who accompanied him to Johnson's dwelling. Upon discovering that his wife and children were not in the house, they arrested him, as above mentioned. Zebly, and the men that Black had brought with him from Delaware, conveyed Johnson to the tavern, and there Zebly left him in charge of those men, while he joined Black and Burkhart in searching for the fugitives.

A few days after this occurrence, a short account of it appeared in the newspapers, by which I have ascertained the time it took place.

NOTES

1. *N.A.S.*, March 24, 1842, 166.

No. LV.
Virginia Slave[1]

A planter in Virginia, held a young girl as a slave. When she was about sixteen years old, being pressed for money, he sold her to a speculator, who made a business of purchasing slaves, and transporting them to the South, or West. This girl had no trace of African descent. Her hair was straight, and her complexion quite as light as the generality of white people; and withal she was uncommonly handsome. Her new master treated her with much kindness, took her as his body servant, and made many promises of what he would do for her. She had discernment enough to discover that his intentions were not of the most honorable character; and taking the advantage of the liberty allowed, escaped to Philadelphia. She had little difficulty in her journey; for her complexion and features bore no resemblance to the African.

After remaining in that city a few years, she married a light mulatto; a sober, industrious man, who for many years, was employed in the shipyard of Joshua Humphreys, a ship carpenter of great respectability, in the district of Southwark. By frugality and industry, they were enabled to build a small, comfortable house on a lot which they had taken on ground rent. Here they appeared to possess every enjoyment their hearts could desire. Their house was neatly though economically furnished, and the floors carpeted; everything about them seemed to denote domestic comfort.

In the year 1808, about thirteen years from the time of her first arrival in Philadelphia, she was arrested as the fugitive slave of her last master, and taken before M. Keppelle, an alderman in Philadelphia. Her former master, and one or two other persons, attended as witnesses. I also attended, with my faithful friend, Thomas Harrison. Her master made his claim, and related the circumstances attending her elopement. The witnesses were examined, and her case appeared hopeless. After consulting together, and being informed by her husband, that Joshua Humphreys would advance one hundred dollars towards purchasing her freedom, we concluded to enter under negotiations for that purpose. Previous to doing so I asked permission to have some private conversation with her; which being granted, I soon learned that she was really their slave. Thomas Harrison and myself took the claimant aside, and proposed purchasing her freedom; but he soon satisfied us that any attempt of that kind was hopeless. He declare with an oath, and in an angry manner, that he would not sell her for *any* price. We endeavored to work on his feelings, by representing to him to the distress he would inflict upon her husband and innocent children; and we finally offered him four hundred dollars for her manumission, which at the time was a very high price. But he continued inexorable, and treated us with the utmost contempt. The magistrate though stupified with wine, (which was commonly the case with him after dinner,) seemed moved with compassion. He asked the woman if she were a slave. I objected to her answering the question, unless he would agree to receive all she might say as evidence. This he declined. I then observed to him that he must be aware that the most honest were liable to be mistaken as to the identity of persons; and it was matter of surprise to me that the witnesses should be so positive in this case; especially as the woman was but sixteen when they said she had eloped, and such long time had since elapsed. That her case was nothing less in importance to her, her husband and her children, than death itself; that for my own part I was not satisfied, by any means; for I conscientiously believed the woman had a *just* claim (of the *legal* claim I said nothing) to her freedom. She stood before the magistrate, holding a little girl and boy by the hand. Her manners were calm and dignified; if she had been educated a lady, they could not have been more so. The children were too young to be fully sensible of the horrible doom that seemed to await their mother; and yet they were old enough to discover that their parents were in trouble, and the tears ran freely down the cheeks of those innocents. I have said the mother was handsome; and she was really so. But on this occasion, the anguish of her heart was plainly written on her countenance. I never shall forget the scene I witnessed that day; it is as fresh before me as though it occurred but yesterday.

At length, a plan was suggested to my mind, that I thought might possibly prove successful; and it appeared to be the only alternative. I proposed that the case should be adjourned till the next day; that we might have further opportunity to inquire into it. I suggested that Thomas Harrison and myself would become security to the United States, in any reasonable sum that might be demanded, for her appearance. The claimant was a stupid looking fellow; and being sure of his game, he made no objection. The case was accordingly postponed. I now began to think I had succeeded; and taking a copy of the recognizance from the docket, signed by the magistrate, I withdrew. The recognizance was to this effect: Thomas Harrison and myself were bound to the United States, in the sum of one thousand dollars, to produce the woman at his office, the next morning, at nine o'clock. Thomas Harrison was quite a humorous character, and had a common saying, when any thing was omitted or imperfect, "There is a hole in the ballad." Upon leaving the office, I said to him, "Dost thou see a hole in the ballad?" He replied, "No." "The recognizance we have just signed is good for nothing," said I: "for the United States have no claim upon the woman."

The next morning, at nine o'clock, we were at the magistrate's office. The claimant and his witnesses were also present; but the woman did not come; the reader can guess whether or not I expected her. After waiting about an hour, the magistrate, said to Thomas Harrison and myself, "Well, gentlemen, I shall be obliged to forfeit your recognizance, as the woman does not appear." I replied, "A thousand dollars is a great deal of money; but if the worst comes to the worst, we must pay to the United States, all the demand they have against her." "United States!" exclaimed the Alderman, and turned to look at his docket. After a pause of perhaps a minute, he said to the claimant, "Mr. _____, There is difficulty here; you had better employ counsel." The man replied that he was a stranger, and did not know who to apply to. The alderman referred him to Thomas Ross,[2] a respectable lawyer, who lived a few doors above. The claimant went for him, and in a few minutes he made his appearance at the office. He asked what was the matter. The magistrate informed him that the gentleman had arrested his slave, and made proof of his property; but as I had wished for further time, and had offered to enter into recognizance to the United States for her appearance, he had inadvertently entered it in that manner on his docket. T. Ross examined the entry, and turning to me, with a look and gesture of comical significance, exclaimed, "Eh!" To the claimant he said, "You must catch your slave again; you can do nothing with the securities." The alderman, who was now sober, saw that he had been misled. Both he and the claimant were much exasperated; they charged me with playing a trick on them, and threatened me with prosecution. But I had no fears on that score. I told them that if I had designedly done all they charged me with, I thought even that was better than that the woman should be torn from the arms of her husband and helpless children.

The magistrate asked me how I could say that I believed she had a *just* claim to her freedom, as I had produced no evidence to prove it. I replied that I believed every human had a *just* claim to freedom, unless he had committed some crime whereby he had forfeited it; and that slavery was founded in the most gross injustice and cruelty. The claimant observed that the laws of the land sanctioned it; and I had no right to fly in the face of the law. I told him if I had broken any law, I was willing to meet the consequences: but no law could make wrong right. The Jews said *they* had a law, and by it Christ ought to die; but that did not justify them in murdering him.

I am aware that some will disapprove of the part I acted in this case, as being inconsistent with the candor which men ought to practise on all occasions toward each other. I can only answer that I never felt condemned in my own heart for it. I could devise no other means to save the poor victim. The claimant spent several days in fruitless search for the fugitive. After giving up all hope of finding her, he called upon me, and offered to manumit her for four hundred dollars. I told him we would at one time freely have given him that sum; but now the circumstances of the case were greatly changed; and we would not give him half that amount. After much bickering, he finally consented to take one hundred and fifty. It was paid, and a manumission duly executed. When the claimant, (I have forgotten his name,) was about leaving my house, he stopped at the front door, and turning toward me, with a most malicious grin, said "I hope I may live till I see you south of the Potomac!" I replied, "Thou hadst better go home and repent of the sins already hanging over they head, instead of meditating the commission of more." I never saw him afterwards.

NOTES

1. *N.A.S.*, April 28, 1842, 186.

2. Thomas Ross, a lawyer, was listed in the *P.D. for 1800*, 105.

No. LVI.
The Foreign Slave[1]

The act of Congress, prohibiting the importation of slaves, took effect at the commencement of the year 1808. I think it was in the, first month of that year, a Frenchman arrived in Philadelphia, from one of the West India islands, and brought with him a slave, whom he took before John Douglass, one of the aldermen of that city, and had him bound to serve him seven years in Virginia. I was informed that this was done under the advice of Dennis Cottineau, a Frenchman, who had resided several years in Philadelphia, and was mostly applied to by his countrymen who needed advice. After the indenture was executed, the slave was committed to prison for safe-keeping. About dusk, one of his keepers called upon me, and informed me of the circumstances; he also said that the master intended to take him to the South early the next morning.

I had not at the time seen the law above referred to; but concluded, from what I heard of it, that the man was entitled to his freedom. In order, therefore, to detain him till his case could be inquired into, I procured a warrant for debt, and lodged it at the prison. Early the next morning, the Frenchman called for his slave; but the keeper refused to discharge him, until he would pay my demand for one hundred dollars. He applied to an attorney, who obtained a habeas corpus, to bring the case before the Mayor's court.

A little after ten o'clock, as I was on my way to the prison, I was met in the street by one of the keepers, who informed me that the colored man was in court. I asked how that could be, as I had received no notice. He said the Recorder did not think it necessary I should be notified; and that he had made some very severe strictures on my conduct. I immediately went to the court, which was thronged with people. I soon discovered that something unusual was going on; for all eyes seemed fixed upon me, and a lane was made for me through the crowd. I soon stood before the court. Mahlon Dickinson[2] was the Recorder, and he was in the act of giving his decision on the case; in closing which, he said that my conduct, upon the occasion, was extremely reprehensible; that the man was not my debtor, and I could have no possible object but to cause delay, vexation, and expense. The lawyers seemed a good deal tickled to hear me so roughly handled. I stood directly before the Recorder, meanwhile, looking him full in the face. As soon as he paused, I embraced the opportunity to address the court. "I respectfully ask the favor of being heard for a few minutes before this case is finally disposed of," said I; "and I presume this request will not be deemed unreasonable, inasmuch as I find I am the subject of pretty severe animadversion; and I think I can soon satisfy the court that it is unmerited." The Recorder paused, and said, "Well, Mr. Hopper, what have you to say in justification of your very extraordinary proceedings?" I replied, "it was true that the man was not my debtor; but the court had greatly erred in supposing that I had any improper motives in taking the steps I had in relation to the business. The court will recollect that Congress had lately passed an act, prohibiting any person from bringing slaves into this country. I had not seen the act, but I had enough to satisfy me that its provisions embraced the case then before the court." Jared Ingersoll, an old and respectable lawyer, who was present, remarked, "Please your honors, I believe Mr. Hopper is correct. I have the National Intelligencer, containing the law, at my office; and will send for it, if you wish to see it." His office was in the same street, and the paper was soon brought into court. J. Ingersoll pointed out the section having reference to the case, and I read it to the court; taking good care that all in the room should hear; and placing a strong emphasis on such parts as particularly related to the case then under consideration.

I then laid the paper on the table before me, and observed that I thought the court must now be convinced that the measures I had pursued were perfectly correct; and that their censures, which had been so liberally bestowed, were quite uncalled for. The counsel for the claimant said that a newspaper was not legal evidence of the existence of the law. I answered that the court knew I was not a lawyer; but I had heard the lawyers talk about *prima facie* evidence; and I presumed that the paper produced was at least of that character; more especially, as it was the government paper, in which the laws were published, for the information of citizens; and that the court would detain the man until an authenticated copy of the law could be obtained. After considerable had been said, the court ordered the man to be detained in custody, until a copy of it should be procured. The attorney for the claimant then abandoned the case, and the man was set at his liberty. There were a large number of spectators, both white and black; and as soon as the court announced their decision, the courtroom rung with "Hurrah, for Mr. T. Hopper!" by which appellation I was frequently called.

Several years afterwards, since I have resided in New-York, as I was returning from Philadelphia, I met with Mahlon Dickinson on board the steamboat; and in the course of conversation, I asked him if he recollected the above circumstances. He replied, pleasantly, "Indeed I do. I thought I *had* you, and I intended to give it to you; but you slipped through my fingers."

NOTES

1. *N.A.S.*, April 28, 1842, 186.

2. Mahlon Dickinson was listed as a lawyer in the *P.D. for 1800*, 2.

No. LVII.
The Fraudulent Indenture[1]

A family in Accomac county, in the State of Virginia, by the name of Stokely, owned a number of slaves. Some members of it embraced the doctrines of the Society of Friends, and joined the Society. Having previously become convinced of the iniquity of holding human beings in bondage, they had manumitted them. About the year 1820, I think, one of those slaves concluded to go to Philadelphia, to seek for employment. Soon after arriving in that city, she made application to Isaiah Knight, who kept an intelligence office, to procure a situation for her. Knight stated that she must pay him twenty-five cents. This was done. He professed great friendship for the woman, and *kindly* invited her to make her home at his house, until he could find a situation; telling her that he would not make any charge for her board. In the course of a week or ten days, he informed her that he had procured a place for her, and had made a good bargain. He also told her that she must go before a magistrate, and sign the articles of agreement, without asking any questions; as he would attend and see that all was right. He was a plausible fellow, and had fully obtained the confidence of the stranger, who had not the least suspicion of any trick in the business. Accordingly, they went before George Bartram,[2] a magistrate of Philadelphia, where they were met by John Huffnagle,[3] who kept a hardware store, at the corner of Market and Fifth streets, in that city. The articles of agreement, already prepared, were duly executed, and the woman went home with Huffnagle. After remaining in his service some time, she asked for the privilege of going out of an evening; this was denied. She was not permitted to put her foot into the street, on any occasion. At length, she asked for her wages; when she was informed that she was an indented servant, for the term of five years, and the Huffnagle had paid Isaiah Knight one hundred and fifty dollars for her. This information greatly alarmed her, but she did not know how to seek for a remedy. After remaining in this situation several months, Huffnagle hired a colored man, who had been a coachman several years for Samuel R. Fisher[4], a relation of Joseph G. Rowland, the husband of the colored woman's former mistress. She made her case known to this man, who communicated the circumstances to S.R. Fisher; and he called upon me, and informed me of them. He also wrote to Joseph G. Rowland, who resided in Delaware, giving the like information to him; in consequence of which, he went to Philadelphia, and called upon me. I accompanied him to see Huffnagle, and asked permission to have an interview with the woman; this was refused. We then informed him that the whole transaction was fraudulent, and that the indenture by which he held the woman, was void. He alledged that the woman had voluntarily signed it; and that if there was fraud in the business, she had made herself a party to it, and must abide the consequences. In reply to this, he was informed, that the woman was ignorant, and had been imposed upon by Knight; and that his refusing to permit her to go out of his house, furnished occasion for suspicion that he was privy to the deception practised upon her.

He appeared much exasperated, and declared that he would hold the woman, in spite of all we could do. I told him we had no wish to put him to any expense or trouble, and advised him to consult some respectable lawyer; with a promise to call again, we left him. The next morning we repeated our visit; when he informed us he had pursued our advice, and had ascertained that the indenture was valid. I asked who was his adviser. He replied, "lawyer Allibone." I told him that he knew Allibone was a very intemperate man, whose opinion could not be relied on; and recommended him to call upon some person who was more worthy of confidence. He, however, declined to follow our counsel; saying he was perfectly satisfied. We then informed him that we would suspend any further proceedings till the next day; being unwilling to institute a suit at law if it could possibly be avoided; at the same time giving him to understand that the woman was free, and that we were determined to secure her liberty. J.G. Rowland represented to him the circumstances in relation to her becoming free; that she had been the slave of his wife, who, from a conscientious conviction of the iniquity of holding her in bondage, had freely given her her freedom; and that he could not now quietly acquiesce in her being defrauded of it. We then returned home, leaving him to reflect upon the matter. In the afternoon, the woman called at my house, and informed me that Huffnagle had discharged her; and thus the matter ended.

NOTES

1. *N.A.S.*, May 27, 1842, 202.

2. George Bartram was listed as a gentleman in the *P.D. for 1801*.

3. John Huffnagle was listed as a merchant in the *P.D. for 1807*.

4. Samuel Fisher was listed as a merchant in the *P.D. for 1810*, 100.

No. LVIII.
The Chattel Restored to Manhood[1]

The following narrative I have written down just as I received it from the lips of a very intelligent and worthy colored man, a subscriber to the Standard. I have thought it prudent to suppress names and dates, lest some innocent person might be brought into trouble. No one who knows the narrator (and he is known and respected by many) will have any doubt of the truth of his statements:

"My father was a free man, but my mother was a slave in Virginia, where I was born. I lived with him until the time of his death, which occurred about the year 1826. He left his brother-in-law executor. Not long after my master's death, his property was divided among his children. I was valued at $425, and became the property of his son Richard, who was nearly my age, and my mother nursed him at her breast. My young master was about 21 years old, when I became his property. During the lifetime of my old master, I fared pretty well; but his son Richard was a very bad man, and treated me with great harshness. I was employed in the field, and notwithstanding I did the very best I could, he often had me whipped very severely. He seemed to delight in cruelty. Sometimes, when a man, old enough to be his father, was sick, he would take a club and beat him out of his house. His slaves were kept almost naked, and were very scantily fed. After a time, he concluded to move to Georgia, and take his slaves with him. I dreaded the very idea of going to that region; having often heard that the slaves there were treated horribly. I determined to make an effort to escape; for it seemed to me I would rather die, than go to Georgia. I made application to the captain of a _____ where my master lived. He refused to take me on board, knowing the laws were very severe, and that he would be made to suffer, if detected in attempting to take me away. He was, however, a humane man, and he gave me some very important information. He pointed out the North Star, and told me to follow it. Before leaving my master, I besought him to sell me to some person in the neighborhood where I was born. He refused to comply with my request, and told me I must go with him. I had been hard at work all day, carting corn to a vessel. This was in the month of January. I had long worked with the oxen I drove on that day, and felt great attachment for them. One was called John, and the other Duke. When I had done my work, it was quite dark. I felt the deepest distress; being determined to set out on my journey to the North that night. I took the yoke off the cattle, but I was in too much of a hurry to feed them. I put my hand on John, and said, 'Farewell, John, I shan't see you again, till the day of judgement.' I then went to the spring, took a last look at it, tasted my last draught of its water, with tears bade that also farewell, and went on my way with fear and trembling. But I had often heard it said that the Lord would be a friend to the friendless; and I believed He would be with me. The corn I had carried to the vessel was for a neighbor. When I went to give an account of my work, my distress was so great that I could not conceal it; and he asked me what was the matter. I answered, 'It is the trouble of this world.'

"He little thought of what I had in view. When I left home, I had about eight dollars. I was badly clothed, and the weather was cold. I took with me a loaf of bread, which was all the provision I could get. It was about nine o'clock when I started. I travelled all night, and laid by in the day. When my bread was gone, I begged some of colored people, whom I met on my journey. One night, about eleven o'clock, a man in the road, called out, 'Who's there?' I replied, 'It is one.' He ordered me to stop. I immediately run, and he after me; but I out-run him, and made my escape. I experienced many dangers and difficulties on my journey; particularly in crossing rivers. I was frequently obliged to traverse the margin a considerable distance, before I could meet with a boat to carry me over; on one occasion I gave a man three dollars to put me over. The weather was cold, and being obliged to sleep in the woods, I became frost-bitten; my feet swelled, and my limbs were so stiff, that I found it very difficult to walk. In about a month after I left home, I came to Pennsylvania, to the house of a Friend. I had often heard my master say that when the slaves run away and got among the Quakers, they could not recover them again; and I rejoiced when I found one. The family treated me very kindly. They placed pie and milk before me; but I had been so long without food, that my appetite was gone; I could not eat. I made but a short stay with those kind people, and then proceeded on towards Philadelphia; where, to my great joy, I arrived in two or three days. I staid there till I recovered my strength, and then came to New-York. In the course of the year, I became acquainted with a gentleman, to whose kindness I am a great debtor. I made known to him my situation, and he opened a correspondence, with my master, through the agency of a friend in Philadelphia. In about two years from the commencement of this correspondence, my master agreed to manumit me for one hundred dollars; which my kind friend and benefactor advanced, and thus obtained my manumission. I have since refunded this money. I have now been in this city about sixteen years, during twelve of which I have resided in the same house; and I am a free and happy man, with a wife and three children.

"About three years before I left home, Mr. _____, had a slave by the name of Harry, whose wife was a slave to Mr. _____, about forty miles off. Harry was in the habit of occasionally making her a visit. His master forbid it; but such was the man's affection for his wife, that he would continue his visits. This so enraged his master that he took him to the public whipping-post, and flogged him till somebody interfered, and he was obliged to release him. His anger was not yet satisfied. He too him from the whipping-post to a blacksmith's, and had an iron collar put on his neck, with a prong, which was bent over his head, so as to project a short distance beyond his forehead; to this he fixed a bell, and then ordered him to run home; he followed, whipping as he run, till the slave became so exhausted that he fell to the ground. The master then ordered my brother to put Harry into a cart and take him home; but he died before they could get there. Mr. _____ was arrested and put in prison, where he remained about three weeks; he was then discharged, and nothing further was done with him.

My mother became the property of Mr. E_____, who treated

her with great cruelty. Her sufferings were so great that she could endure them no longer. Preferring death, to a life of such continued torture, she fled to the woods, where she continued for about a year. She could not have survived so long, had she not been fed secretly by the colored people. She died in the woods, and her body was discovered by means of the buzzards collecting about it."

NOTES

1. *N.A.S.*, June 23, 1842, 10.

No. LIX.
Charles Webster[1]

Charles Webster was a slave to Benjamin Orr, a gambler, in Virginia. Becoming involved in debt, Orr sold him to a person, whom I shall call A.B.; I have forgotten his name, but I remember he was considered wealthy and respectable. About the year 1797, A.B. went to Philadelphia to spend the winter, and took his wife and daughters with him, to enjoy the company and amusements of the city. Charles was their coachman and waiter. They took lodgings in Fourth street, at the Indian Queen; and Inn well known to almost every body in Philadelphia.

After being in the city a few weeks, Charles called upon me, in company with a colored man of the place, and inquired if he was not free. I informed him that the law permitted his master to take him away when he pleased, provided he did not remain *six months*. He supposed his master was acquainted with the law, and of course, would not keep him there so long.

"I never will return to Virginia," said he: "Where can I go, to be safe?"

I advised him to remain with the family until he saw them making preparations for going home; for it was possible A.B. might be ignorant of the law; and if he was not, he might not finish his visit in six months. I told him it was of course better to get his freedom in a legal way, if he could; for if he went off before the expiration of six months, he would be liable to be arrested at any moment, and taken to the South; and then he would probably never have another so good opportunity to escape. Charles concluded to take my advice; though not without some hesitation and anxiety. The time seemed very long to the poor fellow; his fears were continually excited, lest his master should suddenly have him seized and sent home. He was very diligent and attentive, never left home in the evening, and so conducted as not to excite any suspicion of what was passing in his mind.

The very day the six months expired, A.B. informed him that they expected to start for Virginia the next day; and directed him to grease the carriage wheels, and have all things ready. Charles *appeared* quite pleased with the idea of returning; brushed the harness, greased the carriage, as he was directed; and then called upon me. This was an important juncture. It seemed almost impossible to satisfy him that he was now out of danger. I requested him to return to his master, and call upon me the next morning. He was instructed to have an understanding with some of the servants in the house, who would immediately inform me, in case he should be arrested meanwhile.

The next morning, he called again, and I accompanied him to William Lewis, a well known and highly respectable lawyer, who lived within a few doors of me. I stated Charles's case. Wm. Lewis said there could be no possible doubt as to his freedom, provided we had made no mistake about the time of his sojourn in Philadelphia. I had made a note of the time when they came, and fully satisfied him on that point. Wm. Lewis then wrote A.B. a polite note, apprising him that Charles was free, according to the laws of Pennsylvania, and cautioning him against any attempt to remove him out of the State. The note was given to Charles; and at the recommendation of Wm. Lewis, I agreed to see A.B. previous to its delivery.

I was then only about twenty-six years of age, and I felt some delicacy in calling upon a wealthy and distinguished stranger, who was said to be rather irritable in his temper. However, after a few minutes reflection, all considerations of etiquette vanished; and I went to see him. I informed him that I belonged to a society for the abolition of slavery; and had called to inform him that the colored man whom he had brought with him from Virginia was free, and would not return to his service; that I had consulted William Lewis, who I presumed was known to him, by reputation at least; and he had given Charles a note, addressed to him, on the subject. He was exceedingly angry, and charged me with tampering with gentleman's servants. I replied that if his son were a slave in Algiers, he would *thank* me for tampering with him, if I could, by that means, secure his liberty. In the present case, however, I was not obnoxious to the charge. The man had called upon me of his own accord. I had merely made him acquainted with his legal rights; and I intended to see that he was protected in them. I then left him. Charles soon returned and gave his master the lawyer's note. Perceiving that he could not compel his servant to return to Virginia, he proposed hiring him to drive the carriage home. But Charles knew perfectly well that Virginia was a dangerous place for him; and he positively refused. A.B. then told him that if he was free, his clothes belonged to *him*; that he should not take a single garment. In great anger, he cut of his queue, close to his head, and ordered him to strip instantly. Charles complied at once; and was about to leave the room perfectly naked. Astonished to find that this condition was no obstacle to his leaving the house, A.B. seized hold of him, violently thrust him back, and ordered him to dress himself. He again put on his clothes, and walked off. Here ended the connection between Charles and his old master. I think they never saw each other afterwards.

Charles Webster was rather under middle size, and was a shrewd, sensible man. He afterwards lived as a servant in the family of lawyer Lewis; who would never accept anything for his legal services on such occasions. After Charles had been free about two years, he married Amelia, a woman of his own color, who was a domestic in the family of Chief Justice Tilghman. She had been brought up in the family of Captain Miller, in Almond street, and was industrious, tidy, and economical.

Some years after their marriage, they took a lot, on ground rent, of Isaac W. Morris, on George street, between 10th and 11th streets, extending to Juniper alley; and placed upon each front a neat two-story house. They occupied the one on George street, and let the other. Here they resided many years, and were the parents of fourteen children; only four of whom now survives.

This case, with hundreds of others, had entirely escaped my recollection, until I was called upon by Mary Loane, one of their daughters, a few days ago; She perfectly recollected me, though I did not recognize her, until she reminded me of her being a scholar in the school for colored children, established by Anthony Benezet; then kept by Beulah Parker. The school was under the care of the monthly meetings of Friends in Philadelphia, and I was one of the overseers, at the time Mary was a pupil. She attended four or five years, and obtained quite a good education.

Mary married John Loane, and went with him to Nassau, New Providence. They were there at the time of the arrival of the Brig Creole, and partook of the rejoicing, which extended to all classes of the inhabitants, at the escape of so many human beings from bondage. The colored people have formed a society on that island, called the "Friendly Society," to give advice and assistance to people of their own complexion. Upon the arrival of the Creole, the slaves were soon taken in charge by the members of this society. The governor of the island gave them advice how to proceed. It was at first concluded to move the strangers into the interior; but upon more deliberate consideration, it was thought best that they should go to Jamaica; that being deemed a place of greater safety. When the Creole first arrived, three of the women slaves refused to leave the vessel; preferring to remain with their owners; but after being made acquainted with the real state of things, they *all left the Creole*, and are now on the island, where they enjoy that liberty which is the birthright of all the human family. Charles Webster has been dead several years. He conducted reputably--was much respected, and was a kind and affectionate husband and father. About the year 1824 he went to Haiti, and took his wife and all his children, except one, with him. But after a few years, he returned to Philadelphia, where his widow now resides.

NOTES

1. *N.A.S.*, July 14, 1842, 22.

No. LX.
Tom[1]

A colored man, whom for convenience I will call Tom, for I do not remember his name, a slave to Robert Creswell, of Cecil county, Maryland, left his master's service, and went to Philadelphia. He soon after hired with a farmer, near Milestown, about seven miles north of Philadelphia. After remaining there about two years, some person, to whom he had made known his condition, informed Creswell where he was. He forthwith repaired to Philadelphia; taking with him one of his neighbors, and a colored man. Whether the latter was a slave, or a free man, I do not now recollect. They took lodgings at an in inn in North Third street, a few doors above Mulberry, known by the name of the "Golden Swan." This was in the summer of 1809. The day after their arrival, the colored man was sent to Milestown, to decoy Tom into the hands of his master. It seems they were old acquaintances; and upon meeting, they both expressed themselves highly pleased. The stranger invited Tom to accompany him to the city, to spend a day or two with mutual friends. Tom cheerfully complied, and they set off to Philadelphia; the former much pleased with the prospect of enjoying the company of an old acquaintance; little dreaming of the snare the treacherous fellow had laid, to betray him into the hands of his master. When they reached the city, the stranger proposed to Tom to step into the hotel to get something to drink. They entered through a carriage way, alongside of the inn, which communicated with the yard. As soon as they entered the yard, Creswell made his appearance, with a pistol in his hand. He pounced upon Tom, and threatened him with instant death, if he made any resistance. He submitted, as a matter of necessity; his hands were tied together, and he was ordered up stairs.

James Cameron[2] kept the inn at the time. He was a respectable man, and by no means satisfied that his house should be made a prison. He inquired of Creswell and his friend what crime the man had committed, or by what authority they made him a prisoner; but they would give him no satisfaction. He then called upon me, related what had occurred, and said he would not submit to the man's being detained as prisoner in his house, if he could help it. I accompanied him home, and was conducted up stairs. There I found William Master,[3] an indefatigable and efficient friend of the slave, also the two strangers, with the victim of their avarice. We demanded their names, and whence they came; also by what authority they detained the man in custody. They answered us by presenting their pistols, and refusing to give us any information whatever. We remonstrated against the unreasonableness of such conduct, and assured them that it would not be suffered.

Finding entreaty unavailing, I left William Master at the inn, to watch their movements, and departed. On my way, I met Joseph D. Martin. We went together to Jacob Baker, one of the aldermen, and stated the case to him. He was at a loss how to frame a warrant, and we were not enough of lawyers to inform him. It was now after sundown, and there was no time to procure legal advice; and we were apprehensive that unless some energetic measures were immediately adopted, the colored man would be placed out of our reach. I therefore proposed that the magistrate should issue process in this way: commanding any constable to take the two men, that should be shown to him, charged, on *my* affirmation, with intending, as I believed, to take a colored man out of the State contrary to law. The warrant was granted accordingly; and we immediately proceeded to the inn, to have it served upon the men; taking Peter Winn[4] and Thomas North, two city constables with us.

Upon entering the room where those men were, we were met by them, each having a pistol in his hand. The officers exhibited their warrant, and ordered the men to surrender and go with them; but they obstinately refused. I stepped into the room, and while the eye of Creswell was upon me, one of the officers snatched at his pistol. He suddenly threw his hand behind him, to put it out of his reach. I came behind Creswell, and immediately seized the pistol, and jerked it out of his hand. After some parley, they agreed to accompany us to the magistrate, who was in his office, waiting to receive us. The captive also went with us. The first thing which occupied our attention, after getting there, was to examine the pistols, and see whether they were really prepared to do execution, or whether it was a mere sham, to frighten us. We soon discovered the fellows were well prepared. The pistols were heavily loaded, each containing two slugs. The loads were removed, and the pistols put into the magistrate's desk. The men were then called upon to account for their conduct. Creswell stated that the man was his slave; and alledged that he had a right to arrest him, wherever he could find him. In reply to this, it was observed that there was no *evidence* of the man being his slave; and even if there were, they had not proceeded legally; that if such conduct as theirs were tolerated, no colored man would be safe. After a full investigation into the facts, the alderman committed Creswell and his friend to prison. The colored man was discharged, and they never found him afterwards. So our object was attained. Upon their leaving the office, Creswell inquired, "What are you going to do with the negro?" He was answered, "The negro can take care of himself." He added, looking me in the face, "This is your work; and I'll be d----d if I don't pop you over, yet." I replied, "May be not; we don't allow such men as thou art to carry pistols here."

I was aware there was some risk in this mode of procedure; but there seemed to be no other way of getting the fellow out of their clutches; and we concluded to risk the consequences.

The next day, Creswell and his friend made application to Samuel Ewing, attorney at law, who procured their release from prison, and commenced a suit for trespass against Jacob Baker, alderman, and Peter Winn and Thos. North, constables, and Joseph D. Martin, and myself, the warrant being illegal. There exists a law in Pennsylvania, to compel plaintiff or defendant to arbitrate at the option of either party; and we were notified to appear at the office of the prothonotary, to choose arbitrators. James Milnor was our attorney. I shall always respect him for the readiness, zeal, and ability, with which he always advanced the cause of the oppressed, whenever he had the opportunity. He advised us not to attend; in which case, the prothonotary would choose for the party that declined attending.

In a short time, we were informed that John Perot, Thomas

Cumpston, and Joseph Sims, were duly appointed arbitrators, and were to meet at Dunwoody's hotel, in Market street. We attended, and the matter was fully investigated. S. Ewing, who was not remarkable for his modesty, was very severe upon me, and dwelt at considerable length upon the part I was in the habit of taking in such cases. He said I often, by a singular kind of management, took slaves from their lawful owners, and put their masters to much expense and trouble, besides. He said I tainted everything I touched. I replied, "Is that the reason why thou art so offensive? for I have had the handling of thee. There can be no doubt thou art spoiled." This produced a general laugh. Joseph Sims held slaves in Maryland, where he had married; and the other arbitrators were by no means favorable to abolition, though otherwise respectable, clever men. We knew we had no favor to expect from them; and so it proved. They gave an award against Joseph D. Martin and myself, of five hundred dollars; against the magistrate twenty-five dollars; and against each of the constables, ten dollars. From this award Joseph D. Martin and myself appealed; but the magistrate and constables concluded to comply. Creswell appealed as it regarded them, and objected to our appealing; alledging that we could not, without the consent of the others implicated in the suit. This point was argued before the court, and finally determined in our favor. The appeal being allowed, there was an end of the matter. I never heard what was done in the business afterwards. This case, as regards the right of appeal, is mentioned in Brown's reports of cases adjudged in the Court of Common Pleas, for the county of Philadelphia. It was decided in the third mo. 1810.

NOTES

1. *N.A.S.*, September 22, 1842, 62.

2. James Cameron, an innkeeper, was noted in the *P.D. for 1804*, 43.

3. William Master, a shoemaker, was referred to in the *P.D. for 1810*, 190.

4. Peter Winn was listed as a constable in the *P.D. for 1807*.

No. LXI.
What's in a Name?[1]

Wylet was a slave to Benjamin Brannan, inn-keeper in Market-street, Philadelphia. She was born in the family of his wife's father, who registered her under the act of assembly of Pennsylvania, passed in the year 1780, for the gradual abolition of slavery. I believe it was about the year 1808, that Wylet called upon me. She said she was the slave of Brannan's wife, who had always told her that she should be free at her death. That event having occurred, Wylet thought she ought to be free. She was about fifty years old, remarkably smart and active; and withal, not deficient in intelligence, considering her scanty opportunities. After hearing her story, I informed her that slaves in Pennsylvania were considered *personal* property; that when Brannan married her mistress, she became *his* property; and that the promise of her mistress could have no legal effect to make her free. This grieved the old woman greatly; and it was difficult to convince her that I was correct in this opinion. I inquired whether she had been registered; but she was unable to inform me. I then told her I would consider further of the matter, and requested her to call again. In the course of a day or two, I went to the proper officer to examine the record, and there found that she had been registered, by the name of "WYLET." Although the woman called herself by this name, I concluded that it might be attributed to her imperfect dialect, and that her proper name must be Violet; for I had never known any person by the name of Wylet. I then called upon William Lewis, who was not behind the foremost lawyer in Pennsylvania in legal knowledge, and explained the case to him. He agreed with me that the name was doubtless Violet, and not Wylet; and that therefore the registry was defective. He advised that a habeas corpus should be taken out, and the validity of it tested. I accordingly applied to

Chief Justice William Tilghman,[2] and procured one, which was duly served upon Brannan. The judge was a native of Maryland, and I believe, a slaveholder; but of that I am not entirely certain. Many looked upon him with a jealous eye, apprehending that he could not wholly divest himself of the prejudice so common to those who have spent the greater part of their lives in the midst of slavery; but the sequel proved they were, in this instance, mistaken; and I once heard a slaveholder remark, that "Judge Tilghman stood so straight, that he leaned backwards." He was, unquestionably, a very upright judge.

The hearing came on in the judge's chambers, in Chestnut street. William Lewis attended as counsel for Wylet, and Jared Ingersoll for the claimant. Many witnesses were examined, and they all testified that the woman had always been called Wylet. The claimant was of German descent; and although there seemed to be no doubt in the minds of any, that it was *intended* her name should be Violet, yet it was satisfactorily proved that she was *called* Wylet. The woman said she had been baptized; and the church records were thoroughly searched, hoping to find her name there recorded Violet; but it was all in vain; no record of her could be found on the church books. Wm. Lewis managed the case with great ability and ingenuity, and was replied to by J. Ingersoll with much talent. Several hours were spent in examining the witnesses, and in the argument of counsel. At length, the important period arrived when the final decision must be announced; and the countenance of poor Wylet indicated, in no equivocal manner, her deep anxiety. She alternately watched the judge, her counsel, and me. The judge evidently leaned to the side of mercy; but he considered himself compelled to decide that Wylet was a slave. As soon as he had given his decision, Wylet looked him full in the face, her cheeks suffused with tears, and thus addressed him:

"What did you say, Mr. judge? Did you say I am Mr. Brannan's *slave*?"

"Yes, Wylet," replied the judge, mildly; "I said you are Mr. Brannan's slave."

"Well, you should *not* have said so; I ain't Mr. Brannan's slave. I belonged to mistress; and she always told me I should be free at her death. I never did belong to Mr. Brannan."

Then turning to her master, she said, "You are a poor, drunken thing; not fit to have anybody; and I won't live with you."
The judge said, sternly, "Wylet! Wylet! you must not talk so."
She quietly stepped to the door, and walked away. Brannan never troubled the old woman afterwards.

But few days elapsed, before I met Chief Justice Tilghman in the street. He pleasantly remarked, in allusion to the case of Wylet, that the ground we had taken was not tenable. I replied, that we failed to make out our case; that we were not aware we had Germans to deal with. "Wylet and Violet are so near alike," said he, "that it is like splitting hairs to make a distinction."

NOTES

1. *N.A.S.*, September 29, 1842, 66.

2. Justice William Tilghman (1756-1827) was the Chief Judge of the United States Circuit Court of Pennsylvania during 1801-1802, Judge of the Court of Common Pleas for Philadelphia in 1805, Judge of the High Court of Errors and Appeals and Chief Justice of Pennsylvania's Supreme Court during 1806-1827. *Who Was Who in America*, 604.

No. LXII.
William Anderson[1]

William Anderson was a slave in Virginia. When about twenty-five years old, he concluded to "try if he could not do something for himself;" as he remarked to me, when I inquired of him what was the cause of his leaving Virginia. To try this experiment, he left his master, and went to Philadelphia with two of his fellow-servants. After he had been absent a few months, the master "sold them, running," (a common term in the slave States,) to a certain Joseph Ennells, who was in the practice of speculating in slaves. This man repaired to Philadelphia, in search of his newly-acquired *property*. He procured a warrant, engaged a constable, and started in pursuit of the fugitives. It was on a Seventh-day of the week, and they went to the horse-market, where many people congregated. They had not been there long, before Ennells espied the three men standing together in the crowd, and immediately made an attempt to pounce upon them; but happily for them, they saw the marauders coming, and quickly mingled with the multitude, and escaped.

Ennells spent two or three days in search of them, but being unsuccessful, he called upon Thomas Harrison, of whose name I have several times had occasion to make honorable mention. The name always excites pleasant emotions, whenever it occurs to me; for he was the means of rescuing hundreds of unfortunate people from the grasp of avaricious slaveholders. Ennells explained the case to Thomas, and solicited him to assist in finding them; saying he would sell them very low. Not succeeding, he called upon me, and I soon recognized him as a man with whom I had come in contact on a former occasion. I advised him to go home; for his object in coming to the city was, above all things, the most hateful. I reminded him that, on a former occasion, he had been dealt with kindly; and I now wished him to extend a portion of the same attribute to those fugitives. He again called upon Thomas Harrison, and finally agreed to sell the three men to him, for $250. He said this was less than he had given for them. The money was paid, and Ennells returned home. In the course of a few days, William Anderson, one of the three fugitives, called upon me for advice. I informed him that Thomas Harrison had purchased all of them: and recommended him to find the other two, and call upon him and settle the matter. He called, accordingly; but he could give no account of his companions. They had left the city, and he could not tell where they had gone.

William was an honest, faithful fellow, and readily offered to bind himself as a servant, till he had earned money to refund the sum paid by his friend. He was informed that he had a legal right to his liberty, in consequence of a bill of sale having been made to a citizen of Pennsylvania, where slavery was not allowed; but he manifested no disposition to take advantage of this circumstance. On the contrary, he was determined to make full compensation to his benefactor. He said he was thankful for his kindness, and that he should not lose one single cent that had been paid for him. It was gratifying to see one who had been a slave all his life, manifest so much gratitude, and such a nice sense of justice.

Many days had not elapsed, before a place was found, and William was indented to Jacob Downing, a respectable merchant of Philadelphia, for a term of time, for one hundred and twenty five dollars. This was half the amount paid for all of them. William served the stipulated time faithfully. His master told me, he never had a more honest, faithful servant. He became much attached to the family, and often spoke of them with great affection and respect.

After the time of his indenture was expired, he called upon his old friend, Thomas Harrison. After making grateful acknowledgments for his kindness he inquired whether he had ever heard from the other two fugitives. Being answered in the negative, he replied, "Well, Mr. Harrison, you paid two hundred and fifty dollars, and you have not been able to find my companions. It is not right that you should lose by your kindness to us; you have received only one hundred and twenty-five dollars for me. *I am willing you should sell me again to make up the balance.*

This generous and honorable offer was met in the same spirit in which it was made. "Honest fellow!" said Thomas harrison. "Go about thy business. I have no claim upon thee. Thou hast paid thy share. Conduct as well as thou hast done since I have known thee, and thou wilt surely do well."

I happened to be present when this interview took place, and I shall always remember the pleasant glow of heart produced by such honorable, disinterested conduct. William Anderson frequently called to see me for many years after he was a free man; and he continued to conduct in the most exemplary manner. Thomas Harrison never heard of the other two men, and of course lost his hundred and twenty-five dollars.

I once heard a Friend mildly censure this excellent man, for his great activity on such occasions. He cited the story of Mary and Martha, mentioned in the New Testament: "Martha, Martha, thou art careful and troubled about many things; but one thing is needful; and Mary hath chosen that good part which shall not be taken from her."

"All that is very well," replied Thomas; "but Mary would have had a late breakfast, after all, had it not been for Martha."

NOTES

1. *N.A.S.*, October 20, 1842, 78.

No. LXIII.
The Traitor[1]

The following affecting incident occurred, I think, about the year 1810. In relating it, I use the fictitious name of James Austin, because I am unwilling to wound the feelings of his respectable relations, descended from an ancient and worthy family of Friends, in New Jersey. His predecessor filled a highly responsible station under the government of that province, as early as 1703, and was among the first who emigrated to that part of the country from England.

James resided some years in Philadelphia. He removed to Charleston, South Carolina, where he married, and was disowned by the Society of Friends, of which he was a born member. He engaged in mercantile business, and followed it several years, when he returned to Philadelphia, and soon became bankrupt. I was acquainted with him a considerable time. From his plausible conversation and manners, in connection with the respectability of his family, I had formed rather a favorable opinion of him. After his pecuniary difficulties, being out of business and at leisure, he called frequently to see me. He informed me that his wife owned a farm near Charleston, and that he had concluded to remove there and cultivate it; but as he could not conscientiously employ slaves, he found great difficulty in procuring laborers. He, therefore, proposed hiring free people in Philadelphia, and asked my assistance; saying that he could readily engage as many as he wanted, if I would satisfy them that there would be no danger of being reduced to slavery there. The plan appeared plausible, and I concluded to assist him in carrying it out.

In a few days, I was called upon by two colored men, who had agreed to go with him, provided I thought well of it. There was on my mind a strong impression that they had better not go. I could assign no reason for it; but it was so strong, that I resolved to obey it. I, therefore, told the men that I had given James Austin reason to suppose I would assist him in procuring some colored people to go with him to South Carolina; but since then I had changed my mind; and I thought they had better stay where they were. They communicated this to him, and he soon called upon me. He seemed surprised, and dwelt with considerable energy upon the great advantage it would be to the men to go with him. I told him it was all in vain to reason upon the subject; for the more I thought of it, the more uncomfortable I felt; that I had no cause to suspect him of dishonest or dishonorable motives, but the impression of danger was so powerful on my mind that I could not conscientiously have any agency in encouraging colored laborers to go with him.

Not succeeding in this enterprise, he went to New Jersey, and took up his abode with his father, who, as I have said, was a worthy and consistent member of the Society of Friends. While there, an aged colored man who had escaped from the house of bondage in Virginia, was engaged in his service as a laborer on the farm. James soon ingratiated himself in the old man's favor, and obtained his confidence. He promised, if he would tell him to whom he belonged, and the place of his residence, he would write to his owner and buy his time; and then he might work for his father, until the amount he might pay for him should be liquidated. The honest-hearted old man, suspecting no treachery, readily complied, and opened himself fully to this deceitful fellow. He wrote, sure enough; but not with the view of procuring the freedom of his confiding victim. In a short time, a person arrived from Virginia, with full power to arrest the slave and take him to the place whence he had escaped. He was accordingly seized, put in irons, and conveyed to prison in Philadelphia. Being informed that a fugitive was in jail, I went immediately to see him. The poor old man, with a breaking heart, and a mournful countenance, suffused with tears, related to me the circumstances attending his capture. He said he saw the agent of his claimant pay his betrayer fifty dollars, the reward of his treachery. He lamented bitterly that he had been so deceived. "I thought he was a Quaker, and might be trusted," said he. I informed him that James Austin was no Quaker; that I did not believe there was a Quaker upon the face of the earth, who was so lost to all sense of honor and justice. He replied, "There is where I was deceived." The family of James was greatly afflicted when they came to the knowledge of the circumstances.

My heart ached for the poor sufferer; but it was not in my power to relieve him. I bade him an affectionate farewell, for I felt that I loved him. I never saw or heard from him afterwards. I found, upon inquiry, that he was an innocent, good-tempered man, and had obtained the affectionate regard of the family where he had taken refuge.

My indignation was kindled against the perfidious wretch, who, for a few dollars, had been the means of heaping so much misery upon one who trusted him as his friend and benefactor. I now was fully convinced that his motive in endeavoring to prevail on laborers to go to Charleston, was of the same mercenary character; and the impression on my mind was not in vain.

The day after parting with the poor fellow in prison, I wrote a letter to James Austin. I have not a copy; but I remember it, as well as if it were written yesterday:

> James Austin--Yesterday I visited the poor old man in prison, whom thou has so perfidiously betrayed. Gloomy and hopeless as his case is, I would prefer it to thine. Thou hast received $50, as the reward of thy treachery; but what good can it do thee? Canst thou lay down thy head at night, and not feel the bitter goadings of a guilty conscience? Canst thou ask forgiveness for thy sins of our Heavenly Father, whom thou has so grievously insulted by thy hypocrisy? Judas betrayed his Master for thirty pieces of silver, and afterwards hung himself; thou has betrayed thy brother for fifty; and if thy conscience is not seared, as with a hot iron, thy compunction must be great. I feel no disposition to upbraid thee. Thy own heart, I have no doubt, does that sufficiently: for our beneficent Creator will not suffer any to be at ease in their sins.
>
> Thy friend,
> ISAAC T. HOPPER

I never saw James Austin afterwards. He has been dead several years.

NOTES

1. *N.A.S.*, November 3, 1842, 86.

No. LXIV.
The Tender Mercies of a Slaveholder[1]

About the year 1808, a man who had escaped from bondage in one of the southern States, was arrested in Philadelphia as a slave, and committed to prison. He had been in confinement but a very little while, when his master called at the prison with authority to convey him to the place whence he had escaped. When informed that his master had called for him, he appeared greatly distressed. He told the keeper that his master was very severe, and he knew that dreadful suffering awaited him, if he should be taken back to bondage. After some hesitation, he accompanied the keeper to the iron gate, through which he was to pass out of prison; he saw his brutal oppressor standing before it, ready to fetter and take him away. Here he halted, and pleaded, in the most earnest, but humble manner, that he would suffer him to procure a purchaser in Philadelphia, who would pay a reasonable price for him. His master was inexorable, and paid no attention to his pathetic appeals. In a stern tone, and with angry gestures, he ordered him to come out. The slave replied, "Master, I can't go with you." His tyrant exclaimed, "You shall! Come out, immediately!" The poor fellow advanced timidly towards the door, but in an instant stepped back, as though frightened. His agony was so great, that he appeared to have almost lost his reason. The master became irritated, and in an impatient, peremptory manner, again ordered his trembling victim to come forward, and called upon the keeper to *bring* him out. All this time, the keeper stood with his hand upon the key of the iron gate. At last, he unlocked and opened it, and reluctantly told the poor terrified creature that he *must* come out, and go with his owner. For a moment, the slave looked his master in the face--then, in a frenzied manner, he flew to the gate, and as suddenly flew back--seized a sharp knife, which he had concealed about his person, drew it with great force across his throat, and fell lifeless, within a yard or two of his master's feet. The blood flowed freely, and all who witnessed the awful tragedy, concluded that the man must die. Dr. Church was then physician of the prison. Few surpassed him in benevolence, or professional skill. He happened to be at the prison at the time, and his attention was immediately called to this distressing case.

The man was conveyed to a room provided for the sick, and his wound dressed. The windpipe was cut through, though not entirely separated; but little prospect was entertained of his recovery. Soon after the doctor left the prison, the master demanded his victim, but the keeper declined delivering him, until the physician could be consulted. He was sent for, and at once assured the vindictive tyrant that it would be impossible to get the slave outside of those walls alive; that it would be even unsafe to move him at all. The southerner declared that he was *his property*, and he was determined to take him, dead or alive. If he died, it was nobody's loss but *his*.

The keeper felt himself in an embarrassing situation. He was afraid that if he refused to obey the mayor's order to discharge him, he might incur heavy damages; and on the contrary, if he delivered him up, he was certain he would die; and he would thus become accessory to his death. Under these circumstances, he resolved to convene the inspectors, and consult with them. This was done; and the keeper was pleased to find they concurred with him in opinion. They, however, deemed it prudent to lay the matter before the mayor, and accordingly appointed a deputation to wait upon him. Not being a legal character, he sent for the recorder. Upon consulting together, they united in opinion that the slave should not be surrendered to the claimant, until the physician declared he could be removed without endangering his life. Instructions were given accordingly. In the meantime, the master had gone to the prison, and was waiting for the keeper's return. When informed of the result of the application to the mayor, he became perfectly furious. He vociferated that the slave was *his* property, and the officer had no right to interfere with it. After venting his rage, and threatening to prosecute the keeper, he left the premises.

The day the man wounded himself, Dr. Church informed me of the circumstances, and gave me to understand that he had very faint hopes of his recovery. But contrary to his expectation, he lingered several days. I began to think it possible he might yet recover; and I requested the doctor to inform me the moment he considered him out of danger. About a week after the event, he came and told me he now thought he would get well; and that he had given this information to Joseph Price, who was one of the inspectors. The master, however, was kept in ignorance of this fact; and Luke Williams and Joseph Price undertook to negotiate for his purchase. Thinking there was but little chance for his recovery, the southerner sold him for a moderate price; but when he discovered that the slave was made a free man, and was likely to live, he was greatly enraged. The man recovered, and lived many years to enjoy liberty, for the sake of which he had been willing to encounter death; and his exemplary conduct proved that he was worthy of the boon on which he had set so high a value. Patrick Henry's exclamation, "Give me liberty, or give me death!" is applauded to the echo, by thousands who never think how often the terrible alternative is forced upon our poor suffering brethren in bondage.

NOTES

1. *N.A.S.*, November 24, 1842, 88.

No. LXV.
Benjamin Clark[1]

Benjamin Clark was born in Virginia, and was held as a slave till he was about thirty years old, when he escaped from his oppressor, and, about the year 1808, went to Philadelphia. After he had been there about a year, he married, and resided in Middle Alley, mostly inhabited by colored people. He sawed wood, and his wife was employed as a washerwoman. They were industrious, sober people, and being without children, found no difficulty in supporting themselves comfortably. I often employed him, and always found him industrious and obliging. Their house was well furnished, and was remarkably clean and neat. Few white people, in their sphere, exceeded them in this respect. There seemed nothing to mar their comfort.

They were Methodists; and Benjamin was a class-leader, much respected and beloved by those people. He had been in Philadelphia, I think, about ten years, when one of those inhuman monsters, who make a prey of the poor and needy, went to that city, and having procured a warrant from Alderman John Douglass, engaged a constable, by the name of Richard Hunt, commonly called Dick Hunt, who was frequently employed in the infamous business of seeking out fugitives from bondage. His total destitution of honorable principle, and depraved moral character, seemed to fit him well for this employment. The claimant and this vile man broke into Clark's house in the darkness of midnight, seized him as he lay in bed, and were about to drag him off without any garment but his night-dress. He begged for the privilege of dressing himself, which, after considerable demur, was allowed. His wife, almost distracted with terror, run out of the house and screamed, as loud as she could, "Kidnappers! kidnappers!" This soon roused the neighbors; and by the time they got the colored man out of his house, they were prepared for war.

They opened their windows, and let fly a general volley of brickbats. The claimant was badly bruised, and Hunt's head was severely cut; the blow stunned him, and laid him sprawling on his back. By this time, a large crowd had collected in the alley, through which Clark made his escape.

The tumult brought to the place several watchmen. Thomas Davis, an aged, respectable colored man, lived very near to Clark--I think, next door; and he, as it afterwards appeared, was among the active persons on this occasion. Hunt and his co-worker in this wickedness, charged Thomas Davis with rescuing the prisoner: and alledged that he was the person who had wounded him. Thomas was a carter. He owned a horse and cart, and was employed by many respectable citizens. For more than twenty years, he purchased and hauled all the wood I used, and he was universally esteemed faithful and trustworthy. He had acquired a little property, and they pounced upon him, being most able to pay any damages that might be awarded in the case.

Without much ceremony, they conveyed the poor, old man to prison, and locked him up. Benjamin, upon escaping from his assailants, called at my house, and knocked at the door so violently that it startled me. I sprang out of bed, and, throwing up the window, inquired what his business with me could be, to make it necessary to disturb my family at that unseasonable hour. Benjamin was literally slow of speech, and of a stammering tongue; but, notwithstanding, he soon made me acquainted with his case. I immediately went down stairs, and let him in. He was ignorant of his friend, Thomas Davis, having been incarcerated. I invited him to go to bed, but he declined; saying he could not sleep. It was said that he was descended from an Indian woman. This I was satisfied was the case; but as the witnesses resided in Virginia, it would be difficult to procure testimony. After making myself fully acquainted with his history, I retired to bed; but sleep had departed from me, and as soon as it was light I rose. In a little time, a person called and informed me that Thomas Davis was in jail; and I went to prison, and had a conversation with him. At 9 o'clock in the morning, the parties all appeared before the magistrate--viz: the claimant, with his coadjutor, R. Hunt, and Thomas Davis, and myself. The magistrate called upon the two former to state their complaint. I mentioned to him that I had a complaint to offer against the stranger, for an attempt to kidnap a free man; and I hoped we would give the case the precedence, as I had little doubt but the culprit would escape, unless he was closely watched. This alarmed him; he undertook his defense, however, and stated that Benjamin Clark was born in his family, and had lived with him many years as his slave; and that he had absconded from his service. I asked for proof that Clark was his slave. He replied, that he was ready to make oath of the fact. I informed him that that would not do; that I should not be willing to accept the oath of a slaveholder in such a case, even where he was not immediately interested; much less his, who had so much at stake. I inquired why he chose night for his operations, if he knew his claim was legal. He said that the abolition society threw so much difficulty in the way, that it often cost the claimant more than the slave was worth, let his title to him be ever so good; and he adopted that plan to avoid trouble. After much altercation, he requested that his case might be postponed till the afternoon, that he might have an opportunity of advising with an attorney. To this proposition I readily agreed, concluding we should see no more of him; and so it turned out. I saw that the case of Clark was involved in much difficulty, and I was not anxious to test it, if it could be avoided. As soon as the case was adjourned, he left the office.

As soon as that matter was disposed of, the case of rescue, and assault and battery was called up. The claimant having disappeared, the charge was soon disposed of. Hunt testified that, when in the legal discharge of his duty as a public officer, he was surrounded by a mob, and severely beaten; and that the man then before the magistrate, T. Davis, was the person who threw the brickbat that cut his head. After cautioning him to be careful what he said, telling him we also had some witnesses, and reminding him that he was under oath, I asked him if he *saw* Thomas Davis throw the brick that wounded him. He said he saw it come from his window. I several times expressed my doubtss of the truth of his relation. At length he asked me if I thought he would swear to a lie. I replied, "As thou hast asked the question, I confess I think thou wouldst, if thou couldst make anything by it, and do it with impunity." We spent more than an hour in the examination, when the magistrate decided that nothing had appeared that would warrant him in holding Thomas Davis to bail, and he was discharged.

Benjamin Clark resided in Philadelphia many years after this event, and was never more interrupted. The claimant was evidently aware that his case was of a character that would not bear the test of legal investigation, and therefore thought it prudent to abandon further proceedings.

NOTES

1. *N.A.S.*, December 8, 1842, 100.

No. LXVI.
Poor Amy[1]

About the year 1806, a Frenchman resided in Spring Garden, Philadelphia, by the name of _____ Bouilla, who had a small mulatto girl named Amy, about nine years old. He was not married, but he lived with a woman as his wife. Bouilla and his mistress treated the child with great cruelty. I was repeatedly called upon by the neighbors, who were much grieved at the hard usage which the little creature was obliged to endure. At length, I was informed that she was about to be sent into the country. Apprehending she would be disposed of to some person who might make a slave of her, I called to see Bouilla, and made some inquiry as to where the child was to go. He was blind; and upon knocking at their door, the woman opened it, and stood before me, as though she wished to prevent my entering the house. Upon my making known my errand, she called to Bouilla, who stepped up beside her, and they conversed together, perhaps half a minute, in French, when the door was unceremoniously slammed, and locked. Being very averse to adopting coercive measures, I returned home, and addressed a civil note to him, explaining the object of my visit, and asking permission to have a friendly interview. I sent a lad with it, and directed him to wait for an answer. Bouilla and his woman could speak English; she fluently. After reading my note, they told the lad to tell me to mind my own business; that they wanted nothing to do with me. I concluded to take their advice, and believing it to be my *business* to take the child from them, I made application to John Hunter, a magistrate, procured a warrant, and taking an officer with me, proceeded to Bouilla's. On the way, we called upon Thomas Harrison, who accompanied us. Upon arriving at the house, and knocking at the door, it was opened, and we walked in. Bouilla and the woman were in the parlor, but as soon as they were informed of our object in coming, he ran up stairs. After some time spent in parleying with the woman, the officer attempted to go up to execute his warrant; but seeing Bouilla at the head of the stairs, with a gun in his hand, he suddenly retreated, and refused to make another attempt to arrest him. Being urged to take him, he positively refused; saying he was under no obligation to risk his life. We explained the nature of the business, and entreated the man to come down, but he refused, and declared he would shoot the first person that attempted to come to him. After some time, I took off my shoes, and as quick and as softly as I could, I stepped up stairs, laid hold of the gun, and held it over my shoulder. In an instant it discharged. The load struck the plastering of the stairway behind me, and made it fly in all directions; and there arose a loud cry, "Mr. Hopper is killed! Mr. Hopper is killed!" But I was not; as this present writing showeth.

The Frenchman was at last arrested, and we all went to the magistrate's accompanied by several of the neighbors. It was there made apparent that the child had been severely whipped, frequently shut up for twenty-four hours, without any kind of nourishment, and made to stand, hours at a time, on her bare knees, on a brick. The skin on her little knees was extremely thick and hard. The case being fully investigated, the magistrate ordered the child to be given up, and placed under my care. I took her home with me. She was a poor, emaciated object; her very appearance was enough to excite sympathy.

I hastened to my family as soon as possible, lest the report, that I had been shot, should reach them first. My wife often said she expected to see me brought home dead some day. The next day, Bouilla and his woman applied to Matthew Lawler, mayor, and complained of me for taking the child from them. He sent for me. I waited upon him accordingly. He heard their statement, and then called upon me to answer. I objected to his going into the case, and informed him that in the first place, the matter complained of had taken place out of his jurisdiction; Spring Garden not being within the limits of the city; but even if it had not, the magistrate who had already passed upon the case had power concurrent with his own, and of course was as competent to decide upon it as he was. He said he thought he was bound to hear it. I replied, in that case the party dissatisfied with his decision might apply to another magistrate, and so on without end; that I thought the case was too plain to admit of a doubt. After some hesitation, he gave the matter up, and I returned home. I kept the child at my house several days, until I heard of a friend in the country, who wanted a person of her description. I bound her, till she should be eighteen years old, to Thomas Fletcher, of Abington.

I finally ascertained that Amy was the daughter of the woman kept by Bouilla, and her father was a black man. Her mother was a handsome person, and from her appearance and conversation, it would seem that she had been respectably educated.

Amy was a very pretty girl, and served her time out to the satisfaction of the family where she was bound. After she was free, she went to Philadelphia and continued to conduct extremely well. She frequently called to see me, and often expressed her gratitude for the part I had taken in her behalf.

NOTES

1. *N.A.S.*, December 22, 1842, 114.

No. LXVII.
The "Patriarchal System"[1]

I took the following account from the mouth of the sufferer, in nearly her own language. It is but one of many, that have come to my knowledge, all going to show the horrors of slavery:

"My parents were slaves to * * * * who resided in the small village called * * * * in Anderson county, North Carolina. When I was about five years old, my master moved to York, forty or fifty miles from his former residence. While here, he sold my mother to New Orleans, leaving my father at home. We remained here about three years; and during that time I was treated with great cruelty. I was frequently stripped stark naked, locked in the cellar, and while in that condition, severely whipped by mistress; frequently for small omissions of duty, and sometimes without any fault at all. So severe were the whippings, that the blood often run down to my heels, and my clothes were stiff with it.

Upon leaving York, my master removed, with his family, to Alabama. He died about three years after he went there. Being deeply involved in debt, all his property was sold by the sheriff, soon after his decease. He had seven slaves; and Dr. ******, who was a large creditor, bought them all, except my father. I was not informed who bought him, and I never saw or heard from him, after the sale. I lived with Dr. ******** four or five years. He was a good master, and treated his slaves kindly. His step-daughter married J****** A. T******, and at his death he left four of his slaves to her. I was among the number. I lived with J****** A. T****** ten or twelve years; part of the time in Mobile, he having removed there. While I lived with him, I was married to one of his neighbor's slaves. Soon after our marriage, my husband was sold and sent away. I never saw him afterwards.

I carried the key of the store-room. On one occasion, when I was busy baking cakes, one of the slaves asked me for a candle;

and fearing the cakes would burn if I left them, I gave her the key, and told her to get one, and bring me the key again. Just at this juncture, my master happened to come in, and seeing the storeroom open, without saying one word, he took a cane from a colored boy, who was sitting in the kitchen, and beat me over the back and shoulders. He hurt me so dreadfully, that I screamed aloud. This provoked him. He tied me by the two wrists, and drew me up, so that my toes could just touch the ground. He kept me in that condition about fifteen minutes, whipping me at short intervals, all the time, with a cowhide. I was then near being confined; and in two or three days after, I gave birth to twins. They were both dead, and I was very near losing my own life also; I kept my bed five weeks, during which time I suffered extremely.

Sometime after this event, my master moved to Marengo. I was not willing to go with him; and after they had put their goods on board the steamboat, I hid myself, and they were obliged to leave me behind. In about a week, my master returned to Mobile. I told him I was not willing to go to Marengo, and he sold me to a French butcher. Being unacquainted with their language, I could not understand them, nor they me; and after remaining with him a short time, he sold me to a Mr. C. He treated me kindly, but he lived but a short time after I went there. C**** was in debt, and his property was appraised, and sold at auction. They placed me upon a table, that the purchasers might see me. I can't describe the horror I felt for fear some person might buy me who would treat me cruelly. Several persons bid, and at length I was knocked off to a man by the name of ******, for six hundred and fifty dollars. When I found who had bought me I cried aloud. I thought I would rather die than belong to him; for I knew he was very severe with his slaves. He had a woman, who always wore a chain on her ankles, and an iron collar, with prongs, about her neck. He ordered me to leave the stand, and come down. I refused, and he threatened to pull me down. Several gentlemen, who were standing by, seeing my deep distress, persuaded him to give me up; which he did with much reluctance. I was then put up again. Mr. ***** bought me, and a few days after sold me to a gentleman of Mobile. I lived with him several years, and fared little better treatment than I had done with T******. On one occasion, my mistress took offense at one of my fellow servants, and struck her with a bucket. She had also taken offense at me, and begun to beat me with the bucket. She struck me on the arm, and made a deep wound. When she attempted to repeat the blow, I gave her a push, to keep her off. She informed my master, who became greatly enraged, and told me if I ever did the like again he would cut my hand off. He sent me to the guard house, where I was tied up, with my arms stretched out, and whipped with a cowhide; my master standing by, all the time. I was very unwell, and so weak that I could hardly keep about; but I was obliged to work so long as I was able to walk.

An old woman, by the name of Eleanor, was a slave to a person in Mobile, who treated her with great cruelty. One day, she offended her mistress, and she struck her with a spoon, over the fingers, and cut them very bad. She was too old to do much work, and seeing she was so badly used by her mistress, he turned her off, and she went about three miles to an acquaintance. She had been there but a few days, when her mistress sent a constable and had her brought home. Upon her return, she sent her to the guard house to be punished. They beat her naked body with a paddle, with holes in it; after which they beat her with a cowhide, till she was dreadfully mangled. She was then sent home, but her wounds became so offensive that they again turned her away. The poor old creature died a few days after.

I had one brother and three sisters; but they were sold to different persons, and sent to different places. I have not seen them for many years, and do not expect I shall ever see them again.

I have often seen slaves, that have been so badly beaten, they were hardly able to walk. In some instances, to avoid punishment, they would take in the woods. They would hunt them with dogs; and such was their dread of being taken, that they would suffer themselves to be shot down, rather than surrender. They knew too well the sufferings that awaited them. I have known the masters to advertise their fugitive slaves, and offer a reward for them, with directions to take them, dead or alive. In the summer of 1842, my master brought me, with his family, to New-York; in consequence of which I became entitled to my freedom; for which I hope ever to be thankful."

NOTES

1. *N.A.S.*, December 29, 1942, 118.

No. LXVIII.
William Healy[1]

William Healy was a slave in Virginia. When about eighteen years old, his master placed him with a carpenter, in the neighborhood, to learn the trade. He was an active, industrious fellow, and soon became a good workman. After he had got his trade, his master took him home, and hired him out, to work at his trade. At the end of each week, he paid his master the amount he had earned. William became uneasy, and concluded that it would be no more than just that he should be allowed to enjoy the fruits of his own labor. To effect this object, he determined to go to Philadelphia. He was now about twenty-five years old. He was tall, athletic, and intelligent, considering the opportunities within his reach. In pursuance of his plan, he started one moonlight night, and without much difficulty arrived at Philadelphia. For the first few days, after leaving home, he suffered for the want of food; being afraid to apply for it, until he had been several days on his journey. Upon arriving in that city he got employment. After being there a few years, he married a free woman; who, like himself, was industrious and frugal. William took a lot on ground rent, in Moyamensing, near Passyunk road and Fitzwater street, and commenced erecting a frame house on it. He proceeded with his house so far as to get it under roof. Though not plastered, the floors were laid, and he anticipated finishing it in a few weeks. He appeared to enjoy life in a high degree; and there seemed nothing to interrupt their comfort, when some unprincipled, mercenary wretch, informed his master where he might be found. About the year 1810, he went to Philadelphia, and having obtained a warrant, had him arrested, and taken before Richard Palmer, a magistrate, in the district of Southwark. Palmer was not favorable to the colored people. Upon proof, to his satisfaction, he surrendered the poor, afflicted fugitive, as a slave, to be returned to Virginia. He was committed to prison in the evening, and the next morning was carried off, and never heard from afterwards, by his wife, or his friends in Philadelphia.

This circumstance occurred while I was on a visit, for a day or two, to my friends in New Jersey. I had not been home, after my return, more than two hours, when William's wife called to relate her dismal story. It was deeply affecting to hear her bewail her condition. She exclaimed, in her great distress, "O, Mr. Hopper! if *you* had been at home, you could have saved my husband! Oh, how they will make him suffer!" Her lamentations still resound in my ears. I regretted exceedingly, that I was out of the way at the time. I am not aware that I could have been of any service in the case; but it would have been a great satisfaction to have done what I could. It is a source of painful retrospection, to this day.

The spirits of his wife seemed completely broken. From a state of unalloyed comfort, she was at once plunged into the deepest misery. Ever after, as long as I knew her, she was extremely melancholy. Her energy was entirely destroyed. Being unable to pay the ground rent, it accumulated till the amount became considerable, and finally the house was sold to pay it.

I have seldom witnessed a more affecting and painful case. The poor woman was in the habit of frequently calling upon me, to inquire if I could give her any intelligence of her husband; but I was never able to gratify her.

The next day after I returned from the country, I called upon the magistrate who had granted the certificate to remove William. I told him I regretted that he had not detained him a little while, till his friends could have had an opportunity of trying to do something for him. He replied, that he would not be dictated to by me. I informed him that I had no disposition to dictate to him; but I hoped he would not be offended, if I told him that I thought the manner he had permitted the poor fellow to be hurried away, was unchristian, and did not comport with the dignity of the office he filled. He replied, that if I thought to insult him with impunity, I would find myself mistaken; that if I made use of such language to him, he would commit me. I told him I did not wish to insult him; but if he thought to frighten me by such menaces as that, he would find himself in an error; that I disregarded them, and did not think he maintained his dignity by making threats, which I presumed he had no intention of carrying into effect. The fact was, he knew he had acted improperly, and that made him irritable. The magistrates were under great temptation to act arbitrarily, in such cases; for if the slave was set at liberty, they got no fees; but if he were given up to be taken away, they frequently received five dollars for a certificate; and in one instance, I saw a magistrate receive twenty dollars.

NOTES

1. N.A.S., February 2, 1843, 138.

No. LXIX.
Theodore[1]

Theodore, a mulatto boy, the son of a Frenchman, was placed as an apprentice to Stephen Burroughs, of Philadelphia, saddle and harness maker. His father was white, and his mother colored. After he had lived with Burroughs two or three years, his master discovered in the boy's trunk about one thousand dollars, in doubloons. He took possession of the money, and had Theodore committed to prison, on charge of having robbed him. After he had been in prison about twenty-four hours, being at the prison, in the discharge of my duty as an inspector, my attention was directed to him by one of the keepers. I had the lad called, and inquired into the cause of his confinement; when he gave me the following history of himself. He said he came from the West Indies, with his father, who died in Trenton, N.J. a few months after their arrival. That a few days previous to his death, he called Theodore to his bedside, and informed him that a trunk in the room, which he showed him, contained a sum of money in gold; that here was a false bottom in it, where the money was deposited; and after his death, he wished him to take the trunk, but not to let any person, not even his best friend know of his having the money, till after he should be twenty-one years old. He also told the boy that he had bequeathed some property in the West Indies to him, and had appointed his friend ____, a Frenchman, residing in Trenton, his guardian. He could not bequeath the money to the lad, as the laws of France did not permit more than a certain proportion of his estate to be given to an illegitimate child, and this money, in addition to that given him in the will, would amount to more than that proportion.

Soon after the death of the father, the guardian, whose name I do not now remember, bound the lad, as above mentioned. Upon hearing the boy's narrative, I called upon his master, and gave him the information I had received. Burroughs expressed much surprise at the lad's assurance in making such a statement, and said that he had the most positive proof of his guilt. But notwithstanding his declaration to the contrary, I soon became satisfied of Theodore's innocence, and I informed him so. I proposed that the matter should be referred to arbitrators; but he declined taking any step in the business, till he could consult counsel. He engaged M.C. Wells, of Philadelphia, as his attorney. After considerable difficulty, it was agreed to refer the case to Robert Wharton, James Todd, and John Poultney; with an agreement to the following import, viz; they should say to whom the money belonged; if to Stephen Burroughs, they should award it to him; but if to Theodore, they should award it to him. They should also say what the unexpired term of the boy's time was worth and what Stephen Burroughs should be allowed for it. I did not like the agreement, but it was the best we could get. I concluded the arbitrators were at liberty to say his time was worth one hundred and fifty dollars, and, in consideration of Burroughs's improper conduct, he should be allowed only six cents.

After due notice, the parties met. Thomas Harrison and I attended. Burroughs opened his case with much apparent confidence. He said he would prove, by the most positive evidence, that the boy had been leagued with a company of French negroes, and had robbed him to an amount far exceeding, in value, the money found in the trunk. Upon hearing this statement, Robert Wharton, who was an alderman, took Thomas Harrison and myself into an adjoining room, and urged strongly to be excused from serving in the case; saying, that it certainly would become his duty to commit the boy for trial. I assured him that I had investigated the business thoroughly, and was fully satisfied that Burroughs could not make out his case. With much reluctance, he consented to serve; saying, he thought we had better get some person, who was not a magistrate, in his stead.

Several evenings were spent in examining witnesses; I think not less than a dozen. The amount of what Burroughs proved against the boy was, that he had made a small trunk, about a foot long, for his guardian, and had covered it with small pieces of leather, of various colors, which he picked up about the shop, with the consent of the foreman.

After the testimony was closed, Robert Wharton observed, that as charges had been made against Theodore, of a highly criminal character, he thought right to say that nothing had been proved, which in the least affected his integrity; on the contrary, his character for industry, orderly conduct, and honesty, had been satisfactorily established. The reader will readily perceive, that if the boy had robbed his employer, it would have been a very difficult matter to have converted the property taken, into doubloons, and it was never pretended that he had taken the money.

The next day, they furnished Stephen Burroughs and myself each with a copy of their award; which was that the money taken out of the trunk was the property of Theodore; and that Stephen Burroughs should cancel the indenture, on receiving one hundred and fifty dollars. The arbitrators admitted they were of the opinion that, in *justice*, he was not entitled to one cent; but they considered themselves bound, by the agreement, to allow him what they thought the boy's time was worth. I always that the arbitrators took a wrong view of that instrument, and committed an error in allowing anything for the unexpired time of the indenture.

The hundred and fifty dollars were deducted, the balance paid over to the abolition society, and the indenture canceled. Theodore was then placed with Jones & Kinsey, and the money put out at interest. He served his time out honorably, and proved himself honest and faithful. Upon arriving at the age of twenty-one, his money, principal and interest, was paid to him. Soon after, he went to the place of his nativity, and followed his trade, taking with him the esteem and good wishes of all who knew him.

It was common, in those times, for the French, who were emigrating to the United States, to place their money in trunks with false bottoms, to conceal it from the British privateers, with which the seas abounded.

NOTES

1. *N.A.S.*, Februaray 16, 1843, 146; *P.P.A.S.*, Acting Committee Minute Book, Vol. 4, (198-1810) p. 304, Reel 5.

No. LXX.
Caesar King[1]

Caesar King, an industrious colored man, had a daughter that was a slave to a person who resided in Maryland. Caesar was an intelligent, managing man, and had acquired a small property near Pennypack, a few miles north of Philadelphia, where he resided with his family. He was esteemed a man of probity. He informed me, that he never sat down to take his meals, or laid his head upon his pillow at night, without thinking of his daughter; not knowing how soon she might be sold to the speculators, and removed to a part of the country where he could never expect to hear of her.

At length, he determined to make her a visit. He called upon me to furnish him with such documents as would protect him from arrest; for a free man would not be safe in Maryland, without a certificate of his freedom. I procured the necessary papers, and gave him a few lines, stating my knowledge of him, and the object of his journey. His daughter was rejoiced to meet him once more, and he was equally glad to see her again; but a knowledge that in a few days they must part, and probably never meet again, was a great alloy to their comfort.

After spending a day or two with his daughter, he proposed to her master to permit her to accompany him home to visit her relations. I think her mother was then living. Cæsar's respectable appearance, and correct deportment, together with my letter, induced the master to consent. Her father assured him that she should return to his service, when her visit was accomplished, which should not exceed two weeks. They soon set out on their journey home. On their arrival in Philadelphia, they called to see me. She was a fine, healthy looking young woman, about twenty-five years old. Caesar remarked, that her master's having permitted her to come home with him, was an indulgence he did not expect;

but added, that the thought of her returning to slavery was dreadful. The girl was much affected, and wept. Her father purchased a dress for her, and they reached home the same evening.

After Nancy had been under her father's roof about a week, he called upon me in a distressed state of mind. "In a few days," said he, "Nancy must go back. I can't bear to think of it." He suggested that I should write to her master, and try to buy her time; stating that he would rather part with all the property he possessed, than have his daughter return into slavery. "I promised to return her," said he; "and if we cannot prevail upon her master to manumit her, I will send her; for I will not break my promise."

I addressed a letter to the master, in which I queried with him whether he would not consent to manumit Nancy upon receiving a moderate sum. I informed him that her father was not unmindful of his engagement to return her, and that he would do so if he could not be prevailed upon to part with her. I assured him nothing dishonorable was intended, and that the girl would certainly go home if he declined complying with her father's proposition.

He considered this only an evasion, and became alarmed, lest he should lose his slave, unless he took prompt measures to secure her. Without answering my letter, he mounted his horse, and took another with him, on which he intended to carry Nancy home. According to his own account, he traveled with such violence, the weather being warm, and he a heavy man, that he killed the horse, which he valued at $150. Upon arriving at Philadelphia, without calling upon me, he made application to Michael Hillegas, an alderman, for a warrant to arrest his slave; but that magistrate refused to grant one, as it appeared from his own account that she was not a fugitive.

Without delay, he engaged two constables, and proceeded to Pennypack, a distance of about fifteen miles, in search of his slave. When he approached within a few rods of Caesar King's dwelling, he remained behind, concealed in the bushes, and sent the officers to the house. They entered without ceremony, and commenced searching it. Caesar at once suspected what they were after, and demanded their authority for such a rude trespass upon his premises. They informed him they wanted "Nance." He informed them she was not at home; and, taking down his gun, ordered them to leave the place immediately, or he would give them the contents of it. His bold, determined manner, alarmed them, and they withdrew. As soon as their backs were turned, Caesar loaded his gun, which was before empty; but instead of charging it with lead, he pounded in a quantity of coarse salt. They proceeded but a short distance, before he fired in the direction they went. The salt made a tremendous rattling among the leaves, and they were prodigiously frightened, supposing it was shot. They made the best of their way to the city, and the master called upon me to give an account of his adventure at Pennypack, and how narrowly he and his company had escaped with their lives. He was frightened beyond measure, and without hesitation proposed selling the girl. I assured him that Caesar King was a respectable man, and would have returned Nancy, though he was very unwilling to part with her, if he had informed me, as he ought to have done, before pursuing such harsh measures. But now I thought it likely the case was altered, owing to his own imprudence. He asked me if I would assist him in finding her. This I declined. He then asked me if I would buy her. I informed him that if he would take a very moderate sum, I would advance it for her manumission. He was evidently very much excited with liquor, and soon agreed to accept of fifty dollars; which I paid him, and he executed a manumission. He seemed to think it was next to a miracle that he escaped with his life. Nancy came to live with me, and remained in my service till the amount paid for her was liquidated.

NOTES

1. *N.A.S.*, April 20, 1843, 182.

No. LXXI.
Maryland Slave[1]

The following story was printed in the Liberty Bell for 1843; but as many readers of the Standard have not an opportunity of seeing that very interesting little volume, we republish it:

"About the year 1805, a colored man, who was a slave to a Colonel Hopper, of Maryland, (he was no relation of *mine*), left his master and went to Philadelphia, taking with him his wife and children, who were also slaves. He hire a small house in Green's court, running north from Pine street, between Fourth and Fifth. After remaining there some months, his master obtained knowledge of his whereabouts, and followed him. He applied to Richard Hunt, a constable in Philadelphia, who was a notorious slave-hunter; they made application to a magistrate, procured a warrant to arrest the fugitives, and proceeded, in the dusk of the evening, to the house where they resided. The man had just returned from his daily labor, and was peacefully sitting with his wife and children, not dreaming of a visit from his old master, when the door opened, and in he rushed, accompanied by the officer. An instance of greater presence of mind is rarely met with, than was now exhibited. The man immediately rose from his seat, flew to his master, and throwing his arms around him, exclaimed, 'O, my dear master, how glad I am to see you! Will you pardon me for leaving you? I *thought* I should like to be free, but I would a thousand times rather be you slave. I would have returned home, but I was afraid you would sell me to the Georgia men. If you will only forgive me, I will go back with you, and never leave you again. I can't get work, and we have been almost starved. I beg your pardon a thousand times.'

"The master was highly delighted to find his man so desirous of returning home. He readily promised to pass by his offense, and treat him with kindness. The colonel was, by this ingenious manoeuvre, thrown completely off his guard. He informed the constable that he had no further need of his services; but the slave urged him to wait a few minutes. He said he had a little money, for the first time since he had been in Philadelphia, and he wished to get something to drink; for he supposed his old master must be tired. He stepped out, leaving his master and the officer, both of whom were very intemperate men. He soon returned, with a goodly quantity of gin, and they spent the evening inquiring about old friends, and talking on matters that had transpired at home since he had left. In the course of a few hours, the colonel, and his friend, the constable, became insensible to everything around them. The slave made out to lift the former on a bed that was in the room, where they were sitting, and the latter lay stretched upon the floor. Having disposed of his two friends so *satisfactorily*, he cleared out, and retired with his family to New Jersey; where they were comfortably located before the rising of the sun.

When the colonel and his friend awoke, what was their astonishment to find themselves the only occupants of the house! They immediately set out in quest of the fugitives. After a fruitless search of several days, the colonel called to see me. He complained bitterly of the deception practised, and of the man's ingratitude in leaving him. He descanted, at considerable length, upon the slave's folly in deserting his service, and upon the happy condition he and his family enjoyed while in Maryland. He very civilly asked me to lend him my assistance in finding them; promising to treat them as kindly as if they were his own children. I observed, that if the man was happy at home as he represented, I had no doubt that he would soon return voluntarily; and so my services would not be needed. I told him that I did not justify falsehood and deception in any case; but it was no more than might be *expected* of one who was a slave, and had dwelt all his life with a slaveholder; that I was wholly unable to discover upon what pretense he predicated the charge of *ingratitude*; for I thought the man owed him nothing. On the contrary, *he* was indebted to the slave, who had already served him more than thirty years. So far from rendering assistance in finding the poor fugitive, I told him if my services were necessary, I would, with all my heart, assist them in keeping out of his grasp. He asked me if I had seen the man. I answered that he called upon me immediately after leaving his house in Green's court, and that I had given him such counsel as appeared proper and necessary. I told him also that he was the first slaveholder of *my name* that I had ever met. I gravely queried whether he were not an imposter, and had assumed *that* name, as a means of facilitating his wicked project of recapturing the objects of his avarice. He assured me that he had not; that his real name was Hopper. He remained in the city a week or ten days, when he became a victim to *mania potu*. I was informed that he was taken home in a strait-jacket, and soon after died.

"A few months after the colonel had left the city, his man called to see me. While relating the manner of his capture and escape, he laughed till he could hardly stand. 'I knew his weak side,' said he; 'I knew where to touch him.' I asked him if he did not know it was very wrong to tell such falsehoods, and make the men drunk. He replied, 'I suppose it *was*; but liberty is sweet, and none of us know what we would do to secure it, till we are tried.'

"After remaining some months in Jersey, he returned to Philadelphia, where I knew him several years. He supported his family comfortably, and was never afterward molested.

NOTES

1. *N.A.S.*, April 27, 1843, 186.

No. LXXII.
The Slave Trader[1]

About the year 1804, Isaac Sherman went to Philadelphia, in consequence of having received information of several vessels belonging to merchants of that city being engaged in the African slave trade. He was recommended to the abolitionists of that place by some of the abolitionists of New-York. He called upon me, informed me of the object of his visit, and expressed a wish to have an interview with some members of the abolition society. Several of them being notified, met at my house, when Sherman explained the object of his visit. Shortly after, the society had a meeting, and appointed a committee, consisting, I think, of seven persons, to assist him in prosecuting the business. I do not, at this remote period, recollect all their names. Thomas Harrison, Samuel Harvey, and myself, were some of them. Sherman was a native of New England, a shrewd, plausible man, and made an impression on the committee, that his motives were purely benevolent and honorable. Divers persons who, from their character and standing in the world, we should not have suspected, were found to be engaged in the nefarious traffic; upon the enormity of which no man could expatiate more fluently than Sherman. He had been in Philadelphia but a short time, before he informed the committee that the brig Tryphenia, belonging to Maher & McDermot, had been employed in transporting slaves from the island of St. Thomas to Havana. It was determined to commence a prosecution, for the penalty prescribed by an act of Congress. Although the committee were unanimous as to the propriety of instituting legal proceedings, there was much difficulty in prevailing upon any of them to consent to permit their names to be used as plaintiff in the case. At length, rather than the culprits should be suffered to escape, I consented, and a suit was instituted in my name. The case was tried in the circuit court of the United States. Bushrod

Washington presided. The law was as explicit as language could make it; that it should be unlawful for any vessel "to be employed, or made use of, in transporting or carrying slaves from one foreign country, or place, to another." The judge, however, said that Congress could never be such knights-errant as to make a law to prevent a man from taking his property where he pleased; that it was the intention of the law to prohibit vessels from taking *free* people, and making slaves of them; of course, we were defeated. Lewis and Rawle, two eminent lawyers, advised an appeal; but as Maher & McDermot had failed, the case was abandoned. A suit was instituted by Sherman against a certain Captain Towers, which he commuted, as I was informed, by Towers paying seven hundred and fifty dollars. The committee discovered that Sherman's views were entirely mercenary, and withdrew their countenance and support; but he still pursued the business on his own responsibility. He would take his seat in a sailor boarding-house, call for a glass of grog, and when a sailor came in, Sherman would treat him, enter into familiar conversation, and, without exciting suspicion of his object, would often contrive to elicit information sufficient to convict persons engaged in slave trade. He related to me the following circumstance: He had noticed in the newspapers the sailing of a ship, which he suspected was destined for a slaver. Some considerable time after, he saw, by the papers, that she had arrived in South America; I believe at Monte Video. He had no doubt that she had a cargo of slaves; he resorted to the following expedient to obtain proof of the fact. He took his seat in a sailor boarding-house, treated every sailor who happened to step in, and inquire of him where he was last from, what vessel he had sailed in, &c. After spending several days in this way, he happened to meet with one who had been in the suspected vessel. He took the sailor into a private room, and after prevailing upon him to promise secresy, he addressed him thus; I have very nearly his own words: "Well, now, sir, I rely upon your honor, that you will not betray me. I own a part of that ship, and am concerned in the voyage. I have always suspected that the captain made a false return as to the number of slaves, and by that means has cheated me out of a considerable sum of money. I want you to inform me how many you took on board, how many died on the passage, and how many you sold at Monte Video." The sailor, not suspecting his object, gave him a full account of the whole voyage. Sherman then took him an attorney, had an affidavit drawn, proceeded to Richard Peters, judge of the district court of the United States, and the sailor swore to the facts. This was transmitted to New-York, where the vessel was libelled, and, by due process of law, was condemned, and sold.

Another vessel, belonging to P.C. and T.P. of Philadelphia, was discovered, by the same means, to have been engaged in the slave trade. I saw an affidavit of one of the sailors, which stated that she took in about four hundred slaves at Mozambique, and sailed thence for South America; that on the voyage, they encountered a severe storm, which injured the ship, so that they stopped at the Cape of Good Hope to repair. After repairs were completed, they again set sail for the destined port. Soon after leaving the cape, it was found that the rice had been wet during the gale, and had become sour, which produced disease among the slaves, and many died. On one occasion, nine of them were brought on deck, being so ill that fresh air was deemed necessary to save their lives. Weak and emaciated as they were, after being on deck a short time, they exhibited symptoms of mutiny, and refused to go below when ordered to do so. A son of one of the owners, whom I well knew, was supercargo. He had a consultation with the captain, and it was judged necessary to adopt prompt measures to quell the spirit of insurrection manifested among the slaves. The supercargo took his musket, and again ordered the men to go below, which they refusing to do, he took deliberate aim, and shot three, one after another, and they fell dead upon the deck. The others, seeing this, submitted, and went below. This affidavit, I was told, was read to the young man, in the presence of the witness. He asked the witness, "Did you see me shoot three men?" He replied, "I saw you shoot, and the men fall." The parties, finding their case desperate, compromised the matter, by giving Sherman fifteen hundred dollars; and there the matter ended.

A woman by the name of Robbins, belonging to some one of the eastern States, was the owner of a schooner that sailed, I believe, from Newport, directly to the coast of Africa. She went in the vessel herself, managed the whole concern, took in a cargo of slaves, transported them to Havana, and there sold them. She made two or three voyages of the same character. SHe afterwards sold her vessel, and went to Philadelphia. As soon as Sherman heard of it, he procured process, proceeded with the marshal's deputy to her lodgings, and arrested her. Being informed of the nature of the charge on which the proceedings were founded, she inquired of Sherman, "Is this your doings?" "Yes, ma'am," he replied. "Well, I tell you, you had better take care what you are about. A man in Rhode Island got his ears cut off for meddling with this kind of business; and you will get yours cut off, if you don't take care what you are about." Sherman coolly put back the hair from his head, showed the place where ears had been, and answered, "I am that man." Mrs. Robbins, as he called her, gave bail to appear at court; the action was *qui lam.* (the lawyers can tell what that means.) In a few days, however, she cited Sherman to appear before Judge Peters, when it appeared that she had lately been married, and that her husband's name not being included in the proceedings, they could not be sustained; she was therefore discharged. Sherman forthwith renewed the suit, in legal form; but the woman was not to be found. She left the city, and was not heard of afterwards. She was said to be wealthy.

I will now give an account of how Sherman came to loose his ears. For a series of years, he had prodigiously harassed those human hyenas, who fatten upon the tears and blood of their fellow-men. He was instrumental in getting a certain vessel condemned, and sold at Bristol, R.I. When she was put up for sale, the first person who bid was immediately seized by the men with painted faces, and Indian costume. These disguised savages took him to a small island near by, stripped him from the waist up, and severely whipped him. This violent procedure intimidated others, and the vessel sold for a mere trifle. Sherman had rendered himself extremely odious, and a determination seems to have been formed to take his life. He was once traveling to Bristol, in the prosecution of his profession; that of an informer. Observing two men following him in a chaise, he became alarmed; and in order to ascertain to a certainty whether or not he was the object of their pursuit, he turned out of the road usually traveled, and went several miles round about. They kept after him. This circumstance convinced him that they meditated an attack. By hard traveling, he reached Bristol about dusk in the evening; and he soon discovered that his pursuers took lodgings at the same place that he did. A little after ten o'clock, he retired to bed, taking care to lock the door. Although very weary, fear kept him awake. The family retired, and all was still, till about twelve o'clock, when he heard the door of the room on the opposite side of the entry, suddenly burst open. From the noise, he apprehended some person was being murdered. The lynchers, discovering their mistake, released the man whom they had pulled out of bed, and in an instant knocked out the panels of the door in the room where Sherman lay. After beating him severely with a club, they put a rope around his ankles, and five or six men thus pulled him down stairs, and run as fast as they could, over stones and rough ground, till they come to the water's edge. Here they held consultation. Some proposed to tie a stone to his neck, and throw him into the water. Others alledged that if such a plan were adopted, it would not be known what had become of him; but if they were to kill him, and leave him on the shore, everybody would know the cause of his death, and it would intimidate others. The latter suggestion prevailed. They gashed his head with a sharp stone, cut off both his ears, and mangled him in a most shocking manner. After inflicting ninety-three wounds, (the scars of which I have seen,) they left him naked, and, as they supposed, lifeless, on the shore. But after some time he revived, and with much difficulty crawled to the house. The authorities of the city issued a proclamation, offering a reward for the apprehension of the desperadoes who had committed the outrage; but they were never discovered. He gradually recovered his usual health, and renewed his vocation, with increased energy. He possessed superior talents, and was as well acquainted with the laws respecting the slave trade, as any lawyer in the country. He had made them his peculiar study for many years, with great diligence and perseverance.

NOTES

1. *N.A.S.*, May 11, 1743, . 194; *P.P.A.S.*, Case of Thomas Harrison and Isaac T. Hopper, (on behalf of the P.A.S. Acting Committee) v. the Brig Tymphrena, 1805, Reel 23.

No. LXXIII.
William Wright[1]

William Wright, a fugitive from the State of Maryland, informed me that he was a slave at an institution, belonging to the Catholics, called St. Josephs. He was treated with more lenity than usually fell to the lot of persons in his situation, yet he felt the injustice of being held in bondage, and obliged to labor all his life for others, receiving only food and clothing, and that, too, of a very coarse kind. I believe he was about thirty years old when he formed the determination to better his condition if possible, and for that purpose left his oppressors, and went to Philadelphia, about the year 1808. He an his wife hired themselves, as servants, to a Captain Many, of that city. His wife was a free woman; but whether he brought her from Maryland with him, or married her soon after his arrival in Philadelphia, I do not now remember. They were sober, industrious people, and soon conciliated the favor of their employers. After remaining in this situation a considerable time, having acquired some money, William called upon me, and made known his circumstances. He solicited me to endeavor to purchase his freedom; saying that he was in constant dread of being discovered, and conveyed back to Maryland. If that should be the case, he said, he was sure he should not be retained there, but would be sold to the speculators, and taken to the South. His mind was evidently much depressed. I readily agreed to do what I could for him. He left me with sixty dollars towards paying for his freedom, provided those having the ownership would agree to manumit him, upon receiving a moderate sum as a compensation.

Soon after this interview, I wrote to the person having the legal power to negotiate the business, and informed him that the application had been made to me to inquire whether a manumission could be obtained for William upon the payment of a moderate sum; and asked him to state how much would be demanded. Several weeks elapsed, and I received no reply. After waiting some months, William called upon me, said he had occasion for some money, and asked me for twenty dollars, which I gave him; leaving in my hands forty dollars. Getting no intelligence from his claimants, William became impatient, and consulted with his employer, making known his situation. Not long after, he was arrested, and taken to Maryland. I have always suspected that Many betrayed William's confidence, and gave information where he could be found. His wife still remained in Many's service. The first information that I received of William's arrest, I got from Captain Many's wife, two or three days after he was taken away. She inquired how much money William left in my hands. I gave her a statement of the case; but in a few days I heard that it was said that William had placed in my keeping three hundred dollars; and that since he had been taken away, I denied having more than forty dollars. Upon investigating the matter, I traced the story to Captain Many, and immediately called upon him. He readily admitted that he had said so, and referred to William's wife for proof to the fact. She was called, and confirmed the statement. I asked her if she had William's pocket-book, on the blank leaves of which the money transactions between him and myself were written. She replied that she had; but said that I had given some loose receipts, which were not in the book. I soon discovered that I should get no satisfaction from that quarter; and I left the house, somewhat mortified at the ingratitude and injustice of the woman, whose husband I had honestly endeavored to serve. Her object, however, will soon be explained; and although her conduct cannot be justified, yet when I was made acquainted with her motives, I freely forgave her, as far as was I concerned. She had adopted this plan to induce Many to buy her husband; and in this she succeeded. It may be recollected that in the last "Tale of Oppression," mention was made of a suit having been commenced by the abolition society against Maher and McDermott, for being concerned in the slave trade, in which my name was used as plaintiff; and that in consequence of that suit, those men failed. Many was their endorser, and of course lost heavily by them. This had exasperated him against me; and being confident of catching me in a fraud, he sent to Maryland, bought William for four hundred dollars, and brought him to Philadelphia. But his disappointment was not a little provoking, when William told him the whole truth of the matter. He had taken an indenture upon William, for a term of years; and having paid four hundred dollars for him, considered himself entitled to the money which William had placed in my hands. Without any demand being made of me for it, I received a summons to appear before Jacob Baker, one of the city aldermen, to answer John Many for a debt, &c. I accordingly attended, when Captain Many stated the nature of his demand. In reply, I observed that I had never had any dealings with him; but at the same time I admitted that I owed William Wright forty dollars, which I was ready to pay *him*, at any time he would call for it. The magistrate decided that there was no cause of action, and dismissed the business, directing the captain to pay the costs.

But the captain's revenge was not yet daunted; for in a few days I received a summons from the same magistrate, to answer William Wright. When meeting before the alderman, and the case being called up, I asked William if he had ever asked me for the money he had left with me; he replied, "No." "Then, why didst thou sue me?" He said he had not sued me. I asked, "Didst thou authorize Captain Many to sue me?" He boldly and promptly answered, "No." The magistrate then said that he had no further business with me, and ordered the captain to pay the costs. But he was not yet discouraged. In a few days, I received another summons, and attended to answer it. The captain produced a power of attorney, said to have been executed by William Wright; but upon examining it, I found that it had not been executed in due legal form, not having been acknowledged by the proper officer; and I objected to its validity. The patience of Many, by this time, became exhausted. I never saw a man so provoked; he manifested his anger in such manner as drew from the magistrate severe rebuke. The case was again dismissed, he paying the costs I heard nothing further about the business, for two or three weeks; when I received a summons to appear before John Barker, who lived in Sassafras street, more than a mile from my residence. I now concluded that after all the experience the captain had had, I should certainly be defeated.

However, it turned out otherwise; for when I appeared there, and the captain had stated his case, and produced the power of attorney, duly executed, I observed, that this case had been before Jacob Baker several times, and not being able to accomplish his object, and hoping no doubt, to find alderman Barker more pliable, he had now called me more than a mile from home, merely to wreak his vengeance on me. I observed to the magistrate, that if the captain did not gain his point, he might apply to another, and in that way keep me constantly running after him. The alderman asked the captain, "Have you been before Mr. Baker with this business?" "Well," said he, "I wish to explain, sir." "I want none of your explanations. Have you been before Mr. Baker with this matter? Answer the question." I assured him that he had, and that he could not deny it. "Then," said the alderman, "I have no further business with you, Mr. Hopper. Captain Many, you must pay the cost. You are not going to make a cat's paw of me."

I think about three months elapsed, before I heard anything more of the case; at length, William Wright called upon me for the forty dollars, which I paid him. I understood that William and his wife remained in the service of the captain the time stipulated in the indenture, to the mutual satisfaction of all the parties.

NOTES

1. *N.A.S.*, June 1, 1843, 206.

No. LXXIV.
Peter[1]

_____ Stryker, who resided in East Jersey, hoping to improve his circumstances, concluded to move to the city of Philadelphia, and establish an Inn for the entertainment of travellers, and persons having business in the city. Peter was a slave belonging to a near neighbor of Stryker. On becoming acquainted with Stryker's intentions of removing to Philadelphia, he earnestly solicited him to buy him, and take him to that city. Peter knew that he could not be held a slave in Pennsylvania, and he proposed to Stryker to serve him as long as would compensate for the amount he might pay for him. Stryker was well acquainted with Peter's character, and capabilities as a servant, and knew that he would be an important part of his proposed establishment; and a few weeks previous to leaving New Jersey, he effected the purchase for $266.67, and removed with his family to Third street, near Callowhill, in Philadelphia.

Peter had long been desirous of becoming a free man, and now he concluded the way was opening for it. To secure the services of Peter, in legal form, Stryker should have manumitted him before leaving New Jersey, and have taken an indenture for any term not exceeding seven years. But he was not aware of that fact, and took Peter with him as a slave. They had been in Philadelphia but a few days, when Peter unfortunately met with bad advisers. A man who resided in the neighborhood of his new location, soon made himself acquainted with the circumstances of his case, and laid a plan to defraud Stryker, who it appeared, had been influenced more by kindness than by selfish considerations. Peter's new acquaintance informed him that he was now free, and urged him to run away, telling him that if he should be arrested the abolition society would have his freedom established; and that if he did not adopt that course, his master would send him back to Jersey, where he would be kept a slave all his life. Peter became alarmed, and made up his mind to follow this advice. He accordingly left his master, and went to Bucks county. Stryker advertised him, and offered fifty dollars reward for his apprehension.

The unprincipled fellow who had induced Peter to elope, informed Stryker where he might be found, and he was soon arrested and placed in prison in Philadelphia. It afterwards appeared that the sole object of the man who had been the cause of all this trouble was, that he might receive the reward that might be offered for his apprehension; accordingly he applied for it. Soon after Peter's committal to prison, I was informed of it, and called to see him. The poor fellow was much alarmed, fearing that he would be sent back to New Jersey. He gave me his whole history. I addressed a note to Stryker, asking for an interview; he called agreeably to my request, and stated that he never claimed Peter as a slave, but had paid one hundred pounds, $266.67, to redeem him from bondage, at his own request; that he considered him an honest, faithful fellow, and was sure he would not deceive him. He attributed his conduct to some ill-disposed person, who had "put mischief into his head." Stryker's conduct appeared frank and honorable. I informed him that Peter was legally a free man, because he had been brought into Pennsylvania by a person who had removed there with the intention of becoming a permanent resident. I accompanied Stryker to the prison, and we had an interview with Peter, who fully confirmed his statement, and expressed an entire willingness to fulfill his position. I told him he was a free man, and that Stryker could exercise no control over him; but, at the same time, I strongly advised him to fulfill his contract; which he was willing to do. The parties forthwith repaired to the office of Michael Hillegas, one of the city aldermen, where Peter indented himself for the term of three years. Stryker's Inn was much resorted to by people from the country, who came to the city to attend the market. Peter soon gained the respect and confidence of the numerous visitors, and I was informed that his attention drew much custom to the place. He was particularly careful that the horses should be well provided for.

Soon after the three years, for which Peter was bound, had

expired, he, with his master, called upon me. The former stated that he had had a kind master, who had allowed him to go to school evenings in the winter, and that he had learned to read. The latter said he had had an excellent servant in Peter, who still remained in his service as a hired man. The man who had been the cause of Peter's elopement was disappointed; for he never received the reward.

NOTES

1. *N.A.S.*, July 6, 1843, 18.

No. LXXV.
Mary[1]

A colored woman, by the name of Mary, who lived in my family as a domestic, and afterward hired about a year with Matthew Lawler, mayor of the city, became the mother of an illegitimate child by a white man. She applied to one of the city aldermen, and there made oath as to the paternity of her infant. I purposely omit names, being unwilling to wound the feelings of any family. The sins of the father ought not to be visited upon the children.

It appeared that the father of the child was an acquaintance, or friend, of the magistrate, and in order to prevent exposure, he privately communicated to the guilty man, the charge that had been lodged against him. In the course of a few days, Mary called upon the alderman to inquire what provision had been made for her and her babe. He informed her that an arrangement had been agreed upon, and that he would pay her a weekly stipend, which she would receive by calling at his office. She called accordingly, and was regularly paid for some months, until there was a new appointment in the board of guardians of the poor. The father of the child had managed to get one of his friends appointed to that office, who was willing to aid him in conducting the business secretly, and at the same time to avoid giving the security usual in such cases to indemnify the city against any expense they might sustain, on account to the support of the child.

Soon after the new appointment, when Mary called for her weekly allowance, the alderman informed her that he should pay her no more money; that she must leave the child with him, and he would see it provided for. This she refused to do. He attempted to take it from her by force, but was unable to accomplish his object. Mary ran out of his office, and took the infant home. She had been there but a little while, before the magistrate appeared, with a constable, and forcibly took the child from the arms of its mother, and carried it off. In the course of a week or ten days, after several ineffectual attempts to discover where the child had been placed, Mary called upon me, and related all the circumstances. I could hardly believe her narrative. I could scarcely believe that any magistrate in the city of Philadelphia, would be guilty of such an outrage. I waited upon the alderman, who refused to give me any satisfaction, but ordered me to leave his office. I obeyed, and forthwith applied to that excellent man, and upright judge, Chief Justice Shippen, who issued a habeas corpus directed to the alderman, commanding him to produce the child at his chambers. The next morning, at 9 o'clock, was appointed for the hearing. At the time appointed, the parties met. Thomas Smith, one of the judges of the Supreme Court, also attended at the request of Judge Shippen.

The alderman returned to the writ, that "the child, at the time the writ was served upon him, was not in his possession; that he did not know where it was; and that it was not in his power to return it to its mother." He gave as a reason for the part he had acted, that the mother was an abandoned character that she was seen fighting in the street, at 12 o'clock at night, with the child in her arms; and that its life was greatly endangered. He moreover declared she was a thief; that there was an officer then in the room, who had a warrant in his possession to arrest her for stealing silver spoons from a certain Messy Houston; that he had seen the mayor, Matthew Lawler, that morning, with whom she had lived, and he would have attended and testified to her bad character, but was not well enough to leave his house. A watchman was present to corroborate the statement made of her fighting in the street. I asked him if he was sure that she was the woman. He said he was. I asked him if he was sure the child she had in her arms was her own child. He said he was; for that he knew both the mother and the child. I then asked when the circumstance occurred. He stated the night, with great positiveness and precision. I told him the child had been taken from her several days before, and of course he must be mistaken. This settled that charge. We next took up the subject of the theft. I requested the officer to show me the warrant; which he refused to do. I appealed to the judges, and they ordered him to exhibit it; when it appeared to have been issued that morning, by the magistrate who was the subject of complaint. A number of colored people had collected about the door, and among the number was Messy Houston. I called her in, and upon interrogating her, it was discovered that she had lost no spoons, and of course had made no complaint. So that charge was satisfactorily disposed of. I then informed the court that what had been stated respecting the mayor's having given Mary a bad character was as groundless as the other charges made against her. I had seen him that morning. It was true that he was too unwell to leave his house, but it was not true that he had given the woman a bad character. I then took from my pocket a certificate, written with his own hand that morning, stating in substance that she had lived in his family a considerable time, during which she was a faithful servant, and had conducted satisfactorily, and that he knew of nothing against her character, except the circumstance out of which the present difficulty arose. The alderman's plans were completely frustrated. The judges reprimanded him severely, and intimated that they should commit him to prison, till the child should be restored to its mother. At this he gave evidence of great alarm, and said, "If you honors direct it, I will return the child by 8 o'clock to-morrow morning." The case was then adjourned to the afternoon of the next day. A few minutes after leaving the judge's chambers, the alderman stepped up to me, and said that if the woman would call at his office the next morning, she would find her child there, and might have it. I gave him to understand that she would not call at his office; that the child must be returned to the place whence it wa taken; and that he must accompany it in his own proper person, or he must again appear before the judges. He manifested great reluctance to do either; and we parted. The next morning, soon after daylight the child was deposited in the arms of its mother at the place whence it was taken, in the presence of the 'squire, who attended and witnessed the transaction, security being given for its support in due form. Being informed of this result, I called upon Judge Shippen, and gave him the information; and there the matter ended.

NOTES

1. *N.A.S.*, July 13, 1843, 22.

No. LXXVI.
James Williams[1]

I give this fictitious name to the subject of my narrative, because I do not wish to entail reproach upon him or his posterity.

He was employed as a clerk in one of our most respectable moneyed institutions in the city of Philadelphia, and withal, was a high professor of religion. Himself, his wife, an infant, and a colored child about nine years old, constituted his family. He and his wife were in the habit of attending a religious meeting one or two evenings in the week, and the colored girl was left home to take care of the house and the child. Upon their return, they not infrequently found the infant asleep in the cradle, and the girl also asleep on the floor near it. On these occasions, the poor girl was sure to receive severe chastisement; and for trivial offenses, was often confined in the garret for twenty-four hours at a time, without any kind of nourishment.

In consequence of cruel treatment, her health became greatly impaired. On one occasion, she was accused of stealing an apple from one of the neighbors, and the apple was found in her possession. This was considered conclusive evidence of her guilt, and she was severely whipped. Her mother, who lived in the upper part of the city, calling to see her child, and discovering that it had been much abused, spoke to her master, and inquired the cause of such severe treatment. He declined making any explanation, and ordered her to leave the house. She obeyed his orders, but called upon me and represented the case. I observed, that perhaps her daughter had misbehaved. She wept, and said that the child was not of a bad disposition, and even if she had been doing wrong, the treatment was too bad to be inflicted on a dog. I promised to call and see the master, and examine into the matter. I called accordingly. When I knocked, I heard some person in the house say, "walk in." I opened the door, and saw the master standing before the glass shaving himself. He was to me a stranger, but it appeared I was not so to him; for as soon as I entered, he turned towards me and said, "There, Mr. Hopper, you need not come any further; I don't want any thing to say to you." I informed him that I wished to have some conversation with him respecting the little colored girl, whose mother had complained that she was cruelly treated. He replied, "I know your business; if you have anything to say to me, let it be before the mayor." I simply observed, "I will gratify thee;" and forthwith went to John Inskeep, who was then mayor, and kept his office in Mulberry, between Front and Second streets. I stated to him what I knew of the circumstances of the case. He said he would send the master a few lines, requesting him to attend, with the child, at an hour he named, that afternoon, at his office. I attended at the time, and found there the master and the girl. The poor little sufferer looked dejected and broken-hearted, and appeared exceedingly afraid to make her complaint. The master said that when he and his wife came home in the evening, he frequently found the girl asleep, for which he chastised her; but that the occasion of the last whipping he had given her was for stealing. I inquired what she had stolen. He refused to answer me, saying, I had no right to interfere in the matter. The mayor informed him that I had, and that he must answer the question. He then alledged that she had been sent to one of the neighbors for fire, and had stolen an apple. The child denied the charge, declaring the apple was given to her. Her master, however, flatly contradicted her. The girl was afflicted with dropsy, and while she sat in the office the water oozed from the wounds made by the cowskin on her legs, and stood in a puddle on the floor. He made high professions of a conscientious discharge of his duty to the child, and of his desire to do justice by her; and said he considered my interference impertinent. The mayor told him he thought otherwise, gave him a severe reprimand, and informed him that if there was not an amendment in the treatment of the child, he would bind him over to answer at the mayor's court. he promised that there should be no caused of complaint in future. The child was directed to return to the service of her master. We left the office together. In the course of our conversation on the way home, I remonstrated with him for the great impropriety of his conduct; but he still contended that he had only obeyed the dictates of his conscience. I told him his conscience was an evil one, and that he had better try to have it corrected and purified. We parted in the street, and went to our respective homes. the next morning, I think as early as seven or eight o'clock, I was informed by the mother that the child was dead. I was exceedingly surprised and alarmed. I was fearful that, in his rage, he had given her an unguarded blow, which might have occasioned her death. Unpleasant rumors would certainly be set afloat, and I concluded the case ought to be investigated. For that purpose, I wrote a note to the coroner, informing him that a child had died, under circumstances which I thought ought to be investigated; and signed it "A Citizen." The coroner, immediately upon reception of my note, went to the house specified, and found the child in a rough board coffin, just about to be taken away for interment.

A jury was called, Dr. Rush sent for, and witnesses examined. The doctor gave a certificate, stating that "the child's death was occasioned by a dropsical complaint, facilitated by severe treatment and want of sustenance." The master was arrested by the coroner, taken before Alderman Jennings, and bound over to answer at the Court of Oyer and Terminer. I kept out of view, wishing to have no concern in the prosecution. When the court came on, the grand jury indicted him for murder, and the unhappy man was immediately consigned to close confinement. When the trial came on, some of the witnesses mentioned my name, as knowing something of the matter, and I was called upon to testify. This was to me a painful business; but I knew I had no ill-will toward the individual. I had made it my business to inquire respecting the alledged theft, and found that the servant maid where the child had got the fire, had given her the apple, which it was alledged she had stolen. The master was ably defended by the late Joseph Hopkinson; and after a thorough investigation, during which several respectable persons, chiefly of his own religious society, testified to his good character, he was acquitted. I was glad of this result; for I do not believe the man was bad at heart, though he had been so deficient in humanity. He had been educated to expect good results from severity, the effects of which are in fact the reverse of good. Mankind are now generally becoming aware of this, and the pernicious practice of corporal punishment is wellnigh abandoned. Would that it to were wholly so.

NOTES

1. *N.A.S.*, November 9, 1843, 90.

No. LXXVII.
Thomas Harrison[1]

Thomas Harrison was born about the year 1738, in the county of Cumberland, England, where he learned the trade of a tailor. a short time after the expiration of his apprenticeship, he went to London, where he worked a few years as a journeyman, and then emigrated to America, and commenced business in Philadelphia. He was moral in his habits, and religiously inclined, though eccentric in his manners. Becoming acquainted with members of the Society of Friends, he attended their meetings, and eventually embraced their doctrines. Upon his own application, he was, in due time, received into membership with them.

Being a good workman, industrious, and punctual, he soon got into good business, and was for several years at the head of his trade in that city. For many years, he was employed by many of the most respectable of the inhabitants. Among his patrons, were the late Thomas Willing, Benjamin Chew, Richard Peters, and others, who were not only his customers in the line of his business, but were also among the number of his personal friends. His integrity and veracity were never questioned; and nature had given him a strong, energetic mind.

After he had been in business some years, and had got ahead in the world, he connected himself in marriage with Sarah Richards, a virtuous young woman, every way calculated to be an helpmeet for him. She was frugal and industrious, and was much esteemed for her unassuming and humble piety. They had not been married many years, before she appeared as a minister, and was acknowledged as such by the meetings of which she was a member. She traveled extensively, with the unity and approbation of Friends, not only in this country, but in Great Britain, Ireland, and on the continent of Europe.

In the course of a religious visit she made to meetings of

Friends in the southern States, the following circumstance occurred, which may not be uninteresting to the reader:

In passing through Virginia, she and her companion had occasion to lodge at an inn kept by a widow. During the evening, Sarah remarked that she observed a considerable number of female slaves, and but very few men; which led her to inquire if those women did the work of the farm. The landlady replied, that she had but a few acres of land, and it required few hands to till it; that she found it more profitable to keep women than men, as there was always a ready sale for the children, when they were old enough. Sarah inquired if her women were married. She replied no, but that there were men enough in the neighborhood, and there was no difficulty on that account. Sarah remonstrated sharply with her upon the wickedness and debasing consequences of such conduct, and testified, in strong terms, against holding in bondage our fellow-creatures, equally with ourselves the objects of Christ's redemption. The landlady manifested considerable impatience under the cutting rebuke of her guests, but treated them civilly. After spending an almost sleepless night, they pursued their journey early in the morning. This narrative I had from Sarah Harrison's own lips.

Thomas Harrison, from his pacific principles, wa strongly opposed to the American revolution, believing it would be attended with the effusion of much blood, and waste of property. He was often rather free in the expression of his sentiments, which rendered him an object of suspicion, and sometimes brought him into serious difficulty. When going to the State-house, to give his vote at the general election, he saw a crowd of persons near the corner of Fifth and Chesnut streets, who appeared to be much excited. Thomas approached, and inquired what was the matter. He was informed that Joseph Swift, a prominent character in those days, had said that a description of Germans were not entitled to vote. Without intending to give offense, he replied that he did not believe J. Swift had ever so expressed himself; that some one had fabricated the story for political purposes. In an instant, he was attacked by several of those engaged in the dispute, with great violence. Thomas called out, "Fair play! fair play! chose your man, and I am ready for him." A bully stepped up, and said, "I am your man." Thomas found himself in an unpleasant predicament. He knew that reasoning with such characters would be vain, and his principles were opposed to fighting. There was no way to get clear of them, but by stratagem. "Let us choose our seconds," said he, laying hold of one of the company. "This man shall be mine." The seconds were soon selected, when Thomas called upon the company to stand off, and form a ring. He pushed first one, and then another, saying, "Give us room!" till at length he spied a thin place in the crowd, bounced through, and ran at the top of his speed up Fifth street to the corner of High street. He there entered a large store, and close the door, placing a bar across it. He had been there but a few minutes, when the mob burst open the door, yelling like a company of savages. Finding he was no longer safe there, he made his escape through a door that opened into High street; not the one by which he had entered. He ran down High street to an inn kept by a widow Nichols, and upon entering, turned round and barred the door, as he had done in Fifth street. The landlady exclaimed, "Mr. Harrison! Mr. Harrison! you can't stay here." He replied, "We look for no ceremony, in these times. I shall stay anywhere, where I can be safe from those murderers who are in pursuit of me." The words had scarcely escaped his lips, when the door was violently forced open. He then passed through a side door, opening into a court that led to the street. In the bustle and confusion, he proceeded some distance down High street, before he was discovered; when they again set off in full chase. He suddenly turned into Franklin court, and secreted himself in a joiner's shop. After making an unsuccessful search, they gave up the chase and dispersed. He remained till after dark, and then went to the house of a friend. Expecting that the infuriated mob would demolish his dwelling, he had his books and valuable papers removed to a place of safety. He remained at the house of his friend two or three days, till the excitement subsided, when he returned home, and found things as he had left them.

He once received a challenge to fight a duel, from a person who conceived himself offended by something he had said. Thomas replied, ironically, "Tell him I'll fight him; and as the party challenged, has a right to choose his weapon, I shall claim this privilege. Thou mayest inform him that I shall make choice of a red hot goose." There the matter ended.

A number of individuals among the most respectable and peaceable inhabitants of Philadelphia, were arrested, and transported to Virginia, merely on a vague suspicion of being inimical to the American cause, without being allowed a hearing or permitted to defend themselves. Thomas Harrison had many friends among the most zealous and active friends of the revolution. He was among the number of those selected for this persecution; and one of the Committee of Safety, as they were called, gave Thomas this information privately. He straightway informed his wife, and asked her if she could patiently submit to his spending a few weeks in prison; "For," said he, "I don't fear anything they can do to me;" or whether she would prefer that he should "step a one side for a little while." Of the two evils, she chose the latter. He went to work, might and main, to prepare for such an event. A few days afterwards, his friend let him know that the next day was fixed upon for his arrest. When the morning came, Thomas ordered his horse, a fleet animal, to be saddled and bridled, and brought to the door. A man was directed to stand by and hold him, and if he should see any person in military costume enter the street, to give immediate notice. In the meantime, he was busily engaged in preparing work for his men. About the middle of the day, it was announced that three such men had entered the street, from the south end. Thomas instantly mounted his horse, and set off full gallop. The men were but a few rods off, and called out, "Stop that man, stop that man!" But Thomas made good his escape, and soon got among his friends at Abington, about fourteen miles north from the city. Here he remained but a few days, when he returned home and hid himself in his garret, diligently employed in preparing work for his men. He had a number of confidential customers, who furnished him constant employment during several weeks, till the storm blew over. At last, he made his appearance in public again, without being molested.

He remained in the city during the whole of the war; and while the British occupied it, he worked for several of the principal officers. General Howe was among the number. On one occasion, when that officer called upon him, in the line of his business, the conversation turned upon the state of the country, and upon the measures adopted by the British government. Thomas observed to the general, "If one of my journeymen was to serve me no better than thou has served the king, I would turn him out of doors." The general appeared not much gratified with the remark, but manifested no symptoms of resentment.

In the year 1774, a society was instituted in Philadelphia, by the name of "The Pennsylvania Society for promoting the Abolition of Slavery, and the Relief of Free Negroes unlawfully held in bondage." Thomas Harrison was a principal instrument in organizing this society, and wa, till near the close of his useful life, one of the most active, energetic, and efficient members. In the year 1789, it was enlarged; Benjamin Franklin was chosen president, James Pemberton and Jonathan Penrose, vice-presidents, and Benjamin Rush and Tench Coxe, secretaries. These names gave respectability and weight to the enterprise. Soon after the organization of this society, Thomas Harrison was appointed a member of "the acting committee," and was made their secretary. The duties of this committee were very laborious. They met once a week, in the evening, at a schoolhouse belonging to the Society of Friends, for colored children. Whatever changes took place in it, he remained at his post, and continued a member until old age and infirmity rendered him incapable of being useful. It was the business of the acting committee to transact such business as should occur in the recess of the society, and report the same at each quarterly meeting. An act was passed in the third month, 1780, for the gradual abolition of slavery. It required that all owners of slaves should cause them to be registered in the office of the clerk of the country, where the owner resided, before the first day of the eleventh month, then next ensuing. This law opened a wide field of labor for the acting committee. Some neglected to furnish the clerk with the necessary documents to make the registry, until it was too late to make the entry; others again made informal returns. And as the committee met once each week, the time and place of their meeting became known to the colored people generally, and it rarely, if ever, passed without more or less applications for advice and assistance. Very many, who had been held in slavery, were liberated through their agency.

The society kept a book for recording manumissions, and another for recording indentures. The originals were filed; and when occasion required, the parties were furnished with certified copies, with the seal of the society affixed. Those records and papers were kept at Thomas Harrison's, and he cheerfully rendered the services necessarily attendant upon them during many years, and always without any pecuniary compensation.

There was not a magistrate or judge in the city or county, before whom this indefatigable friend of the oppressed had not appeared as their advocate; and his integrity and uprightness of character, gave him much influence. Hundreds, and perhaps thousands, were rescued by him from the grasp of the avaricious slaveholder. He was feared and respected by those wretches, who make a prey of their fellow-man, by hunting out and arresting fugitives from slavery. I have heard the following anecdote related, which is very characteristic of the man. The case of a poor fellow, who had made his escape from bondage, and who had been for some time under the protection of Thomas Harrison, was before the supreme court in Philadelphia. Moses Levy was employed as counsel for the claimant. Levy, in the course of his speech, took the liberty to reflect very unjustly and severely upon the character and conduct of Thomas Harrison, who sat and listened to him, until he could bear it no longer. He called out, "Hold! hold! I will not sit here and hear my character abused with impunity, by anybody." One of the judges said, "Mr. Harrison, do you know where you are, sir?" He immediately replied, "I thought I was in a court of justice; but certainly no court of justice would permit this." Any other man in the court-house, who should have used such language, would have been punished for contempt; but instead of that, the chief justice rebuked the attorney. I do not recollect the particular ground on which the fugitive claimed his liberty; but I remember that he was discharged. No man was ever more disliked by slaveholders, than the individual of whom I am now writing.

Thomas Harrison generally exercised his privilege of voting at the election, for the different officers of the government; at least, for representatives in the city council, and in the general and State legislature. About the year 1800, when there was much excitement among politicians of the day, Thomas concluded that he would not attend the election. Some time in the course of the day, a person called and informed him that it was said at the State-house, where the election was held, that he, and several others whom he named, would not be permitted to vote. Thomas quickly replied, "I will try that." He immediately went to the State-house. The subject of his not being permitted to vote, had become a topic of general conversation. People were curious to see how he would fare, and the way was soon cleared for him. He stepped upon the platform and offered his ticket, when the following short dialogue took place between the inspector and himself: "Mr. Harrison, have you ever been attainted?" "Search the records, and ascertain for thyself," replied Thomas. "Have you ever taken the test of oath to this government?" "No; nor to any other government on earth." "Were you here when the British were here?" "Yes, I was here before they came, I was here while they staid, and I remained when they went away; and that's more than thou dared to do." The by-standers set up a laugh. The vote was received, and Thomas quietly returned home.

A southern slave-trader once went to Philadelphia, in pursuit of three slaves that he had purchased. He procured the assistance of an officer, and went in search of them. Upon going to the horse market, he saw the three men standing together. He had but just fixed his eyes upon them, when they saw him, and immediately made good their escape. After spending some time in hunting for them, he applied to Thomas Harrison, who paid him two hundred and fifty dollars for their manumission; not doubting but he could find them, and that they would be willing to bind themselves for a period sufficient to refund the amount he had paid; but in this he was disappointed. Two of them cleared off, and never were heard of afterwards. The third, hearing that Thomas Harrison had purchased them, called upon him, and was indented to Jacob Downing, of Philadelphia, for a term of years, for which Thomas received one hundred and twenty-five dollars; just half of the sum he had paid for the three. The slave's name was William Anderson. He served his time out, to the satisfaction of Jacob Downing, and soon after called upon Thomas Harrison, and thus addressed him: "Mr. Harrison, you paid two hundred and fifty dollars for three of us. Two have gone away, and cannot be found; for they did not know you had done anything for them. You have received only one hundred and twenty-five dollars for me. It is not right that you should lose your money. I am willing you should sell me again, for the balance." Thomas replied, "Honest fellow! honest fellow! Go about thy business. Thou hast paid thy share, I have no claim upon thee. Only conduct thyself as well as thou hast done heretofore, and thou wilt do well."

A slave left his master, in the State of Delaware, and went to New Jersey. He applied to me to negotiate for his freedom, and I wrote to the master, whose name was David McAlmont. Soon after receiving my letter, he called upon me, in company with Levi Hollingsworth, a respectable merchant of Philadelphia, and endeavored to prevail upon me to persuade James, the slave, to return to him, or to inform where he might be found. He assured me that he was much happier at home, then he could be anywhere else. They could not, however, prevail upon me to comply with their wishes. They then called upon Thomas Harrison, and solicited him to use his influence with me to inform them where James might be found; at the same time telling him how well he lived at home; that he was well clothed, and well fed, and not overworked. Thomas was busily engaged at his shopboard, cutting out clothes; for he never stopped this, let who would be talking. He, however, listened attentively to their statement. When they had got through with their fine story, he turned to them with one of his roguish, quizical looks. "Oh yes," sid he, "the condition of the slaves in that part of the country is well understood. We all know very well that they are treated most kindly. They sleep on feather beds, while their masters' children lie on straw; they eat white bread and their masters' children eat brown." Then turning to Levi Hollingsworth, who was an ardent politician, and had written much in the newspapers, in relation to the election of governor, which was then near at hand, he said, "I'll tell thee what, my friend, fence in with a good substantial wall, ten acres, and plant it with Lombardy poplars, and the most beautiful shrubbery; build an elegant mansion in the middle; fill the cellar with the choicest wines, and furnish thy table with every dainty; have a coach and four to drive round it at they pleasure; and pen, ink, and paper, to write about the governor; but after all, thou wilt want to get out." They soon discovered that nothing was to be gained from him, and withdrew.

An old man who lived near the falls of Schuylkill, and who had once been a clergyman, but having a become a devotee of Bacchus, had resigned his station, called upon Harrison, saying that his servant, a colored man, had absconded, and he wished to know if Thomas could give any account of him. Thomas was busily engaged cutting out garments of his men to make up, for he was remarkable, for his diligence in business. He replied without stopping, that he had not seen him, and knew nothing of him. The old quandam clergyman appeared to be in some measure under the influence of alcohol. He became much excited, and made use of very opprobrious language, alledging that if it were not for such men as Thomas Harrison, people would not have so much trouble with their servants. Immediately at the door wa a large iron grate, covering a deep vault. Strangers were somewhat cautious in walking over it. As the old man continued to rail abusively, Thomas raised his large shears, wide open, and stepped towards him, saying, "Get out of my house." The man was prodigiously alarmed thinking that he was about to do him personal violence; though he had in fact, no such intention. He made a sudden retreat, and attempting a long step over the grate, stumbled and fell flat upon his back in the gutter, splashing mud and water against the window. "There, thou old vagabond," said Thomas, laughing, "that is the right place for thee." He shut the door, and the old man went away muttering.

Few men understood human nature better than Thomas Harrison. There was a natural drollery about him, which he well knew how to use to promote his purposes. He would often sit with his spectacles on the top of his head, and put on such a quizical look, and accompany it with such humorous expressions, as would set the whole court in a roar of laughter. Even the judges on the bench could not always maintain their gravity on such occasions. Judge Yeates once remarked that an excellent comedian was spoiled, when he was made a tailor. Yet, when occasion required, he could assume a serious, stern countenance, and his keen piercing eye seemed as if it would penetrate the inmost recesses of the heart.

One of his sons became connected with a chemical establishment, which required the investment of considerable capital. His father became his endorser. This establishment was accidentally destroyed by fire, in consequence of which, both the father and son became insolvent. This was a severe affliction to Thomas, who was now an old man. He forthwith laid his case before his creditors, of which the banks were the principal. A committee was appointed to confer with him on the occasion. They met at his house, where he laid a statement of his affairs before them. After examining into it, they inquired of him what propositions he had to make. He seemed not to understand their meaning. They asked him if he did not expect to retain something for his own support, as he was an old man, incapable of doing business. "Retain something," said he, "why I have not enough to pay my debts!" "But how do you expect to live?" "Go to the almshouse round yonder," said he, pointing to the Friends' almshouse, near by. They requested him to withdraw a few minutes, while they consulted together. After a short conference, they recalled him, and informed him that they had agreed to give him the use of the house in which he lived, during the life of himself and his wife, and the furniture, household goods, &c, they wished to give him outright. The tears started in his eyes, as he exclaimed, "Thank ye, friends! Thank ye, friends! Sally and I *would* like a few shingles to shelter us from the storm, in our old days." The house was a good three story building, a few doors south of Girard's bank. He owned a share in glass works, near the river Schuylkill; and to prevent his partners from being involved in his embarrassments, he had prepared and executed an assignment to them of his interest in that concern; but he had not delivered it. This document he exhibited, and stated his reasons for making it, assuring the committee that if they thought there was anything dishonest or dishonorable in the transaction, he would throw it in the fire. They commended him for what he had done, and inquired what he supposed his book debts would amount to. He replied, "five hundred pounds, more or less." After another brief conference, they informed him that they had concluded to give him his share in the glass works, and also to make him a present of his book debts. This was far beyond his expectation. It rejoiced his heart, and was sufficient to supply the necessities of the honest couple as long as they lived.

Thomas Harrison and myself had been co-workers for many years, in the cause of the colored people. He often suggested the idea that I was to succeed him in that concern. For several years we resided within a few hundred yards of each other, and were often together. One day, he took occasion to remark that he was an old man, and nearly worn out, and he felt glad that I had entered with so much feeling into the cause in which he had been so many years engaged. He said that he already felt the burden in a great measure taken from his shoulders, and hoped when he was removed from the stage of action, that I would fill his place. I have endeavored to fulfill his dying wishes.

I believe no man ever engaged in any cause with more pure and disinterested motives, than this friend did the cause of the oppressed colored people. He spent much time and money, without prospect of any other reward than what arose from a consciousness of duty discharged. "Then shall the King say unto them on his right hand, come ye blessed of my Father, inherit the kingdom prepared for you from the foundation of the world. For I was hungered, and ye gave me meat: I was thirsty, and ye gave me drink; I was a stranger and ye took me in; naked and ye clothed me; I was sick and in prison, and ye came unto me. * * * Verily I say unto you, in as much as ye have done it unto one of the least of these my brethren, ye have done it unto me."

He died the 5th of the 11th month, 1815; aged seventy-seven years. An immense crowd of colored people followed him to the grave.

NOTES

1. *N.A.S.*, February 8, 1844, 142.

No. LXXVIII.
Tom[1]

A person by the name of Wallace, a wealthy planter in Virginia, took a tour to the North and East, accompanied by his wife and two daughters. After visiting Quebec, and some of the cities in New England, they arrived in Philadelphia, in the autumn, about the year 1804, and took lodgings at the well-known inn, called the "Indian Queen," in South Fourth street. They concluded to spend the winter in that city, for the purpose of enjoying the popular amusements of the place, among the fashionables of the city. They had with them a favorite family servant to wait upon them. During their sojourn there, they were careful to keep him from forming acquaintance with any of the colored people, fearing they might induce him to leave their services. They remained in Philadelphia till late in the ensuing spring, when they made preparations for returning to Virginia. I shall call the servant Tom; for I believe that was his name, though it is so long since the circumstances occurred, that I am not certain. Tom had been long enough in Philadelphia to become attached to the place, and his master discovered that he was extremely reluctant to return to Virginia. To prevent difficulty, he had him arrested, and placed in prison. He was committed in the evening. The next morning, the keeper sent and informed me that a colored man had been committed to prison as a slave, who he thought had a legal right to his freedom. Soon after receiving this information, I had an interview with the prisoner. He was about thirty-five or forty years old, and had resided with Wallace from early childhood. He made no complaint of hard treatment, but was very desirous of being free. I inquired of him why he was so unwilling to return to Virginia, inasmuch as he did not complain of bad usage. He replied, "Everybody wishes to be free. If master dies, I shall be sold, and may be sent to Georgia." I discovered, on interrogating him, that he had been in Philadelphia more than six months. I then informed him that he was a free man, and that I would protect him. He clasped his hands with deep emotion, and in an instant his face was suffused with tears. His joy was inexpressible. I stepped into the keeper's office, and drew up a petition for a habeas corpus. While I was writing it, the keeper informed me that his master had gone to the magistrate who committed him, to get a discharge; and that he intended to send him off immediately. He added, "Be as expeditious as possible. If he comes with it, I will detain the man till you return, if you don't stay more than an hour." I proceeded forthwith to the courthouse near by, where the supreme court was then in session. I gave my petition to Joseph Hopkinson, who was then in court, to present. It was addressed "To Edward Shippen, chief justice of the supreme court of the State of Pennsylvania, and his associates." Hopkinson, after looking over it, remarked, "you must let me add 'To the honorable.'" This I declined, and he refused to present it to the court. I then stepped up and said, "I hold in my hand a petition for a habeas corpus; I gave it to my friend, Joseph Hopkinson, to present; but he declined doing so, because it is not couched in the usual terms, 'To the honorable.' I presume I have as honorable an opinion of this court as my friend Hopkinson; but it is an epithet that is often misapplied, and one which I have conscientious objections to using. I hope this court will not deny justice to the man, on whose behalf I make this application, on account of my conscientious scruples. Unless the habeas corpus is issued immediately, the man will be taken out of the jurisdiction of this court." As soon as I took my seat, Sampson Levy, counsel for the claimant, rose and said, "I hope the court will not suffer that petition to be read. The proceeding is irregular. The court have been told that Mr. Hopkinson had declined to present it. Mr. Hopkinson is one of the counsel of the abolition society, and if there had been no objection, but that mentioned, he doubtless would have cheerfully attended to the business." Levy commenced a speech, which I soon discovered was likely to occupy considerable time. I rose, and asked the court to permit me to interrupt the counsel for one minute. I remarked, "I repeat that unless a habeas corpus is issued *immediately*, the man will be out of the jurisdiction of the court.

I suppose his claimant is now at the prison, waiting to take him away." Judge Yates, as soon as I had done speaking, said, "Read your petition." I read it. He then said, "Take your writ." I was soon furnished with it, and immediately went to the prison, where I found Wallace, and Richard Hunt, a constable, with their manacles ready to fetter Tom and carry him off. Upon exhibiting the writ, I received, as was customary in such cases, a volley of abuse from Wallace and his officer. They demanded their man, and threatened the keeper with prosecution, unless he immediately gave up the prisoner. As soon as he could make out the return to the writ, we all proceeded to the court-house. Upon arriving there, J. Hopkinson said, "Now I will attend to the case for you." I replied, "I thank thee, I shall not need thy services."

I had in court, one of the servants from the hotel, where Wallace and his family lodged, to prove the length of time they had been in the city. I had also subpoenaed the bar-keeper. Upon looking round the room I saw the landlord. Wallace had anticipated difficulty, and had previously provided himself with counsel. Soon after the man appeared in court, the case was called on. In the meantime, the bar keeper made his appearance. He testified most clearly the time of their arrival in the city, and that they had remained there ever since. I then called upon the landlord, who with much reluctance confirmed the same facts. I observed that if it was necessary, we could produce additional testimony, but that I presumed the court was now satisfied. Levy asked the witnesses no questions. After a few minutes, the man was discharged.

As I was leaving the court-room, J. Hopkinson said to me, "Isaac, you have got the impudence of the devil: They should have made a lawyer of you." "Is that a necessary constituent in the character of a lawyer?" replied I. And so we parted.

NOTES

1. *N.A.S.*, February 29, 1844.

No. LXXIX.
William Dixon[1]

William Dixon was arrested on the 4th of 4th month, 1837, by virtue of a writ of habeas corpus, founded on the oath of Doctor Walter P. Allender, of the city of Baltimore, that he was his slave, and had absconded from his service, in April, 1832. He was taken before the Recorder, Richard Riker. ____ Phenix and John A. Morrill, attended as counsel for the claimant, and Horace Dresser on behalf of Dixon.

Dixon denied being the slave of Doctor Allender, or that he had ever resided in Baltimore. The case was adjourned, in order to give the parties an opportunity to procure testimony, and Dixon was committed. The case produced tremendous excitement, and occupied the attention of the Recorder, at intervals, during three or four months. Many hundreds, perhaps thousands, of persons of all colors, crowded round the court-house, and filled it to overflowing.

When the case was again called on, it was clearly proved that Dixon was in New-York some years previous to the time of his alledged elopement. The investigation had proceeded but a little way, before I became convinced that the doctor could not succeed in establishing his claim. Seeing the great excitement which prevailed, and feeling some sympathy for the doctor, I proposed to him to abandon the case; telling him that if he pursued it, he would involve himself in heavy expenses, and be disappointed at last. He treated me respectfully, but declined taking my advice.

Doctor Allender brought on from Baltimore several persons as witnesses. Thomas J. Messach, a merchant of Baltimore, was sworn for the claimant. He testified that his brother-in-law, claimant's father, had a slave named Jacob Ellis. The prisoner was the man, beyond all doubt. He would risk his life on the identity. He was in the habit of seeing him almost everyday. He knew him for twelve years. The prisoner drove him to the claimants wedding, in November, 1830. He was missing in warm weather. He thought it was in the summer of 1831. He had not seen the prisoner since he was missed, till he took his seat in the court. The claimants father had sold a servant, two or three weeks before prisoner eloped."

The Recorder here asked Mr. Demerest of Boston, (who had, on previous examination, sworn to having known the prisoner, in Boston, in 1828) whether he could not be mistaken in the prisoner. He answered that he could not.

Walter Price, of Baltimore, deposed that he knew the family of Dr. Allender, sen., many years. He married one of his daughters, in 1834. The prisoner was the property of claimant's father. He was certain of it. He could not be mistaken. He had not seen the prisoner till to-day, since he eloped. He ran away in 1831. He could not state the month, but it was before October. The prisoner was the property of Dr. Allender, sen., when he eloped. Dr. Allender, sen'r., died in 1834, leaving the prisoner to his widow, who gave up her right and title to the claimant.

It would be tedious and uninteresting to detail all the testimony given on behalf of the claimant. There were not less than fifteen or twenty witnesses, who testified as positively as those above named. Several of them were persons of unquestioned veracity, and doubtless fully believed what they said.

There was a profligate fellow of this city, who said he had resided in Baltimore, and knew the prisoner. He offered himself as a witness; but just before he was examined, I made an appearance in court. Upon seeing me, he exclaimed, "I won't be examined in this case. Yonder is old Hopper. He will impeach my character." I had previously come in contact with this man, in a case not very honorable to him, and he was unwilling to encounter me again.

In a private conversation with the Recorder, in his office, in the presence of the counsel for the claimant, I suggested that the rule of evidence in criminal cases should be observed in this; that the matter at issue was as important to Dixon, as if he was on trial for his life; and if any doubt existed, the prisoner ought to have the benefit of it. The Recorder said he would hear an argument on that point. The claimant's counsel threw much ridicule on the suggestion. But, at the opening of the court, the next morning, the

Recorder observed "that he had considered the suggestion offered the previous day, and he should certainly be governed in this case by the criminal law of evidence. In a case involving the liberty of a person, he held the criminal law of evidence must govern. The superior weight of evidence must of course, carry the case; but if there was a reasonable doubt as to the identity of the prisoner, that doubt was certainly the prisoner's property, and should be raised in his favor."

Testimony on behalf of Dixon. Arthur Jones, black, sworn. "Lives No. 145 1-2 Ann street, Boston; has lived there twenty-one years. Knows Dixon; first saw him in Boston, twelve years since. He went by the name of William Dixon. (Jones produced several testimonials of character from Boston.) The prisoner lived with him, and he shipped him about eleven years since. Dixon was in Boston a year before he boarded with witness. He sailed in a brig to some port in Europe, does not remember which. Dixon had no wife then. He was with witness eleven days. Witness was on the wharf when Dixon came home to Boston, in the brig Oak, belonging to Tobias Lord; and he took him home to board with him. Before that, he had seen prisoner at Mrs. Brown's in Brighton street, near Charlestown bridge. After shipping Dixon, he did not see him again till now, in this city." Here counsel for Dixon produced the certificate of Mr. Henshaw, collector of the port of Boston, that William Dixon shipped from that port in May, 1827. Witness was not sent for, from this city, that he knows of. He read in the papers about Dixon's trouble here, and came on voluntarily, at his own expense. He called on Mr. Dresser, and went with him to the prison, and saw Dixon. He has not the least doubt of Dixon's identity. Dixon recognized witness when he first saw him, in prison, before witness spoke. This wa not three minutes after he made known his errand to Mr. Dresser. Dixon owed witness, and it was to get his money that he came to this city, if the prisoner was the same. The vessel that Dixon shipped in, at Boston, was cast away. The name of the brig was the John Gilpin; it was her first voyage.

The recorder then proposed to have a separate private examination of Jones and Dixon, as to the circumstances, and the persons, their appearances, ages, &c. mentioned by Jones, to test the correctness of the identity of the prisoner. Dixon expressed his willingness to take such a course; but Mr. Morrill, counsel for the claimant, solemnly protested against it. The Recorder entered his protest, and expressed his conviction of his perfect right to go into such an examination, and his determination to prosecute it.

Jones to the Recorder: "The John Gilpin was a bright sided brig, without painted ports. She was about the size of the brig Delta, which was about 180 tons. The John Gilpin was owned by Mr. Curtis, and his partner.

Richard Livingston, a servant in the family of Mr. Hicks, a respectable Quaker gentleman up town, deposed that he was positively well acquainted with the prisoner in this city, in 1831--that during the absence of Mr. Hicks, at a quarterly meeting in Philadelphia, in 1828, he employed the prisoner to whitewash two rooms in his master's house, and had been in the habit of seeing him since.

_____ Demerest deposed that he knew the prisoner, in Boston, in 1828.

Many other witnesses, both white and colored, were examined, who all testified that they had known Dixon both in this city and Boston, long before the time of the elopement alledged by Dr. Allender.

There was another colored man in the city who so strongly resembled Dixon that few could tell them apart. If the case had not dropped as it did, he might have been smuggled into the prisoner's place, and produced fine confusion among the witnesses.

The Recorder stated that in the power of attorney, in which the prisoner claimed, his elopement was stated to have been in April, 1832, whereas it was proved beyond doubt, that the prisoner was here in 1831.

Some of the Baltimore papers came out most violently against the proceedings in this case. This brought forth the following pertinent remarks in one of our daily papers:

> *The Pending Slave Case.* We regret that the Baltimore Chronicle should have perpetuated so unjust and inflammatory an article in relation to the slave case, now at issue before the recorder, as appeared in its columns on

Tuesday. The information upon which it hurls its threats northwardly, we assure it, is wholly incorrect. It is *not* true that Dr. Allender is charged, or suspected, even by the most devoted abolitionists amongst us, of an attempt to *kidnap* the man he claims; nor that there are any "barefaced and horrible prejudices" by which the claim of Dr. A. is sought to be defeated. If the sorrow expressed by the Chronicle, at its discovery of too much credulity in ministers of the law in the eastern section of the country, "to the fabrications of unscrupulous and conscienceless negroes," has been excited by the adjudication of the case in point, it has made a lamentable waste of sympathetic grief. We can assure our sorrowing correspondent that the strongest testimony as yet elicited in behalf of the alledged slave, has been uttered by white citizens--citizens of as pure and honorable a character as that of the much lauded claimant can possibly be. The Chronicle need feel under no apprehensions that Baltimore will be called upon to revenge herself upon this city for "any harsh measures adopted toward the doctor." His rights and safety will be as faithfully guarded both by the legal authorities and citizens of New-York, as will be those of the man he claims -- *but not more so*, though the latter may be black. Whether, as the Chronicle avers, "there cannot be the slightest doubt" in the case, will be better known when the oaths of respectable white citizens to their acquaintance with William Dixon years before Jacob Ellis is said to have eloped from Dr. A. are proved to be forgeries. In conclusion, we advise the Chronicle to "keep cool," and not lose its temper, and not again burst forth in braggadocia, before it knows what it is talking about.

This case, as has been already mentioned, was continued before the Recorder several months; and as it was impossible to conjecture when it would be terminated, unless it should be removed to another tribunal, it was concluded to take it to the Court of Errors. A law had been enacted some years before, giving persons who might be claimed as fugitives the right of a trial by jury. This law had been adjudged by the Supreme Court unconstitutional; and this was thought to be a proper case to carry up to the Court of Errors, that their decision might be had upon it. To accomplish this object, H. Dresser, counsel for Dixon, drew up a protest against the Recorder's proceeding any further therein. Bail was given to the sheriff, and a writ of homine replegiando, issued out of the Supreme Court, was served upon the keeper of the prison, and Dixon was set at liberty. Arrangements were made, and the case was taken to the highest tribunal in the State. After Dixon had been at liberty some months, the counsel for the claimant taking no measures to bring the case to a final issue, Dixon was returned to prison. Doctor Allender had been obliged to pay two dollars a week for Dixon's support, while in jail, and finding it rather onerous, declined to contribute. The sheriff was not disposed to maintain him at his own expense, and he was discharged. He has been ever since pursuing his business without molestation. The case was never brought to an issue, and is never likely to be.

During the examination of the case, there was much confusion. On one occasion, after the court adjourned, as the officers were taking Dixon to the prison, a crowd surrounded them, and rescued him. J.M.B. a police justice, hearing the tumult, ran out of his office toward the scene of action. He had gone but few steps, when a fat colored woman came behind him, threw her arms round his neck, and amid shouts of laughter from the bystanders, brought him flat to the ground. Dixon, however, was recaptured, and conducted to Bridewell. When taken, he had a dirk and knife in his possession.

Before the examination commenced, the next morning, the Recorder said, in reference to the rescue, that he was fully convinced that the escape of the prisoner was altogether the work of violence on the part of the mob, who compelled him to fly, and forced upon him the weapons found upon his person. The Recorder fully exonerated him form any blame on account of that transaction. H. Dresser, counsel for the defense, stated that it was reprehended and regretted by the respectable portion of the colored people, and by their abolition friends.

A day or two after this occurred, I went to the police office, and inquired if J.M.B. was there. The man whom I addressed replied, "My name is J.M.B." "I was acquainted with a friend in Philadelphia," said I, "who often used to say, 'if thou knowest any good of a man, tell it to others; if thou knowest any evil of him, tell it to himself.' In conformity with this rule, I have come to mention something I have heard about thee, if thou art willing to hear it." He replied that he was willing to hear anything I had to say. I then told him I understood he had expressed regret that he had not his pistols about him, when treated roughly in the Park, a day or so ago; for if he had, he would have blown out the brains of some of his assailants. He answered, "I did say so; and I would have done it." "I am sorry to hear it," I replied. "Permit me to say that I think the city of New-York is disgraced in having a man on the justices' bench, thirsting for the blood of his fellow-men." He said, "I am not thirsting for the blood of my fellow-men." I told him his expressions seemed to convey such an idea, and recommended him to cultivate a more Christian spirit. I observed that the colored people saw such a savage disposition exhibited towards them by the police, that it was no wonder they should attempt to retaliate in the same spirit; that if the police had conducted with the dignity and propriety becoming the station they occupied, those riots would seldom, if ever, occur.

The Recorder has long since been called to render his final account at that bar where he has certainly received the reward of his works. It may not be amiss to say, that if he had been as prompt to render justice to those accused of being fugitive slaves, as he was to deliver them to the oppressor, this case could not have occupied him as long as it did.

NOTES

1. *N.A.S.*, May 23, 1844, 202.

BIBLIOGRAPHY

Aptheker, Herbert, *Documentary History of the Negro People in the United States* (4 vols., New York, 1951-1974).

Blackburn, Robin, *The Overthrow of Colonial Slavery, 1776-1810* (London, 1988).

Blassingame, John, *The Slave Community: Plantation Life in the Antebellum South*, Rev. and enl. ed. (New York, 1979).

_____ *Slave Testimony: Two Centuries of Letters, Speeches, Interviews and Autobiographies* (Baton Rouge, 1977).

_____ Mae G. Henderson, *Antislavery Newspapers and periodicals* (5 vols., Boston, 1980-1986).

_____ et al., eds., *The Frederick Douglass Papers* (5 vols. New Haven, 1975-).

Brown, Ira V., "Pennsylvania's Anti-Slavery Pioneers, 1688-1776," *Pennsylvania History* LV (1989).

Brown, Margaret, *Lamb's Warrior: The Life of Isaac T. Hopper* (New York, 1970).

Campbell, Stanley W., *The Slave Catchers: Enforcement of the Fugitive Slave Laws* (New York, 1970).

Child, Lydia Maria, *Isaac Hopper: A True life* (London, 1853).

Curry, Leonard P., *The Free Black in Urban America, 1800-1850, The Shadow of a Dream* (Chicago, 1981).

Davis, Charles T., and Henry Louis Gates, Jr., eds., *The Slave's Narrative* (New York, 1985).

Drake, Thomas E., *Quakers and Slavery in America* (New Haven, 1950).

Elkins, Stanley, *Slavery: A Problem in American Institutional and Intellectual Life* (Chicago, 1969).

Fogel, Robert W., and Stanley Engerman, *Time on the Cross: The Economics of American Negro Slavery* (2 vols., Boston, 1974).

Fogel, Robert W., *Without Consent or Contract: The Rise and Fall of American Slavery* (New York, 1989).

Frey, Sylvia R., *Water from the Rock: Black Resistance in a Revolutionary Age* (Princeton, New Jersey, 1991).

Gara, Larry, *The Liberty Line: The Legend of the Underground Railroad* (Lexington, Kentucky, 1961).

Genovese, Eugene D., *Roll, Jordan, Roll: The World the Slaves Made* (New York, 1974).

Harding, Vincent, *There is a River: The Black Struggle for Freedom in America* (New York, 1981).

Huggins, Nathan Irving, *Black Odyssey: The Afro-American Ordeal in Slavery* (New York, 1977).

James, Sidney, *A People Among People: Quaker Benevolence in Eighteenth-Century America* (Cambridge, Mass., 1963).

Kolchin, Peter, *American Slavery, 1619-1877* (New York, 1993).

Konkle, Burton Alva, *Benjamin Chew, 1772-1810* (Philadelphia, 1932).

Litwack, Leon F., *North of Slavery: The Free Negro in the United States, 1790-1860* (Chicago, 1961).

Meaders, Daniel, *Dead or Alive: Fugitive Slaves and White Indentured Servants Before 1830* (New York, 1993).

McFreely, William S., *Frederick Douglass* (New York, 1991).

Morris, Thomas P., *Free Men All: The Personal Laws of the North, 1780-1861* (Baltimore, 1971).

Nash, Gary B., *Forging Freedom: The Formation of Philadelphia's Black Community, 1720-1840* (Cambridge, 1988).

_____ Jean R. Soderlund, *Freedom by Degrees: Emancipation in Pennsylvania and its Aftermath* (New York, 1991).

Phillips, Ulrich, B., *American Negro Slavery* (New York, 1918).

Quarles, Benjamin, *Black Abolitionists* (New York, 1969).

Rawick, George P., *From Sundown to Sunup; The Making of the Black Community* (Westport, CT, 1972).

Siebert, Wilbur H., *The Underground Railroad From Slavery to Freedom* (New York, 1898).

Soderlund, Jean R., *Quakers and Slavery: A Divided Spirit* (Princeton, NJ, 1985).

Stampp, Kenneth, *The Peculiar Institution* (New York, 1956).

Turner, Edward R., *The Negro in Pennsylvania* (Washington, DC, 1911).

White, Shane, *Somewhat More Independent: The End of Slavery in New York City, 1770-1810* (Athens, GA, 1991).

Winch, Julie, "Philadelphia and the Other Underground Railroad," *Pennsylvania Magazine of History and Biography*, 111 (1987).

Woodward, C. Vann, "History from Slave Sources," *American Historical Review*, (1974).

Yetman, Norman R., ed., *Voices from Slavery* (New York, 1970).

Zilversmit, Arthur, *The First Emancipation: The Abolition of Slavery in the North* (Chicago, 1967).

Newspapers and Journals

Genius of Universal of Emancipation	1821-1837
Herald of Freedom	1835-1846
Liberator	1831-1865
National Anti-Slavery Standard	1840-1872
Pennsylvania Gazette	1728-1815
Pennsylvania Freeman	1836-1844
Pennsylvania Packet	1771-1790
Poulson's American Daily Advertiser	1800-1820
Philadelphia Gazette	1794-1802
Philanthropist	1817-1818

INDEX OF PLANTERS' NAMES

Planter's Name	Tale #	Title of Tale
Allender, Dr. Walter P.	79	William Dixon
Bishop, John	24	Pegg
Boots, Perry	10	Daniel Benson
Bouilla	66	Poor Amy
Brannan, Benjamin	61	What's in a Name?
Brown, Captain James	31	Philadelphia Apprentice
Buckmaster, Charles	43	Phebe Numbers
Burroughs, Stephen	69	Theodore
Caulker, James	53	Self-emancipated couple
Chew, Benjamin	9	Richard Allen
Coates	35	James Poovey
Collins, James	24	Pegg
Creswell, Robert	60	Tom
Darg, John P.	16, 33	Thomas Hughes
De Boudee, Peter	19	Wagelma
Dobson, Betsey	1	Haitian Slave
Dobson, Widow	1	Haitian Slave
Donahue, Benjamin	15	Phebe
Downing, Jacob	62	William Anderson
Ennells, Joseph	62	William Anderson
Gales, Littleton	34	Anne Garrison
Gibson, Judge	45	James Hall
Gover, Gideon	21	Prince Hopkins
Gover, Priscilla	21	Prince Hopkins
Halliday, Henry	34	Anne Garrison
Hamm, Charles	43	Phebe Numbers
Hanson, John	28	Solomon Clarkson
Harris, Samuel	21	Prince Hopkins

Planter's Name	Tale #	Title of Tale
Harrison, John	24	Pegg
Hess, Christain	24	Pegg
Hollinsworth, Samuel	34	Anne Garrison
Holmes, George	26	George Cooper
Hopper, Colonel	71	Maryland Slave
Hopper, Isaac	75	Mary
Hutchins, Thomas	1	Haitian Slave
Laird, Samuel	26	George Cooper
Lamaire	18	Stephen Lamaire
Lawler, Matthew	75	Mary
Leigh	1	Haitian Slave
Lewis, William	59	Charles Webster
Lloyd, Frisby	32	Ben
Low, Samuel	40	Maryland Slave
Lucas	17	Emery Sadler
Many, Captain John	73	William Wright
McCalmont, David	49	James
Moses, T.I.	2	Peter Johnson
Orr, Benjamin	59	Charles Webster
Peacock, Nathan	8	A Maryland Fugitive
Pigot, John	22	Germaine
Purnell, Joshua	42	Maryland Slaves
Read, Jacob	44	Red Betsey
Read, Samuel	1	Haitian Slave
Reynolds, George	24	Pegg
Rich, Dr.	27	Maryland Slave
Rinker, Casper	24	Pegg
Roach, J.	2	Peter Johnson
Salaignac, Anthony	7	Romaine
Salter, Capt.	1	Haitian Slave
Sears, John	46	Mary Holliday
Spear, Joseph	11	Samuel Curtis
Stokely	57	The Fraudulent Indenture
Stone, James	1	Haitian Slave
Stryker	74	Peter

Index of Planters' Names

Planter's Name	Tale #	Title of Tale
Tatum, John	45	James Hall
Vandegriff, Abraham	24	Pegg
Wallace	78	Tom
Welton, David	24	Pegg
Williams, James	76	James Williams